Maximizing the Impact of Comics in Your Library

MAXIMIZING THE IMPACT OF COMICS IN YOUR LIBRARY

Graphic Novels, Manga, and More

Jack Phoenix

LIBRARIES UNLIMITED®

An Imprint of ABC-CLIO, LLC

Santa Barbara, California • Denver, Colorado

Library of Congress Cataloging-in-Publication Data

Names: Phoenix, Jack, author.
Title: Maximizing the impact of comics in your library : graphic novels, manga, and more / Jack Phoenix.
Description: Santa Barbara, California : Libraries Unlimited, [2020] |
   Includes bibliographical references and index.
Identifiers: LCCN 2019056103 (print) | LCCN 2019056104 (ebook) |
   ISBN 9781440868856 (paperback) acid-free paper | ISBN 9781440868863 (ebook)
Subjects: LCSH: Libraries—Special collections—Comic books, strips, etc. | Libraries—Special collections—Graphic novels. | Libraries—Activity programs—United States.
Classification: LCC Z692.G7 P48 2020 (print) | LCC Z692.G7 (ebook) |
   DDC 026.7415—dc23
LC record available at https://lccn.loc.gov/2019056103
LC ebook record available at https://lccn.loc.gov/2019056104

ISBN: 978-1-4408-6885-6 (paperback)
         978-1-4408-6886-3 (ebook)

24 23 22 21 20   1 2 3 4 5

This book is also available as an eBook.

Libraries Unlimited
An Imprint of ABC-CLIO, LLC

ABC-CLIO, LLC
147 Castilian Drive
Santa Barbara, California 93117
www.abc-clio.com

This book is printed on acid-free paper ∞

Manufactured in the United States of America

Dedicated to . . .

My mother, who bought for me my first comic book
from a drugstore spinner rack.
My grandmother, who helped me cultivate
my comic book habit for years after.
My husbeast, who supports my comic
book addiction even still.
And to the London Public Library in London,
Ohio, my first library home.

Contents

Foreword by Sina Grace — ix

Acknowledgments — xiii

Introduction — xv

Chapter 1. What Is a Comic? — 1

Chapter 2. A Brief History of Comics in Libraries — 49

Chapter 3. Acquiring Comics — 69

Chapter 4. Making Comics Accessible — 93

Chapter 5. Comic Programs — 129

Chapter 6. Hosting a Comic Convention — 153

Chapter 7. Promoting Comics — 173

Chapter 8. Comics and the Curriculum: School and Academic Libraries — 181

Chapter 9. Comics as Professional Development — 203

Chapter 10. Conclusion — 213

Appendix A. Love Comic Books? Then Take This Survey! — 217

Appendix B. Arlington Heights Memorial Library Project Proposal — 221

Appendix C. Recommended Comics — 225

Bibliography — 231

Index — 237

Foreword

Sina Grace

I almost don't know what to write here because Jack Phoenix did all the heavy lifting. The history and necessity of comic books/graphic novels in libraries is masterfully detailed in the pages following. He did an absolutely aces job of taking a very complicated subject that others would fail at tackling with big words and run-on sentences . . . and he made it a fun read. What Jack couldn't do, however, is get down to the personal of it all.

My first memories at the Santa Monica library involve me scouring through Astrid Lindgren's work, hoping to find books that could match the awe and wonder I felt when reading the illustrated versions of *Pippi Longstocking*. Aside from *Mad Magazine* (which may be an imaginary memory—more on that in some other book), I don't recall there being any graphic novels or collected editions at the public library. For me personally, this wasn't a huge problem as the comic store (Hi De Ho Comics) was located literally across the street from the library, so when I reached an age where I didn't want to read books, I could mosey over to Hi De Ho. The library lost me right at peak middle grade years. Jack gets into the nitty-gritty of the symbiotic relationship between nonprofit and for-profit businesses, but suffice to say, I had a positive opinion of both, but assumed they were to remain separate.

While comics and graphic novels have had a tenuous relationship with legitimacy in the book market and library system, there is without a doubt a positive correlation between literacy and kids who read comics. Again, because Jack so succinctly details all the facts, I get to focus on the personal. When I was in sixth grade, a lonely kid who enjoyed drawing

Spider-Man's clone Ben Reilly over playing basketball, I spent countless lunch breaks re-reading Stephen King's *Creepshow* collection, a comic book so divine and horrifying it's a tragedy that it was out of print for so long. The city library still didn't have many offerings in the graphic novel department, and I was so exhausted from the Shilohs and Shabanus of literature, that I still yearned for the accomplishment one feels from finishing a book, and I was too old for *Goosebumps* to scratch that itch. All this is to say, I was a middle grade reader without many options beyond the handful of meager comic book offerings and my go-to selection of Lois Duncan novels.

Thanks to the efforts of Raina Telgemeier, Jeff Smith, and so many more, serialized graphic novels have found their way to YA readers' hearts. *Maus*, *Persepolis*, *Diary of a Teenage Girl*, and others, have taught tastemakers that comics is a space for high art. Manga has been accepted and appreciated by American readers (and they're also super easy to organize). Much like the embrace of digital technology, the tides have changed for how comics are perceived in libraries and bookstores, and it's time for everyone to do their part by making sure that the comics section doesn't look like the ghettoized cluttered corner no one wants to go in. I can imagine the plethora of excuses each and every librarian has . . . but we're nine steps ahead of you. This book will give you the vocabulary, the glossary, the index, and the source code to better understand, appreciate, and maximize a comic book section in any library.

Maybe now's a good time to talk about my personal opinion of Jack's work in *Maximizing the Impact of Comics in Your Library*. While I've spent the last few paragraphs detailing my love and history of comic books and libraries, it's been with the utmost awareness that you, dear reader, may lack your own history with the above. In a way that only a chief librarian could handle, this book accomplishes the near-impossible: it explains the history of comics and its relationship with pop culture, organizes a means for figuring out how to sift through tens of thousands of superhero yarns for the most valuable books to stock in every county, and does all of this in a way that feels conversational and never didactic. This is no easy task, and as someone with an extensive history in comics, I've got to say that this book truly does cover it all.

I personally owe a great debt to the libraries of America. My *Iceman* series at Marvel—one that followed an openly gay male protagonist fighting his way through Manhattan while sorting out his personal life—was cancelled because of low direct market sales ("direct market," a phrase you'll learn a lot about in this book). Had it not been for librarians embracing the book in its collected edition form, and putting it on shelves for YA reading or for LGBTQ+ selects, the series would not have been picked up for a revival in 2018. Now, more than ever, comic books need libraries for survival.

Sina Grace is a writer and illustrator living in Los Angeles. He's best known for his work on the iconic Iceman *series for Marvel Comics, as well as his graphic memoir at Image Comics.*

Acknowledgments

I would like to offer a very sincere and hardy "thank you" to the following for their assistance and support of this book: My editors Jessica Gribble and Barbara Ittner for all their editing prowess, their wisdom, and for providing me with this opportunity, as well as everyone at Libraries Unlimited and ABC-CLIO; Tom Gaadt and the staff at Cartoon Books for enthusiastically supporting me and providing images; Jack Baur who probably should have been the one writing this book; Valentino Zullo whose input and assistance were invaluable; Cindy Orr and Tish Lowry for their encouragement and support, for this could not have happened without them; Becky Spratford for being an inspiration; Ashley Dallacqua and David Kohl for the information and encouragement; Amie Wright, Tina Coleman, and every member of the GNCRT for being such wonderful resources; Brad Ricca for the publishing advice; the staffs of Carol and John's Comic Shop and The Laughing Ogre for supporting my comic habit; Alice Son and Clare Kindt for guidance; Christian Wildgoose for helping me to include his work; the staff of the London Public Library for helping me grow; the staff of the Willoughby-Eastlake Public Library for cheering me on; Michael Ritchie for the valuable cataloging information; all the librarian experts on comics who have come before me, including Michael Pawuk, David Serchay, Steve Weiner, Randall Scott, Robert Weiner, Francisca Goldsmith, Matthew Wood, and anyone I'm missing; Dr. Miriam Matteson for overseeing my project on comics in grad school; DC Comics, Judd Winnick, Terry Moore, Gene Ambaum, and Pat Coleman for permitting me to use their material; all my contributors, including Karen Green, Hope Larson, Mark Waid, Tony Isabella, Raina Telgemeier, Andrew Tadman, Bryn Wolanski, Jessica Lee, Lucas McKeever, John Dudas, Chloe Ramos, Rachael Bild, Carolyn Paplham,

Violet Jaffe, Sean Gilmartin, Natalie DeJonghe, Shivon, Megan Zagorski, Sina Grace, and anyone I may have missed; and my wonderful husband, who supported me during this process by bringing me food and letting me go on and on about what was currently happening in the world of comics.

Introduction

"Fifty percent of the circs, zero percent of the respect," said the teen librarian as the others in the room nodded in solid agreement. This I overheard at the American Library Association (ALA) Graphic Novels Interest Group Meetup (now the Graphic Novels and Comics Round Table) in the spring of 2018 at the Chicago Comics and Entertainment Expo, better known as C2E2. The unanimous nodding was indicative of a common frustration for those in librarianship who love comics; the materials they love are popular and circulate very well, but many others in the field cannot be bothered to take them seriously. The data would support that comics are more generally accepted, if not thoroughly embraced, by public libraries across the country now more than ever before (Osicki 2018). Yet librarians who love comics know that comics could circulate *even better* if they had more wholesale support. All comics librarians want is to see the medium they love find its way into the hands of eager readers.

What if I told you, though, that it's not only those librarians resistant to comics who may be holding them back? What if there are many well-intentioned comic-loving librarians out there who are still not quite allowing comics to reach their full potential? How could this be, you ask? A multitude of reasons from misunderstandings to terminology to an insistence on shelving and classifying and cataloging the same ways that we librarians always have without making much room for something new. This, my fellow nerds, is where I ask you to trust me for the next few hundred pages of this book as we explore together how you can truly maximize comics in your library. This is my passion, and this is why I'm here.

Comics is a complicated medium with which librarians have a long and sordid history. The complication begins right off the bat with the name, "comics." "Comics" can be plural, indicating multiples of a comic, or it can be a collective noun used singularly for the entire medium, hence the sentence "comics is a unique medium" is grammatically correct (McCloud 1994). Believe me, we'll be discussing the comics lexicon plenty during our time together. Yet despite the apparent complications with comics, there is also something conversely simple about them. Comics are, as writer, artist, and comics scholar Scott McCloud says, simply "words and pictures" (1994). But it's that exact simplicity that led many librarians to not take comics seriously until it was, perhaps, too late, and now the field of librarianship is trying to play catch-up, leaving some librarians who have yet to understand these "words and pictures" in the dust and others still not quite aligned with the readership.

When I entered the field of librarianship, I decided early on that I wanted to help with this problem, that I wanted to help all librarians appreciate or at least understand comics. I'm not sure that such a lofty goal can truly be achieved. After all, librarianship is huge and there are far too many materials for all of us to be fully versed in. But this book is my best effort. Librarians are, at the very least, experts at finding information and guiding others, so perhaps this guide can be a handy tool for those who still find that they just don't understand these "words and pictures." Librarians tend to be perfectionists when it comes to their information, they tend to be service-oriented, and they want to put the patrons first. I hope to show you that, since comics is a unique medium, it is deserving of unique treatment to best suit the readers' needs.

Librarians who love comics would argue that, if we were genuinely prioritizing, far more in the field would give comics more respect and

---

FIGURE I.1 [*opposite*]. Proposed cover by Tom Gaadt featuring images courtesy of Jeff Smith, Judd Winnick, and Terry Moore. (Bone © and ® Jeff Smith. The material reprinted in this book was originally published in the comic book BONE ©2019 Jeff Smith. RASL™ is ©Jeff Smith. The material reprinted in this book was originally published in the comic book RASL ©2008 Jeff Smith. Used by permission of Cartoon Books, Inc. All Rights Reserved. Illustrations from HILO BOOK 1: THE BOY WHO CRASHED TO EARTH by Judd Winick, copyright @ 2015 by Judd Winick. Used by permission of Random House Children's Books, a division of Penguin Random House LLC. All rights reserved.)

put more effort into learning about them. After all, comics-related media is dominating the cultural landscape at this moment. Comic-based movies are bringing in billions of dollars at the box office, as *Avengers: Infinity War,* based on the Marvel Comics characters, has grossed over 2 billion dollars worldwide and its sequel, *Avengers: Endgame,* made 1.2 billion dollars in its opening weekend of April 2019. Not to mention the films *Captain Marvel* and *Shazam!,* based off the Marvel and DC characters, brought in over a billion dollars collectively just a couple of months earlier. TV networks are pumping out comic-based shows as fast as they can, running the gamut from *Sandman* offshoot *Lucifer* to *Legion,* which is based on an obscure *X-Men* character, and there is even a DC Universe streaming service, with shows and digital comics dedicated to DC characters. Oscar-winning actors are turning to comic properties and comic movies are getting Oscar buzz, and even, perhaps, reshaping the Oscars themselves (Romo 2018). Comics are making the *New York Times* bestseller list as well as other bestseller lists around the world. Comics are being used in the classroom and have become the topic of college courses and academic discourse. Comics are winning prestigious awards previously reserved for traditional books, such as *Nimona* by Noelle Stevenson being nominated for the National Book Award in 2015. Essentially, comics have become mainstream.

It's true that there are librarians who need to get on board the comic wave and embrace this medium. But it's also true that some of the librarians who have embraced comics may still be engaging in practices that are not conducive to providing comics to patrons. Libraries were designed to house traditional books and the profession of librarianship was primarily designed, with all of its classification and shelving systems, to organize traditional books. Comics, though, are not traditional books. By shoe-horning comics into systems that were designed to support traditional books, librarians may be inhibiting access to these materials while trying to provide it.

There are three main factors that keep libraries from maximizing comics, and each stem from a lack of understanding about the material. Those factors are:

Misnomers: Using an identifier that is unfamiliar to the comics-seeker and may exhibit intellectual bias, such as labelling all comics as "graphic novels"; Cataloging: Strictly adhering to typical cataloging standards for books can lead to insufficient and inconsistent metadata when applied to comics; Shelving: Comics are unique among print materials, so filing them with traditional print materials by Dewey Classification or shelving them under other standards applied to typical books (such as by author), can inhibit access; "comics are unique for they are both a content and a format and should be treated with appropriate speciality." (Phoenix 2015)

So, put on your cape and tights and fasten your utility belt. We're going to dive into comics and learn how we can help each other maximize these weird and wonderful things in our libraries and fully reward our weird and wonderful patrons!

What Is a Comic?

If you're reading this book, you probably already have an idea what a comic is. You probably know that comics, which can also be called sequential art or graphic narrative (Chute 2006), is a narrative format that tells a story through panels of words and pictures. You likely know that comics come printed in paper and ink, sometimes in black and white, sometimes in color, but that they can also be digital. You may have heard in the past the frequently vocalized motto of librarians and academics: "comics are a format, not a genre"; though there are certainly those who would debate such a statement (West 2013). But if you're reading this book, there's also a significant chance there's a lot you *don't* know about comics. If you're a comics newbie, then you may very much enjoy this chapter. If you're a current comics expert, you'll likely shake your head disapprovingly at the information that this book leaves out. That's why it's up to you, dear comics-fan librarian, to fill in the gaps for your staff and patrons.

DEFINITIONS

Here are some of the common words and phrases one may encounter when dealing with comics. You may encounter a few of these quite frequently or you may encounter them a whole whopping never, but you will definitely encounter *some*. Keep in mind, when it comes to comics, many of the commonly used terms and their definitions can be nebulous and subjective, as comics scholarship and authoritative bodies are still relatively new. The definitions listed here are typically agreed upon by most comics scholars, fans, and, of course, many librarians.

FIGURE 1.1. Quick Tips for How to Read a Comic! (Original comic by Sina Grace.)

Comic: Also known as sequential art or graphic narrative, a comic is a narrative told through pictures, usually accompanied by words displayed in bubbles or boxes, which flow primarily left to right, panel to panel, often through multiple panels on a page (a feature that distinguishes them from children's picture books). This includes comic strips, comic books, graphic novels, manga, webcomics, and more. "Comics" refers to the plural of comic or is used as a grouping noun for the name of the medium (e.g. "Comics is a fascinating medium"). Note that in this book, when discussing something that can apply to any and all in the medium, the word "comics" will be used. If discussing only a particular type of comic, one of the terms below under Formats and Genres will be used.

Formats and Genres

These are the different types of comics you may encounter.

Comic strip: A small, quick narrative told within a few panels, often printed in newspapers and magazines. The first comic books were collected versions of comic strips that were reprinted in their own magazine-style publication. They are sometimes referred to as "funnies" or "cartoons" (the latter especially when it's a single panel comic). Examples: *Garfield*, *Peanuts*, *Funky Winkerbean*, *The Phantom*.

Comic book: The most well-known and popular form of comic, a magazine-style publication that tells a graphic narrative, often serially,

Library Comic by Gene Ambaum and Pat Coleman   librarycomic.com © 2018 Ambauminable LLC

FIGURE 1.2. A Library Comic that shows comics are for everyone. (©2018 Ambauminable LLC, used with permission.)

and is typically published monthly. Most superheroes come from comic books. Comic books are sometimes referred to as "monthlies" or "floppies." Other types of comics, such as graphic novels, trade paperbacks, and manga are also sometimes referred to as comic books, but for the sake of this book, comic book will refer to "floppies." Comic books usually come with an issue number. Often when people use the word "comics," this is the format to which they are referring, which is accurate, since "comics" is an umbrella term. Examples: *Action Comics, Captain America, Archie, or Savage Dragon.*

- *Ongoing series:* A comic book that is designed and intended to be published *ad infinitum* and meant to tell stories for years, even decades. Most monthly comics published by the major comics publishers and carried in comic shops are ongoing series, often shortened to "ongoing."
- *Limited series:* A comic book that is intended to be published for but a finite number of issues and designed to tell a single story from beginning to end.
  - ○ *Miniseries:* A limited series that usually lasts 11 issues or fewer. Examples: *Iceman* (Marvel, 2018), *The Infinity Gauntlet* (Marvel, 1991), *Angela* (Image, 1992).
  - ○ *Maxiseries:* A limited series that lasts 12 issues or more but is not designed nor intended to last *ad infinitum*. Examples: *Crisis on Infinite Earths* (DC, 1985), *All-Star Superman* (DC, 2003), *Afterlife with Archie* (Archie, 2013).
  - ○ *One-shot:* A single issue story. One-shots were popular in the 1990s with the establishment of prestige format comic books, which were comic books published without ads with glossy paper and used glue binding instead of staples. Most one-shots during the 1990s were prestige format. Examples: *Dazzler* (Marvel, 2018), *Batman: Mr. Freeze* (DC, 1997), *Team Sonic Racing* (Archie, 2018).

Trade paperback: Often abbreviated as "TPB." This means something a bit different with comics than the rest of the book world, as it connotes something more nuanced than just the type of binding. A trade paperback can also be referred to as a "collected edition" and is frequently just shortened to "trade." This is a collection of single-issue comic books, often 6 to 12 issues, that are then collected and reprinted under a single binding to resemble a graphic novel and are sold through the typical book market and vendors, unlike monthly issues. Trade paperbacks found their popularity boom in the 1990s. They are often published with a volume number. They are also the primary culprit in people's confusion of the lexicon, since "TPBs make up 95% of what many librarians refer to as 'graphic novels'" (Fee 2013).

Hardcover: Often abbreviated as "HC." This is the clothbound edition of a trade or graphic novel. A typical question overheard in a comic shop may go something like, "Is the *Red Goblin* story from *Amazing Spider-Man* out in hardcover yet?" Currently, comic books are often collected and reprinted as hardcover first and then released as trade paperbacks shortly after.

Graphic novel: This term comes with some baggage. A graphic novel is typically a longer, thicker comic that is originally published with traditional book binding and tells a single story from beginning to end, like a traditional prose novel (Goldsmith 2010). A good example would be *This One Summer* by Jillian Tamaki and Mariko Tamaki (First Second, 2014). A graphic novel can sometimes be originally published as a miniseries or maxiseries, such as *Watchmen* (DC, 1986), before being bound in novel form. Because graphic novels are typically self-contained, they do not usually have volume numbers; however, some do tell serial stories in multiple volumes, such as *My Favorite Thing Is Monsters* (Fantagraphics, 2017), which is intended to be a multi-volume set.

Original graphic novel: Abbreviated to "OGN," this is a term used to specify that a graphic novel is published as is, not in serial format first. "OGN" has increased in use over the past decade as a way of distinguishing graphic novels from trade paperbacks and is frequently applied to graphic novels featuring characters that are normally published serially, such as *The Punisher: Intruder* by Mike Baron, Bill Reinhold, and Linda Lessman (Marvel, 1989).

"Graphic Novels": a Problematic Term? If you work in libraries, there's a significant chance that nearly all of your encounters with comics have been under the term "graphic novels." Libraries and bookstores often use this term for their comics collections, and you may think graphic novels is *the* preferred and official term for all comics. Indeed, many librarians are under the impression that the term "comics" is perhaps old-fashioned or even obsolete. The confusion between "comics" and "graphic novels" and the nebulous definition of the latter has led to a lot of delieberation. This book is not suggesting libraries shouldn't use the term "graphic novels," but it's important for librarians to know that its definition and use are not concrete, nor is it an interchangeable term. Comics scholar

Brenna Clarke Gray explains, "I have had variations of this conversation with colleagues ('But you're teaching graphic novels, right? Not comics.') and people on the internet ('I just read the best graphic novel memoir!') and fellow serious-book-people-turned-serious-comic-people ('I don't read comics. But I loved *Maus* and *Fun Home*.')." She continues, "Somewhere along the way, we decided to accept that 'comics' are silly ephemeral reading material for children, and 'graphic novels' are the serious things that get reviewed in the *New York Times*. We need to reject this distinction for three reasons . . . 1. They Are Not All Novels . . . 2. They Are All Comics . . . 3. You're Reifying an Arbitrary (and probably snooty) Distinction" (2014). It seems what is old is now new again, with "comics" being the preferred term, or, sometimes, "graphic narrative" but libraries continue to dominantly label all comics as "graphic novels."

The term "graphic novel" was popularized (not coined, contrary to popular belief) by legendary creator, Will Eisner. He also used the term "sequential art." At the time, comic books, comic strips, and the term "comics" had garnered a negative connotation and were thought of as kid stuff and low art, after being connected to juvenile delinquency in the 1950s. Eisner used "graphic novel" to distinguish his works from other comics in the hopes that they would be taken seriously, but even Eisner shifted in the terms he used, including using the catch-all to describe the medium/process, sequential art. "It's a meaningless term," says Karen Green, Curator for Comics and Cartoons at Columbia University's Rare Book & Manuscript Library, "Honestly, it's meaningless because it's a marketing term. It's a term designed to market comics in a way to make them seem more palatable to adults; to seem more sophisticated. When Will Eisner popularized the term, he was trying to market his books to bookstores rather than comics shops."[1]

The major difference between traditional comic books and graphic novels was that comic books were serially published in magazine format and graphic novels were finite stories (beginning, middle, and end) published in a book format. These graphic novels were often called "original graphic novels," and this difference remained mostly consistent throughout the 1980s and much of the 1990s, as publishers like Marvel and DC also began publishing prestige format comics or original graphic novels featuring their characters such as *X-Men: God Loves, Man Kills* by Chris

Claremont (Marvel, 1982) and *Batman: The Killing Joke* (DC, 1988). Comics, though, was the name of the medium itself, and still is, encompassing all styles and genres within the medium.

The confusion came about when comic publishers began reprinting monthly comic books in collected editions as trade paperbacks and hardcovers that resembled traditional books. Though these are significantly different from original graphic novels, the term graphic novel was gradually applied to these as publishers, taking a cue from Eisner, used it as a marketing term so that the titles would be taken more seriously. Whether or not collections of monthly comic books or collections of comic strips and, indeed, works of nonfiction should be referred to as "graphic novels" is up for debate and is not decided, depending on whom you ask. Currently, "graphic novels" seems to be the preferred term for libraries, bookstores, and those occasions when publishers and vendors are selling comics to those organizations, while academics and most in the comics industry primarily use the term "comics" (consider that they are referred to as "comic shops" and not "graphic novel" shops). Though, as John Dudas, co-owner of Carol & John's Comic Shop says, "The terminology is always changing, so I don't think the difference matters too much."[2]

So, what is a *true* graphic novel? Let's look at some examples of why this is confusing:

- Is *My Favorite Thing Is Monsters* by Emil Ferris a graphic novel? It was published by Fantagraphics in traditional book form at a whopping 416 pages and tells a self-contained story, which could continue in another book. There are few who would disagree that this is a graphic novel.

- Is *Bone* by Jeff Smith a graphic novel? It was originally published in serial, comic book form and then later combined into larger volumes. When taken as a whole, this is a single, self-contained story that has a beginning, middle, and end. Despite being originally published serially, most would agree this is a graphic novel.

- Is *Superman: Action Comics Volume One: Invisible Mafia* a graphic novel? This is a hardcover collection of monthly *Action Comics* issues 1001–1006. *Action Comics* has been printed in comic book form on a near-consistent monthly basis since 1938. In order to fully understand the events of this story, one would have had to have read the events of the previous *Action Comics* runs in a story called "Rebirth" and the runs before that. It's hard to argue that this is a self-contained story with a beginning, middle, and end, since this publication is designed to last into perpetuity. Some would call this a graphic novel, and some would not.

- Is *The Dark Knight Returns* by Frank Miller a graphic novel? *The Dark Knight Returns* was originally published in comic book form as a limited series by DC Comics and later as collected editions. Though it features characters who appear in monthly superhero comic books, it is mostly a stand-alone story, requiring only general knowledge of Batman to read it. One could argue that it fits the criteria for a graphic novel like the abovementioned *Bone* but simply features DC characters.

- Is *Garfield at Large* by Jim Davis a graphic novel? This is the first collection of *Garfield* comic strips that originally appeared in newspapers reprinted in book form. It does not tell a single, longform narrative. It is unlikely that many would call this a graphic novel.

- Is *Fun Home* by Alison Bechdel a graphic novel? This is longform narrative and published as a single volume, but it is a memoir. It is the true story of someone's life. A work of nonfiction does not qualify as a novel, so should it qualify as a graphic novel?

- Is *Maus* by Art Spiegelman a graphic novel? If *Fun Home* is disqualified from being a graphic novel because it is nonfiction, then surely *Maus,* a biography about the Holocaust, is, too. Karen Green says, "Art Spiegelman was one of the first to grouse about the term graphic novel, since he felt it wasn't accurate for *Maus*. It's simply not a novel."[3] However, during a panel discussion,[4] Regina Shapiro, cataloging librarian of Queens Library, observed that if the same story were told in prose (a story about people who actually lived but are portrayed in the work as anthropomorphic mice), it would be labeled as a *fictionalized* telling of actual events and, therefore, fiction, further, a novel.

See? It's confusing. It's messy. But it's worth noting that there is one word that applies to every single example listed above: they're all "comics." Comics is the name of the medium itself and remains so to this day, which includes graphic novels, comic strips, comic books, and so on. Is it time for libraries to avoid the confusion by embracing the actual term for the medium?

Let's look at the argument from both sides:

Pro-"Comics"

- "Graphic novel" is a genre of comics, a genre within a medium. Think fictional, long form, comics storytelling. Comics is an umbrella term and is more inclusive. After all, all graphic novels are comics, but not all comics are graphic novels. Using "comics" allows comics in all formats to be allowed equal opportunity for merit.

- There are certain criteria that make a work a novel. For starters, a novel is long form fiction that has a beginning, middle, and end and deals with the human condition. Original graphic novels fit these criteria, but not trade paperbacks or hardcover collections of comic books and comic strips or nonfiction titles.

- If most experts (scholars, historians, academics, and creators) refer to them as "comics," why would librarians differ? It's worth noting that most organizations that specialize in the medium refer to them as comics, such as the Comics Studies Society.

- "Graphic novel" displays an intellectual bias. To those who would prefer to call them "comics," it may seem that the library is correcting them, especially if the comic they are looking for is not a graphic novel but the library has it labeled that way. The library shouldn't be making value judgments on a work by suggesting that referring to it as a comic makes it somehow lesser.

Pro-"Graphic Novels"

- The term may sound more appealing to those who aren't already fans of the medium.

- Many traditional novels were first published serially, so perhaps trade paperback and hardcover collections of monthly comic books should count. Perhaps serial, superhero stories are now being written as sequential novels.

- The terms are all a bit nebulous and ill-defined, between comics, graphic novels, sequential art, and so on, so why can't libraries choose which one they prefer?

- Comics is still a young medium and the terms associated with it are frequently changing.

Here is what comics historian Tim Hanley says about the topic:

I hear both [terms] the same amount, and interchangeably, really. The distinction between the two is pretty fuzzy. For me, I generally use "comics" when talking about monthly single issues or the collections thereof, and "graphic novels" for standalone books that haven't been previously released in a serialized format. But I'm not hard and fast about it. "Comics" can be more of an umbrella term, too. In the same way that every novel is a book but not every book is a novel, every graphic novel is a comic but not every comic is a graphic novel. In the end, though, I feel like getting too hardcore about the semantics of the terms can turn into a gatekeeper situation. Just call them what you want![5]

Manga: Comics originally published in Japanese and then translated to English. Manga, despite the series, creators, or publishers, tends to have a distinctive style that is shared across titles, such as characters with disproportionately large eyes. This is not to be confused with anime, which shares these distinctions in style but is animated for film (it's worth noting that much manga has an anime counterpart and vice versa). Manga is unique among comics, especially to American audiences, as it is a sort of blend of American comic books and graphic novels; it is typically published as an ongoing series like a monthly comic book, but its binding more closely resembles a graphic novel but in a "digest" size. Most manga is read right to left and is published in black and white. Be advised that manga specifically refers to titles that are originally Japanese, but the term is often erroneously applied to other Asian comics, such as manhwa (Korean comics). Note that in this book, when discussing manga, we will be referring to the North American editions. Examples: *My Hero Academia* (Viz Media, 2014), *Attack on Titan* (Kodansha USA, 2009), *Fullmetal Alchemist* (Yen Press, 2001).

- Shojo: Manga that is targeted to the teenage, female reader.
- Shonen: Manga that is targeted to the teenage, male reader.

Webcomic: Webcomics are comics that premier in an online, specifically web-based, format. Most of these resemble comic strips, but they can also take narrative forms closer to comic books or graphic novels appearing on websites such as Buzzfeed or personal blogs. Some web-comics become so successful, they eventually find their way to print form. Examples: the works of Adam Ellis (AKA adamtots), *Phoebe and Her Unicorn* by Dana Simpson. Recently, it was announced that Marvel will be joining with Serial Box, which publishes weekly installments of original books and audiobooks online, to release original, serial, digital works featuring Marvel characters (Lee 2019).

Digital comic: The opposite of the above, this is a comic originally created and intended for print but is also released in a digital version. At this point, nearly all newly-printed comics are given a digital release the same day as print.

Other Terms

Here are some other words you may encounter while providing comics materials to your patrons. Some of these may occasionally pop up in reference or readers' advisory questions. Note that I have restricted these to the search terms most likely to actually come up while trying to help a patron find or identify a comic, so we'll not be covering words such as "editor."

Story arc: A continuing storyline told through multiple issues of a comic book or comic strip. Story arcs have a beginning, middle, end, and, thanks to the serial nature of most comics, lead into a new story arc upon completion. Many creators, especially writers, begin a new story arc when joining a comic title. Most trade paperbacks and collected edition hardcovers are collections of the issues that make up a single story arc.

Series: This is simply the name of the particular comic that has multiple entries, such as ongoing monthly comic books or multi-volume graphic novels. However, this is also often referred to as simply "title" or "book," especially in regards to monthly comic books. Example; "Mark Waid joined that title in September as writer" or "which of the *X-Men* books that launched in the summer is your favorite?"

Crossover: A crossover can mean any time that characters in a particular series appear in another series, which is common within a single publisher's titles, but can also happen inter-company (such as *JLA/Avengers* by Kurt Busiek and George Perez). A crossover is also the word used for big event stories, usually annual and usually in the summer, that span multiple titles within a company, such as *War of the Realms* (Marvel, 2019).

Writer: Sometimes called the plotter, or credited in the comic as "story by" or "plot by" or "script by," this is the creator who comes up with the narrative being told that is then illustrated by the artist.

Artist: Often called the penciller, this is the primary illustrator of the comic.

Inker: Sometimes credited in the comic as "inks by," the inker uses ink to solidify the artist's pencil illustrations on the page.

Colorist: The colorist is responsible for providing the variety of colors and shades for the artist's illustrations, sometimes done with ink but more frequently these days with digital software such as Photoshop.

Creative team: All of the above and more. All the individuals who pool their creative talents to create a comic.

Run: This refers to the time that any creator, usually the writer or artist, spends on a particular series. For example, "I really loved Ed Brubaker's run on *Catwoman*."

Volume: This term may not be as obvious as you think. "Volume" can mean two different things when discussing comics, and it all has to do with the type of comic you're talking about. For graphic novels or graphic nonfiction, an example such as *Maus* Volume 1 and Volume 2 is self-explanatory. For trade paperbacks and hardcovers, it means the next sequential trade paperback or hardcover of that series, but it gets confusing because of how "volume" is defined for floppy comic books. See the discussion about the word "Volume" and learn how the word can be the bane of a comics librarian's existence in Chapter Four.

Indie: Just as with movies, indie is short for independent and refers to comics that are creator-owned or self-published. Sometimes, these comics can have a mainstream distributor, such as Image or Top Shelf; other times, they are sold by hand, such as at comic convention booths or by the creator's local comic shop. There are even indie comics that are so successful that they are sold and distributed by the thousands and still remain self-published, such as the works provided by Cartoon Books.

Comix: Occasionally you may see this stylization of the word. This usage became popular in the 1970s through the 1990s to specifically denote underground comics that were self or otherwise independently published and distributed. The term still has some connotation for independent works, usually intended for adult audiences, but it is now sometimes, though rarely, used as the collective noun for the medium as opposed to the clearly plural "comics."

Direct market: The term that describes the sale model of comics being sold through dedicated comic shops who purchase the items from dedicated vendors as opposed to the newsstand model similar to that of magazines.

DISTINGUISHING FEATURES OF COMICS

Undeniably, comics' bread-and-butter is the superhero. Comics did not begin with the superhero, but since the release of *Action Comics* #1, comics and superheroes have been intrinsically linked, and it shouldn't be a surprise. Superhero fiction, as a genre,[6] provides escapism for the reader that is unique and unmatched, often colorful, with grand adventures and strong moral cores. Superhero stories have often provided fantastic settings, dashing characters, and even a fair amount of wish-fulfillment, all while leaving plenty of social and political commentary. The earliest Superman stories portray the Man of Steel taking on corrupt slumlords and domestic violence, so social commentary and, more arguably, social justice are in the very DNA of comics. Comics can provide life lessons and establish moral compasses with messages of compassion and civil duty, and the protection of the public good, which, according to comics scholar Valentino Zullo has shifted from public health to agents of security.[7]

But that's just the superhero genre. What about all the other comics that are out there, including nonfiction? Comics provide reading as well as visual stimulation in a way that neither reading a traditional book nor film can. Lucia Cedeira Serantes, who is an expert on the effects of reading on children and young adults and their interaction with public libraries, says, "Comics are often characterized as a 'quick read' and are therefore often recommended for reluctant readers," but there is a "duality" to them since "there is the possibility both of reading fast and of taking time when reading" (2018). Sheila Heinlein, school librarian and resident comics-in-the-classroom expert at OverDrive has said, "Comics engage by imparting meaning through written language *and* images, convey large amounts of information in a short time," and allow readers "to recall the content better and transfer learning to other content areas."[8] Reading comics can exercise the mind in a way unique from the comics' prose or fine art counterparts, often enhancing a reader's skills in other areas, such as writing and other types of reading (Dallacqua 2018). Comics teach beginner readers to follow a sequence of events, and they learn quickly to fill in the gaps of the action between the panels, allowing them to make associations and connections. Comics can teach narrative structures in a way that is different from prose books, sometimes allowing readers of different levels of ability to keep up with core concepts that they may lose if made to read traditional prose texts.

In 2009, expert and lecturer on comics, Laura Jimenez, noted that the different type of reading that comics offer can enhance a reader's vocabulary, which is especially beneficial to young readers (Ehrlich 2014).

FIGURE 1.3. RASL by Jeff Smith can get teen readers hooked on
STEAM topics, thanks to the references to the life and discoveries of
Tesla throughout. (RASL™ is ©Jeff Smith. The material reprinted in
this book was originally published in the comic book RASL ©2008 Jeff
Smith. Used by permission of Cartoon Books, Inc. All Rights Reserved.)

Disguised within seemingly mindless action fare, comics will use words and concepts that many other books that are targeted toward kids will avoid. Young readers may not know a certain word and are forced to look it up in order to follow the story or are able to decipher its meaning through context. Words like "gamma radiation," "plasma," "quasar," and more, are not unusual for comics, even those aimed at younger readers, and such concepts can attract children to STEAM topics. In fact, Dan Hurley credits comics, especially *The Amazing Spider-Man*, for putting him on the path to become one of the country's leading science writers (Riggs 2016).

Of course, mythology, history, folklore, literature, and other multicultural concepts also pop up. Children reading comics may encounter quotes, concepts, and characters from classic literature (*Moby Dick* is frequently referenced in Jeff Smith's *Bone*), world mythologies (hello, Wonder Woman, hello, Thor), Shakespeare, and more. Art Spiegelman once said, after all, "comics are a gateway drug to literacy" (Toon Books). But do not allow such positive attributes to limit comics to simple "gateway" reading that will lead to more complicated books. True, that may very well happen, and it's wonderful if comics can lead readers to other types of reading, but the uniqueness of comics means that not all comics are "easy" to read. Comics, like traditional books, have differentiating levels of complexity. Some comics are for more advanced, mature readers, and some comics are well-matched for beginner readers. Take the obvious differences between a comic like *Johnny Boo* by James Kochalka, primarily intended for younger audiences with but a few word balloons on each page, and *Jimmy Corrigan* by Chris Ware, a highly complex narrative that interchanges narrative styles, illustration methods, time periods, and more.

What the research from experts in education who specialize in comics shows us is that we should not consider comics valuable simply because they might lead to other forms of reading (Ehrlich 2014). Rather, comics are valuable reading unto themselves, and so libraries should support them and try to get them into as many interested hands as possible. Comics is a "visual medium," so the experience of reading a comic is quite literally unlike any other type of reading or any other way of absorbing a story, and comics deserve our respect (Baker 2019). As defenders of learning, enrichment, and intellectual freedom, providing and supporting the comics medium is a librarian's responsibility.

WHO PUBLISHES THESE THINGS?

As we'll discuss later, one of the many things that make comics unique is the importance of the publisher to the readership. Unlike many

FIGURE 1.4. Comic readers may be inspired to read other literature such as *Moby Dick*, just like Fone Bone. (Bone © and ® Jeff Smith. The material reprinted in this book was originally published in the comic book BONE ©2019 Jeff Smith. Used by permission of Cartoon Books, Inc. All Rights Reserved.)

traditional books and publications, the publisher can really matter to comic readers, with some readers pledging their loyalty to one publisher over others (there are many "Marvel vs. DC" conversations that take place as well as those who refuse to read either and want only indie comics; just hop on comic-related web pages for a minute and you'll see what I mean). Let's quickly review some of the major comics publishers that you'll likely encounter in the library. Please note, there are many, many wonderful publishers out there, from small to large, so this list is but a sampling.

DC Comics

Established in 1934, DC is justifiably credited with popularizing the superhero in the late 1930s and 1940s, thanks to Superman. DC took its name from *Detective Comics*, one of its many comics offerings that is still in print today and the very comic that gave us Batman. DC's repertoire of superheroes includes some of the most recognizable characters in the world, such as Wonder Woman, the Flash, and Green Lantern. Their licensed characters appear in movies, television, billions of dollars' worth of merchandise, and traditional novels. DC is owned by Warner Bros. and their publications are distributed by Penguin Random House, Diamond Comics Distributors, and digitally by Trajectory.

Marvel Comics

Technically, Marvel has been around for nearly as long as DC if we include its precursor, Timely Comics; however, it first appeared as Marvel Comics in 1961. Marvel helped reignite readers' passion for superhero comics in the 1960s and forever changed the way that comics stories were told. Over the past 20 years, their characters, such as Iron Man, Captain America, Spider-Man, and the X-Men, have become household names, rivaling DC characters in recognition, thanks to blockbuster movies. Marvel is now owned by Disney.

Image Comics

Formed in the 1990s by creators from Marvel who wished to maintain the rights to their works, Image functions more similarly to a traditional publishing house than most comics publishers. All of the comics Image publishes are creator-owned, with the creators retaining the copyright. Along with some superhero titles, Image publishes a wide variety of genres, including science fiction, comedy, fantasy, horror, crime, and memoir. Image tends to be very library friendly, with many of their books reasonably priced as well as a library liaison on staff. Some Image comics you may recognize are *Spawn, The Walking Dead* originally created by Robert Kirkman and Tony Moore,[9] *Bitch Planet* by Kelly Sue DeConnick and Valentine De Landro, and *Saga* by Brian K. Vaughan and Fiona Staples.

Spotlight on Chloe Ramos-Peterson, Library Market Sales Representative of Image Comics

Can you explain for us what your role is with Image Comics and what your position entails?

I oversee everything that Image Comics does involving libraries. I think the simplest way to describe my role in library terms is as a combination Readers' Advisory and Programs Specialist. I act as a source of both information and physical resources for libraries looking to utilize our books not only as items to be acquired but also as keys to facilitate increased patron engagement. I also manage our presence at library conventions and professional conferences nationwide, be they in-person or virtual in nature.

In terms of information, I provide book previews, recommendations and title lists (both general and individually tailored), and more. In addition to on-demand advisory, I also engage in passive advisory through a digital newsletter, which provides samples of these services on a bimonthly basis.

In terms of physical resources, I coordinate with libraries looking to organize their own programming, be it a simple book display or a county-wide comic convention, and provide support through free services ranging from materials donations to creator appearances. These appearances also span a wide array of complexity, from one-shot lectures to repeating art/writing workshop events.

Are you a comics fan yourself? If so, can you tell us about how you first got into comics? What are some of your favorite titles? Do you read anything on a monthly basis?

I've been reading comics since I was a kid. I did stop reading them for a while in the beginning of my tween years. It was not a very welcoming time to be a young girl who liked comics. The one local shop was pretty unfriendly and my library didn't carry graphic novels at all . . . They were a real rarity. Thankfully, a woman-owned comic shop opened in my hometown and it allowed me a venue to explore titles like *Kabuki, The Maxx, Milk and Cheese, The Tick, Too Much Coffee Man,* and other weird indie books in a supportive atmosphere. And then manga became more widely available in the US and my fate was sealed. In terms of what I read now, it's hard to pick a favorite title, but I do have authors and artists that I follow and I will run, not walk, to get anything they publish. My current "pull list" includes Moyocco Anno, Kiyohiko Azuma, Jordie Bellaire, Ed Brubaker, Afu Chan, Johnnie Christmas, Leila Del Duca, Warren Ellis, Jonathan Hickman, Marjorie Liu, Joe Quiñones, Gabby Rivera, Greg Rucka, Shinsuke Sato, Kit and Cat Seaton, Kyle Starks, Rumiko Takahashi, Brian K. Vaughan, J. H. Williams III, and Ron Wimberly . . . I think I mentioned having trouble picking favorites?

For your position to exist, Image must see libraries as valuable. Can you tell us a little about Image's philosophy when it comes to libraries?

Image has always pursued a very open ideal when it comes to who should be able to create, own, and access content, and I believe that philosophy extends to our relationship with libraries. The library is the one place where no personal, philosophical, or socioeconomic factor can act as a barrier, where books belong to everyone, and free expression is championed, and that is something Image will always work to support. In addition, many of the staff, myself included, have backgrounds in the library world. Our experience working to bring literacy to the public has stayed with us, and that influences the way we think about bringing books to readers.

Have you learned anything new about libraries and librarians since taking this position?

I was, somewhat naively, surprised to realize that just like me, there's a generation of librarians who grew up reading comics and are passionate about bringing the medium to the library mainstream. With them at the helm, the number of professional development events offered at comic and fan conventions has grown exponentially. It's creating this amazing professional overlap where comic creators, library professionals, and educators can share information, offer different perspectives, and inform each other's fields. It's really stunning and I think it's elevating the discourse and the content in a way that doesn't get nearly enough attention.

What are some services that you and Image can offer libraries through your position?
We offer the following:

- Creator Appearances—Authors, artists, colorists, editors, and letterers offer demos, lectures and Q&A sessions, book club visits, career talks, writing workshops, and more. These visits are done free of charge and in-person when possible. If no one is within range of the branch, our creators can "visit" via a virtual platform such as Skype or Google Hangouts.
- Galleys and ARCs—In addition to offering books samples and information on Edelweiss, Image provides digital and/or physical review copies upon request for libraries looking to preview before purchase.
- Readers' Advisory—Librarians can reach out to Image for title lists and recommendations tailored to their specific needs. From novice to expert, sometimes everyone needs a little direction, and we're happy to provide information on plot summaries, appeal factors, age appropriateness, etc.
- And more!

Do you have a ballpark guess of how much of Image's or the comics industry's annual sales can be attributed to libraries?

That's a tough one, since the vast majority of libraries do not order direct and will often order from multiple distributors to get their books. What's even harder to ballpark, but is quite possibly the *greatest* impact of library purchases, are the overall circulation figures any given sale translates to. Most of the books we sell through retailers will belong to the buyer. Some might be shared or resold, but the library copies are *intended* to be read multiple times. The impact that this has on discovery of other series and growing the fanbase is as immeasurable as it is important.

What are some of the more unique partnerships you've engaged in, such as professional development events? What are some of your favorites?

There have been two recent programs that really resonated with me:

- The first was a panel we presented in partnership with the San Diego Public Library for CCEL@SDCC in 2018 entitled, *Border Narratives: Voices from Beyond the Wall*. Latinx comics professionals gave a talk on their work, the state of the industry, the state of the nation, and how libraries can partner with artists and authors to help serve their Latinx patrons. To have an event like that take place in Southern California, mere miles from a section of contentious border wall, was a truly powerful experience. To be in the same room with Latinx comics luminaries like Johnnie Christmas (FIREBUG, *Angel Catbird*), Marco Finnegan (CROSSROAD BLUES), Ricardo Padilla (executive director and co-founder of the Latino Comics Expo), Zeke Peña (illustrator at The Nib, *Photographic: The Life of Graciela Iturbide*), and Isabel Quintero (*Gabi, A Girl in Pieces, Photographic: The Life of Graciela Iturbide*) *and* to be surrounded by a standing-room only audience of library professionals passionate about the community? That was more than just a program, that was an honor.

- The second event was a partnership between Image Comics, Pop Culture Classroom, New York Public Library, and New York Comic Con. With the direction of comics education phenomenon Dr. Katie Monnin (PCC Education Director) and the ever-knowledgeable Adam Kullberg (PCC Education Program Manager), we offered a workshop that provided instruction on how educators and librarians can deconstruct Marjorie Liu's title, MONSTRESS, in order to build their own teaching guides and curricular resources to support teaching the title to diverse populations. We hope that this will be the first of many such partnerships aimed at helping librarians and teachers unpack our graphic novels to build engaging and educational programming for patrons and students, alike.

Besides simply buying more books, is there anything you think libraries can do to help support the comics medium?

I think the most important way to support comics is to continue to reinforce the fact that they are a genuine artistic and literary medium (and not a genre). If your patron is looking for a book on a particular subject, include a graphic novel or two in your reader's recommendation. If they've checked out every crime novel you've got but they've never read an Ed Brubaker book, they're missing out on a whole segment of modern noir classics. After all, the lasting power of comics and graphic novels lies not in their ability to spawn blockbuster movies, but in their unique way of doing the most human thing of all, telling a story. If you can be the bridge that connects them to a whole new world of stories, the comics medium will flourish.

As you may know, comics are a relatively new phenomenon in libraries, and librarians resisted the medium for decades. What would you say to any librarians who are still hold-outs and think that comics don't belong in libraries?

I could talk about this for a literal eternity, but I'll demur in favor of offering a bit of context: In the early 19th century, the novel faced criticism similar to that which we now see directed at the graphic novel. There were some who felt that fiction failed to offer any instruction or enlightenment to the reader and that it would degrade the intellect and erode the moral character of society. This argument was later directed at genre fiction in the 20th century, as a new canon of classic literature cemented to exclude subjects like romance, science fiction, and fantasy. Most recently, we've seen gatekeepers regard graphic novels as the new threat to "real reading." And yes, even as comics and graphic novels have taken over popular culture, even as they begin to be taught on college campuses, even as they are increasingly the subject of scholarly examination, there continue to be those who look upon the medium as something unfit for libraries. I would ask that anyone resistant to the idea of comics as literature consider the aforementioned historical comparisons when they think about whether to include graphic novels in their collection. I would also ask that they remember one of the key mandates of being a librarian: *To provide a book for every reader.* We have to meet our readers where they are. If your patrons are being denied something they want or need based on your personal preferences, you're doing them a disservice, no matter how well intentioned you may be. Consider this an exercise in moving beyond your sphere to provide quality material that you may not be interested in or even strictly approve of, and remember that comics can be a gateway into non-graphic literature, if that is your priority.

Image seems to offer a lot of diversity in its titles from diverse creators. Would you say that diversity is a value at Image, or does it happen naturally since it is a company that fosters creator-owned content?

Diversity is a core value at Image Comics. Be it race, ethnicity, gender identity, sexual preference, religious or philosophical outlook, making a space for creators to bring any and every aspect of themselves to bear in their work is something that we encourage as part of our inclusive philosophy. For now, I think creator-owned and independent publishers are doing a better job at fostering representative content, simply because "individual voice as value" isn't a concept that is universally compatible with the "comics as commodity" business model of the larger publishing houses. Thankfully, the diverse purchasing habits of libraries working to reflect their patron demographics in a more equitable manner has a positive effect on the publishing landscape overall, because those habits reinforce the need for more representative content to be produced in order to keep pace with demand.

Have you seen any changes come about, either in libraries or in comics, from librarians listening to comics creators and comics creators listening to libraries?

I've seen the level of engagement grow and blossom quite a bit in a relatively short time. It's really encouraging. In many instances, creators are shocked that libraries know or even care about their content and librarians are shocked that creators want to collaborate on programming. When you put the two groups together, they naturally complement and strengthen each other's work. In some ways, it's been like watching two people realize they were always destined to be friends . . . and that's pretty fantastic.[10]

Archie Comics

Archie Comics is one of the oldest comics publishers still in business, nearly as old as DC. Archie's selection of family-friendly titles that focus mostly on teenage characters didn't diversify much over the decades, offering characters such as Archie Andrews and friends, Sabrina the Teenage Witch, Josie and the Pussycats, and, until 2018, Sonic the Hedgehog. Recently, however, Archie has offered adult comics featuring new twists on their classic characters, including horror favorites like *Afterlife with Archie* and *Chilling Adventures of Sabrina*, both written by Roberto Aguirre-Sacasa with art by Francesco Francavilla and Robert Hack, respectively, and even *Archie vs. Predator* by Alex de Campi and Fernando Ruiz! Archie characters have appeared in movies and on television, such as teen drama hit *Riverdale* and the hit Netflix series *Chilling Adventures of Sabrina* based on the above mentioned title.

Dark Horse Comics

Established in 1986 by a former comic shop owner, Dark Horse publishes a wide variety of comics including superhero, noir, manga, and much more. Some of the more popular franchises to sprout from Dark Horse are *The Mask* by John Arcudi, *Hellboy* by Mike Mignola, *Sin City* by Frank Miller, and the publisher is well-known for their licensed works such as *Buffy the Vampire Slayer, Aliens, Avatar: The Last Airbender,* and even *Star Wars* before Marvel purchased Lucasfilm. Dark Horse releases many of its comics in hardcover Library Editions, which are perfectly sized and priced for library acquisition.

IDW Publishing

IDW offerings are incredibly diverse for various genres and age groups, thanks to the company's many imprints including Top Shelf Productions, which publishes many creator-owned titles such as *March* by John Lewis, and *The Library of American Comics,* which reprints classic comic strips of yesteryear, including those owned by other comics publishers such as Disney and Archie. IDW also heavily relies on licensed material for their comics, such as Transformers, My Little Pony, and Godzilla, and they even announced a recent partnership with Marvel to publish YA comics featuring Marvel characters (IDW 2018).

Valiant Comics

Often regarded as an underdog in the superhero comics world, Valiant was formed in 1989 by former Marvel creator, Jim Shooter, and it is a publisher to keep your eye on. They have been receiving much recognition lately with multiple Harvey nominations, YALSA highlights, and more, and their characters, such as Zephyr from the series *Faith*, a female superhero who breaks the mold by being plus-sized, may be headed for stardom as Valiant has signed a four-picture deal with Sony to make movies about Valiant characters (McNary 2018).

First Second Books

This publisher is possibly the most library friendly, especially to you school libraries out there. First Second offers the widest array of comics in particular subjects that would otherwise be considerable gaps in comics collections. They publish fiction that is often diverse and fits the #OwnVoices movement, as well as an impressive amount of nonfiction. Some of their notable titles are *American Born Chinese* by Gene Luen Yang, the *Science Comics* series, and *The Prince and the Dressmaker* by Jen Wang. If you're looking to fill the subjects on your shelf, whether those be nonfiction or diversity offerings, such as LGBT, take a look at First Second's catalog.

Fantagraphics

This publisher doesn't have a lot of kid's stuff, and that's just fine. Fantagraphics prides itself on offering alternative comics that fit the independent beat, including erotica through their Eros Comix label, which often results in a very diverse catalog. They are also prone to collecting and reprinting old comic strips, such as *Peanuts* and *Little Nemo,* which are perfect for nostalgia readers. Fantagraphics is well known for originally publishing Chris Ware's *Jimmy Corrigan, the Smartest Kid on Earth* in its serial format and has had recent success with *My Favorite Thing Is Monsters* by Emil Ferris.

Graphix

Graphix is an imprint of Scholastic, and their just-for-kids graphic novels are very popular with juvenile readers. Graphix got its start by publishing the color editions of Jeff Smith's *Bone* and since then has gone on to publish other popular titles such as *Smile* by Raina Telgemeier, *Dog Man* by Dav Pilkey, and *Amulet* by Kazu Kibuishi. These graphic novels are very library friendly, usually available in hardcover, which is no surprise since they are published by a traditional publishing house.

Humanoids

Beginning as a comics magazine with roots in France, Humanoids is best known for publishing *Heavy Metal.* Humanoids content is generally for adult audiences with emphasis on speculative fiction. Along with the magazine, Humanoids also publishes original graphic novels from well-known creators as well as debut creators.

WHO READS THESE THINGS?

Comics are often thought of as kids' stuff. While it's true that many, if not most, comics are created to be at least youth-accessible, if not youth-friendly, the vast majority of comics fall into what we in the library and publishing worlds would consider the YA category. However, the vast bulk of comic readers are not young adults. The majority of comic readers are actually in their thirties (Pawuk 2007). According to surveys conducted of comic shops, most comic shop visitors are also in their thirties (Rogers 2017). And according to a similar survey, most comic convention attendees are ages 30–49 (Macdonald 2014a). If this surprises you, you're not alone; this is yet one other way that comic readers are unique. A medium that began primarily for kids and is now published mostly for a young adult audience is primarily read by an adult audience bordering on middle age. There is a bevy of theories of why this is, ranging from the effect of the direct market to the ever-rising price tags to competition from video games, which now also provide the complexity of storytelling and escapism that comics provide. Is there another medium that libraries carry that is dominantly targeted to an audience of one age group but dominantly read by another? Not one this writer can think of.

This oddity in readership can create opportunity, however. This is both part of the weirdness and wonder of comics. People within wildly different age groups, potentially parents and their children, can travel to the comic shop or library for the exact same comic, anxious to find out what happens next in the serial adventures of their shared favorite character. Comics are reading material that can act as an intergenerational bridge, but in a strikingly different way than other media; these current adult readers didn't grow up and grow out of comics, they simply got older and kept reading. Compare this to, say, picture books. A parent may share a picture book that they read as a child with their own children, but the parent has likely grown far beyond reading picture books. Comic-loving parents may very well buy two copies of a comic; one for themselves and one for their child, both enjoying the same material, often with the same exuberance. Comics invite adults to stay young. The trick for the comics industry right now, though, is attracting newer, younger readers and maintaining their loyalty as they did with the previous generation. Libraries may be in a perfect position to help with this, as we will discuss throughout this book.

Comic readers are just as unique as the medium they love. As expert and librarian, Francisca Goldsmith, says, "they are sophisticated consumers of image-based communications" (Goldsmith 2005). Comic readers have a tendency to be very informed about their particular brand of reading material, often knowing more background information of the particular comic they are enjoying than a reader of traditional novels would about their preferred work. Many comic readers will come to the library knowing exactly what they are looking for and will often know who wrote it, who illustrated it, the story arc title, and sometimes they'll even know roughly when it was published and the issue or volume number. This isn't always the case, though. Not all comic readers are as informed as others. Some comic readers may need your help finding a title. They may have bare minimum information, such as plot points or even just cover details. It is not unusual for a comics seeker to ask a question such as, "Do you have the book where Norman Osborne becomes the Red Goblin?" or "Can you find the book that has the Joker holding his own severed face on the cover?" Many comic fans will have just enough information to get you started, just like typical readers' advisory scenarios.

Of course, answering the question of "Who Reads These Things" is actually a bit of a trick question. You see, the answer should and could be everyone and anyone. As librarians, you must remember a very important type of comic reader; the *potential* comic reader. Someone who has never picked up a comic in their life can become the next big comic reader. Ask any lifetime comic geek and they'll tell you, it can all start with a single issue. All it takes is one story, or, often, just a snippet of a story, to get a reader hooked. You may find a potential comic reader in the young child who is just learning to read, or in the science fiction lover, or in the older child who is a struggling or reluctant reader. You may find that fans of nonfiction and memoir can suddenly become hooked on comics when they pick up a memoir in graphic style and are willing to try something new. Because comics is a format, exposing traditional readers to comics can open a new world for them and bring a new champion into the comic realm.

PROFESSIONAL/SCHOLARLY ENTITIES

There may be those who still think comics are just for kids, but there are professional and scholarly organizations composed of very educated experts who would disagree. The members of these organizations have dedicated their time, energy, and critical minds to proving that comics deserve to be taken seriously and are an artistic and literary force worthy of attention. Comics studies has become an accepted field of academics in many colleges and universities around the world. See Chapter 3 for a list of scholarly sources and Chapter 9 for a list of professional organizations.

Awards

Just like other media, the comics industry and comics critics have awards that are bestowed upon the best that comics has to offer. Here are a few examples.

- **Bill Finger Award:** Named after the co-creator of Batman, this award is specifically for comic writers. First awarded in 2005.
- **Harvey Awards:** Named for comic creator Harvey Kurtzman, there are a variety of Harvey Awards for different roles in comic creation, which are voted upon by comic professionals. First awarded in 1988.
- **Ignatz Awards:** This award is given during the Small Press Expo (SPX), which focuses on independent comic creators. First awarded by Small Press Expo in 1997.
- **Inkpot Awards:** This is an award for comic creators but also for those who contribute to pop culture in general and is given by Comic-Con International during San Diego Comic-Con. First awarded in 1974.
- **Pulitzer Prize for Editorial Cartooning:** This Pulitzer is dedicated to political cartoons and political comics, sometimes a single cartoon or sometimes multiple cartoons throughout a year. First awarded in 1922.
- **Reuben Award:** Granted annually by the National Cartoonists Society to a nominated creator for a specific work. First awarded in 1946.
- **Will Eisner Comic Industry Awards:** Often referred to as the "Eisner Awards" or simply the "Eisners," this is often considered the most prestigious of awards for comic creators. Like the Harvey Awards, there are multiple categories for works and creator roles and they are voted upon by industry professionals. Named after legendary creator Will Eisner and first awarded in 1988. In 2019, the GNCRT was kind enough to divide the Eisner Award nominees by age group to make them more relevant for librarians.

Spotlight on Mark Waid, Eisner Award-Winning Creator and Library Supporter

Mark, you've been in comics for a long time. What would you like librarians and educators to know about you, your career, and about comics?

That comics are not just superhero comics. Those terms are not interchangeable. Comics is a medium, superheroes is a genre. I fear there are librarians who still think all comics are all "bam, pow, and zap," unaware how drastically that paradigm has changed in the last 15 years or so.

As far as my career goes, I started reading comics when I was 4 years old, Batman specifically, and that was my introduction to literature and the written word. I formed a love for those characters at an early age, and it stayed with me, even after I discovered girls and cars. I always knew I wanted to be involved professionally with comics somehow, but I pictured myself as an editor not a writer; it never occurred to me that I would be capable of coming up with stories every month. I did, in fact, begin as an editor in '87, and it was a writing boot camp. So many scripts from good writers came across my desk that I learned more about writing in my two years as an editor than I would have in ten years on my own. Once I left and went freelance, I've been insanely lucky that I haven't had to look for a job since. I've worked for every single major comic company, even some that aren't around anymore. I've even worked in the self-published and creator-owned area with *Thrillbent,* which is an online company I started with Hollywood writer John Rogers that features original webcomics.

How have libraries had an impact on your life and career?

They've had an enormous impact. I read comics growing up, but they weren't the only things I read. I grew up in rural Alabama in the '60s, bookstores weren't everywhere, and my family didn't have near enough money to keep me afloat in all the books I could read. I spent countless hours in school libraries. I would spend a couple of hours after school every day in the public library waiting for my parents, scarfing down books the entire time.

Do you believe comics can be a source for social change?

Absolutely. They speak to readers at a young, impressionable age in a way that other media don't. The beauty of comics as a medium is that it's a very private experience, unlike watching a TV show or movie. With other visual media, the story sets the pace uniformly, without regard to how quickly or slowly an audience member can (or wants to) take in the story. But comics are designed to be read at your own pace, which makes it more personal and thus more penetrative. That makes what you receive from the experience—a moral message, an emotion, something to think about, whatever— even more meaningful.

Having been in the industry a long time, you have no doubt seen a lot of change in comics. Which of these changes make you happy, and which of these changes are you perhaps not so fond of?

I'll start with the negative, which would be the continuing narrowing of distribution of comics. When I was introduced to comics, they were still available on the newsstands and could be found for sale in many places. Now in the 21st century, we've unfortunately successfully turned a mass medium into a niche market. Now, you have to find comics exclusively in comics shops (or better libraries!) to become an avid reader. Fortunately, digital access is slowly changing this. On the other hand, the biggest positive change I've seen has been the huge rise in comics diversity among creators. There's a long, long way to go, but when I first started as a professional, almost all comics were done by—and made for—white males. I must say it's not like there was gatekeeping happening *on purpose* in the past, but most comics were also produced by people who grew up loving comics. That created a vicious cycle. The industry wasn't diverse, but why would you expect a huge number of women or people of color to be banging on the door to get in when for decades this stuff wasn't written with characters in which they could see themselves? The good news is that in the last ten years especially, things have improved, and more readers are being represented and thus new creators are more diverse; it's a new cycle. While I cannot stress strongly enough that there's still huge room for improvement, it's all trending in the right direction.

For you, what is the difference between a comic and a graphic novel?

To my mind, the only difference is the physical format. When we say "comic book," we mean the monthly, flimsy periodical magazine, whereas "graphic novel" is the general term for a bound collection of those flimsy comic books into a single volume. That, however, isn't completely accurate; a true graphic novel tells us a story from beginning to end, like the works of Raina Telgemeier, which I know are popular in libraries. Comics by and large are serial storytelling in action, and superhero graphic novels in particular tend to be installments in the lives of characters.

I understand you are an avid library supporter. Have you participated in any library events?

Many times. I've been lucky enough to be invited by libraries to speak about comics and how the medium has evolved. There was an event here in LA a few years back that was attended by hundreds of people, and that was very exciting. It was a discussion about the origins of comics, a brief history, and most critically how they are relevant to today.

As you may know, libraries resisted carrying comics for decades. As a library patron and a comic creator, what would you say to librarians who are still reluctant to support comics?

I would encourage them to try and shake off the misconception that comics are just for adolescents or just for boys or just superheroes. Look at a wider range of materials. There is really no difference between what Raina does and what other comics creators do—it's all storytelling. I've noticed some librarians will latch onto her work or Alison Bechdel's, for instance, and I'm thrilled—when I was growing up, librarians all had blue hair and saw comics as sub-literature (and they weren't necessarily wrong). Today's librarians are the same men and women who were reading comics as kids, and they know there are comics and graphic novels for every age, demographic, and interest.

Is there something more you would like to see libraries do for the comics industry?

I think that libraries are doing enormous work on our behalf now. It encourages me that sales to libraries have become a crucial part of comics publishers' business models. Humanoids, DC Comics, Marvel, and others are working hard to be accessible to that market, a change from the past 10 years when comics publishers didn't find it inviting. The best thing that libraries can do is to continue to buy graphic novels.

Is there something more you would like to see the comics industry do for libraries?

I would like us to continue to publish a greater variety of graphic novels that are original and not just collections of already existing material, but for most publishers it's not economically feasible. Right now, the publishers' main source of income is from comic stores, and comic stores' lifeblood is the monthly comic books. That's what keeps the vast majority of their customers coming in—the need for that "weekly fix." Humanoids is publishing original graphic novels with libraries in mind, but that's only because comic stores aren't essential to their business model, giving them more flexibility than major publishers like Marvel and DC.

What do you think the future holds for comics?

I think the future really is a shift away from the monthly periodicals and into the graphic novel format. I think that arc is longer than is ideal, but it is the future. We are now a culture that is trained to be binge-watchers. Monthly comic books don't allow for that unless they're collected as graphic novels, and as the consumer base becomes more and more acclimated to that format, original graphic novels can become more economically viable.[11]

A BRIEF HISTORY OF COMICS

The Golden Age (1938–1954)[12]

If you want to maximize comics in your library, it's important to understand them. As librarian and comics historian Alicia Holston says, "In order to understand something, one has to study its history. Likewise, understanding the history of graphic novels and how they developed is key to understanding the medium in its current form, and its cultural impact" (2010). Take, for example, the different "Ages" of comics. According to William T. Fee, a leader in the discussion of how to best provide library access to comics, he proclaims that knowledge of the different "Ages" of comics is important to take into account when choosing how to organize them (Fee 2008). Some "Ages"[13] of comics tend to be filled with darker, more violent material. Some older comics have become dated in their sensibilities, meaning that though they may have been inoffensive and kid-friendly during their time, they may not be considered suitable for a school-age reading level now, for a multitude of reasons. These comics, which would likely show up at a library as a trade, should probably not be shelved in "juvenile," even if it does feature Superman with an old-fashioned appearance. Considering this, let's use the next few pages to learn a very brief and summarized version of the rich history of comics so to further our understanding of them.

The first comic character and first example of a comic as we know it, sequential art, is Richard F. Outcault's *The Yellow Kid*, which appeared in 1895, and from these humble beginnings sprung an artistic revolution, providing new opportunities for artists such as cartoonists and writers to explore a new medium (Van Lente and Dunlavey 2012). Comic strips swiftly became popular in publications across the United States, and soon enough these comic strips were collected and reprinted in a magazine-style format, becoming the first comic books around 1933. Before long, publishers sought to create original material to be published in comic books rather than reprinted strips.

In 1933, two Jewish Cleveland high schoolers had an idea. Jerry Siegel, the writer, and Joe Shuster, the artist, had an idea for a character they called the Superman. Inspired by the look of circus strongmen, they sketched a chiseled-chinned human-like alien immigrant-to-America with incredible strength. This powerful immigrant would fight against injustice and stand for those who cannot stand for themselves, with each of the young men injecting a little bit of himself into the character: Jerry's desire to prevent the type of crime that he believed killed his father and Joe's desire to be strong (Ricca 2013). He is the Man of Steel, the Man of Tomorrow, who "fights for Truth, Justice, and the American Way" with the help of his secret identity, mild-mannered reporter Clark Kent.

Though comics did not begin with the superhero, superheroes can call comics their home medium and helped push comics into what they are, the two being forever entwined. For all intents and purposes, Jerry Siegel and Joe Schuster created the superhero and this, as far as libraries are concerned, is where the story of the comic begins.[14] The publication of *Action Comics* #1 in 1938, the first appearance of Superman, kicked off what we call today the Golden Age of Comics. This was when comics became dominated by superheroes and were, by and large, intended for children. By the 1940s, 90% of all the children in America were reading comics of some sort (Tilley 2014). Some were regaling to the adventures of these colorful heroes who battled crime and injustice, including those with a particularly patriotic persuasion, battling real-world villains like Nazis, or giggling over more comical comic fare like the antics of Archie Andrews.

FIGURE 1.5. A comic book that was released in 1938, the same year as Superman's debut. Comic books featured genres of all kinds, including crime, Western, science fiction, and more.

As it became clearer that the Allied forces were going to win the war, interest in the superhero began to wane. The world was at relative peace, and there was no longer a need for men and women of superior strength and skill to fight the good fight. The comic readers were growing up, and their comics began to grow with them, the content becoming more mature. Superheroes were pushed aside to make way for crime and horror stories, featuring buckets of violence, glorified sex, and gore galore. The trouble was, the readers of these newly matured comics still included many, many children who were irresistibly drawn to the mature content, as children are wont to do.

Enter Dr. Fredric Wertham, a psychiatrist who made a (now oft-regarded erroneous) connection between comics and juvenile delinquency. Wertham made it his singular goal to discredit comics and to reveal how harmful he believed them to be, appearing before Congress and testifying to the medium's detrimental effect on children.[15] The public turned against comics, and comics publishers, particularly those who still published superhero comics, devised a solution that would win back the public's trust as well as allow them a chance to capitalize on the current situation. These publishers created the Comics Code Authority in 1954, a self-regulating board that dictated what content could, and could not, be published in comics. Some of the banned material included various forms of crime, violence, horror, sexuality, and more. The publishers of superhero comics found a way to suppress their competition as well as protect comics from the threat of government intervention. The issue was complicated, to say the least.

The landscape of comics changed, with horror and crime comics being affected the most by the Comics Code, and just a few superheroes (notably Superman, Batman, and Wonder Woman) keeping superhero comics afloat, along with wholesome kids and teen titles like *Archie* and comic strips that were still popular in newspapers. Many of these remaining superhero titles were saturated to fit the new Comics Code Authority standards, with any perceived offensive material or any content that was perceived to espouse nontraditional values removed. Wonder Woman, in particular, was altered immensely during this period, to be less of an independent emissary who preached to change the world of Man with a message of love, and instead fading into a sort of reverse-Superman; her alter ego, Diana Prince, sought nothing more than to marry her love Steve Trevor and one day set the superhero stuff aside (Hanley 2014).[16] The Golden Age of Comics had passed, and comics, especially superheroes, weren't what they used to be.

The Silver Age (1956–1970)

With the Comics Code Authority firmly in place and its influence cemented, its effect on comics was evident. Unable to do superheroes the same way and unable to do horror stories at all, comics publishers needed new directions to take their tales and freshen them up. This new direction came in the form of science fiction. The beginnings of the space race were taking place, with stories of space adventures dominating most other media since the launch of Sputnik (Van Lente and Dunlavey 2012). Science fiction became the new go-to adventure for children, with fantastic space-spanning fare becoming a genre unto itself. It was only natural for comics to follow suit.

Superheroes had changed, but some writers found the opportunity in the challenge, and began turning their superheroes toward science fiction. Batman and Wonder Woman found themselves faced, more and more, against sinister space monsters, cosmic robots, criminals from other planets, and other extraterrestrial threats. This turn in narrative wasn't as jostling for Superman, whose origins were already science fiction-based before science fiction was fully understood as its own genre. But soon, other heroes would take a turn to science fiction, heroes that were no longer around and would be resurrected quite unexpectedly in the fledgling realm of sci-fi adventure.

The Flash was a Golden Age superhero possessed of superspeed who was retired from publication in 1951. But thanks to creators who could read the new terrain, the Flash was brought back with a new science fiction-filled origin. This, along with the sci-fi resurrection of fellow hero Green Lantern, kicked off what would come to be known as the Silver Age of Comics. The Silver Age of Comics was marked by notable differences in tone and content that would influence superheroes, and more importantly comics as a whole, for decades to come.

During the Golden Age, one of the many comics companies that emerged was Timely Comics. Timely brought us characters such as Namor the Sub-Mariner and Captain America. But Timely didn't survive as well as DC and Archie, and it slowly withered away. That is until an editor, already a middle-aged man, had some ideas. Ideas that he was able to get off the ground and into print. He went from being a lowly mailroom worker to essentially the face of what would become Marvel Comics, which he remains, unofficially, and not without criticism today.[17] That man was Stan Lee.

Stan Lee and artist Jack Kirby developed an idea for a new group of superheroes that would put a spin on the genre in 1961. They created superheroes with normal human problems, making their heroes deal with everyday issues that readers could understand, especially those Golden Age readers who were now adults. But these heroes would still engage in fantastic, space-faring, derring-do that thrilled the younger readers. The first heroes of this kind were called the Fantastic Four, and they were four super-powered beings who were also a family. This came with all the familial complications of bickering, jealousy, and so on, and their superpowers were not always beneficial. Lee and Kirby could have no way of knowing just how their new brand of hero would change the comics industry forever.

This was the beginning of the Marvel Comics we know today. Lee would continue to collaborate with the likes of Kirby, Steve Ditko, and more in creating superheroes that would go on decades later to become household names and billion-dollar blockbusters at the movie theater. This includes Spider-Man, the X-Men, Iron Man, the Hulk, Thor, Dr. Strange, and the Avengers, to name just a few. Marvel characters typically aren't the larger-than-life modern myths that the DC heroes of the Golden Age were. The characters were written as grounded, many street level, living in real-world cities like New York instead of fictional cities like Gotham or Metropolis, and these heroes dealt with real-world problems such as dating, paying the rent, getting to work on time, and other mundane, grown-up things. Some of the characters are known and loved just as much for their alter egos as they are for their superhero identities, and their everyday drama, such as their love lives, relationships with supporting characters, their day jobs, and so on, brought in the readers each month just as often as their world-saving adventures.

DC Comics lit the fire that began the Silver Age, but it was Marvel who cranked up the burner. What resulted was a decade of invigorating comics trends that shocked the medium for the better. Comics had become more sophisticated, more personal, more mature, with a science fiction bend, and these changes were just the beginning. This superhero renaissance became something of an arms race between the two big comic publishers, with each trying to up the ante on the other with sophisticated stories that became edgier and darker. The Comics Code began to feel the first instances of resistance and push-back as comics creators decided to use comics as canvases for sociopolitical messages and new American values.

Comics have always been political. It's safe to say anyone who suggests otherwise simply doesn't know their comic history.[18] Many of the Golden Age superheroes have their very roots in the war effort as anti-Nazi propaganda. Captain America's first appearance portrays him famously punching Hitler, an image that has seen a resurgence in recent years, and his two Jewish creators, Joe Simon and the just-mentioned Jack Kirby, were quite possibly using art to promote the idea that the United States should join the war effort against the Nazis (Ackerman 2017). The politics of Marston's Wonder Woman were his own politics, as he believed in women's superiority; she is an immigrant ambassador to man's world, here to show us the way to peace, which involves, appropriately enough, also tossing around Nazis. And then of course there is Superman; a man who immigrated to this planet, but more specifically the United States, as a baby and contributes his many talents to the betterment of society. Superman is the ultimate pro-immigrant story which, many would argue, makes it a very American story. Comics and political cartoons are cousin artforms, after all (Van Lente and Dunlavey 2012).

And the political posturing of comics simply exploded during the Silver Age, as this was now the 1960s, a hotbed of political activity from equality movements, anti-war sentiment, and so on. Race relations were a near-constant topic being tackled across the country, and comic creators began to use their medium to throw in their two cents. The X-Men are one perfect example of these politics at play, as the merry Mutants who fight to protect a world that fears and hates them are, according to Stan Lee himself, an allegory for the Civil Rights Movement and the oppression of minorities (Karpf 2017). Superheroes of color began to appear, such as the Black Panther and the Falcon and more would follow in the 1970s. More female characters began to appear in comic books; they were not generally headlining their own series, like Wonder Woman, but they were increasing in number and appearing as members of super teams like the X-Men and Avengers. Wonder Woman herself spent much of the 1960s pining over Steve Trevor, but a new era was approaching for her and other female superheroes[19] on the horizon.

The Silver Age, thanks to the influence of Marvel in particular, molded comics and especially superheroes into the forms that we know them today; rather than being larger than life, the characters are every-day people who are granted incredible powers and must reconcile those powers with their ordinary lives in stories that are often socially relevant and grounded in reality. Silver Age superheroes are superhumans with human problems, and comics have rarely looked back since.

The Bronze Age (1970–1985)

As comics entered the 1970s, they maintained many of the same conventions established in the Silver Age, such as superheroes who faced everyday human problems, real-world settings, and tackling relevant social issues. This latter quality would escalate in the Bronze Age, as would a darker tone for many of the stories appearing in comics. Social issues such as racism, sexism, poverty, and drug abuse became more frequent and were less and less being written with veiled, kid-friendly symbolism.

The 1970s saw the introduction of even more superheroes of color, including Luke Cage (AKA Power Man), Vixen, Storm, Blade, John Stewart (AKA Green Lantern), and Black Lightning. Many of these characters' stories tackled racism and inequality head-on, while still finding time to include a supervillain or two. Wonder Woman and other female characters saw a roller coaster of changes during the Silver Age,[20] as the feminist movement kicked in to full swing and the female superheroes began to reflect the very tumultuous issues of real-world women, even if it was sometimes unintentional.

Comic creators were gradually pushing back against the Comics Code, and this became evident in the way comics tackled the issue of drugs. Famously, the US government approached Marvel Comics about publishing a comic that would warn young readers about the dangers of drug addiction. Agreeing, *The Amazing Spider-Man* featured a story in 1971 that sees Harry Osborn, best friend of Spider-Man alias Peter Parker, become addicted to drugs, and the issue was printed without approval from the Comics Code. The creators behind the Green Lantern/Green Arrow comic followed suit and published a story in which the heroes discover that Green Arrow's sidekick, Speedy, has become addicted to heroin. Rather than a scourge upon society that the government sought to neutralize, as comics were often seen by the end of the Golden Age, comics had become a cultural source of powerful morals through story, and the government recognized its potential as a force for sending messages to the youth of the country.

Thanks to these powerful stories that sought to be forces of social responsibility, the Comics Code's rigidity began to wane. Other content banned by the Code, especially the portrayal of vampires and other monsters, began creeping its way back into comics. Thanks to this, the 1970s saw the return of vampires, werewolves, and other monstrosities in comic form with such titles as *Tomb of Dracula, Werewolf by Night, Swamp Thing,* and more. In retrospect, this was the beginning of the end for the Comics Code, though it still had a few decades left. Hard-hitting social issues and drugs were evident of comics becoming darker, but they were the tip of the iceberg, as the stories "The Death of Gwen Stacey" in *The Amazing Spider-Man* and "The Dark Phoenix Saga" in *The Uncanny X-Men* featured murder, suicide, and saw superheroes (and their readers) suffer incredible loss by portraying the deaths of long-standing characters.

The Modern Age (1986–present)

In the Modern Age, deconstruction is the name of the game. Alan Moore's *Watchmen* and Frank Miller's *The Dark Knight Returns,* two superhero comics that acted as deconstructions of superhero comics, kicked off the Modern Age in 1986 and have had a lasting impact on comics ever since. These books and their many imitators later declared that comics were no longer for kids, and the stories, tones, themes, and characters became much darker. Comics, despite the Comics Code still in place, were stepping further and further into adult territory, with increased violence, adult language, politics, and sexual content. Much of this has to do with comics becoming far more critical of themselves, with comic creators deconstructing the staples and tropes of the characters as well as the industry itself right in the pages. Though Moore and Miller were hardly the first to deconstruct superheroes in superhero comics, as it had been done decades earlier, they absolutely popularized the grisly route of doing so (Van Lente and Dunlavey 2012). The theme that developed in the Silver Age, superhumans with human problems, met its logical but extreme conclusion with these works, which portray superheroes with such human failings as emotional and psychological disorders, corruptive hubris stemming from their great power, and simple human pride and jealousy.

The 1990s carried on many of these dark and serious tones, but also brought what many would consider to be hyper sexualization, especially of female characters (Hanley 2017). The 1990s featured comics full of violence, guns, a turn to characters who were considered antiheroes, and the female characters were often drawn and portrayed in objectified ways, including very revealing outfits and unrealistic measurements. Franchises that were once bright and optimistic found themselves diverting to the more violent trend, including the *X-Men* franchise, which saw the addition of a spin-off, *X-Force,* featuring a lead character (called Cable) with big guns and a cast of other characters baring claws and a variety of bladed weapons. This is also the era that brought us the character who would become an R-Rated superhero movie sensation, Deadpool.

Something far more important happened to comics besides the ubiquity of the darkness and gritty violence, and that is the acceptance of the idea that comics had literary and artistic merit. Art Spiegelman published his work *Maus* in book form in 1986, and it would go on to win the Pulitzer Prize and have its own influence on the medium. Though the term "graphic novel" is often credited to legendary creator Will Eisner as early as 1978 (Levitz 2015), it was the Modern Age that saw the term become popularized as an alternative to "comics," which sounded more sophisticated. We discussed this term earlier in the chapter, but it was during this time that reviewers, bookstores, and, yes, many librarians began using "graphic novel" in their fields to grant the medium legitimacy. What really matters, though, is that *Maus* and its contemporaries helped solidify the idea that comics were worthy of critical attention and had intellectual merit (Cavna 2016).

This is also the era when the idea of comics collectability hit its peak on a national scale, to the detriment of the industry. Comics had, for some time, been known as a hobby and as collectible items, with many older comics selling for hundreds or even thousands of dollars. But during the 1990s, this concept truly hit the public consciousness, and the comic industry took notice and capitalized on the idea. Single issue comics were created that were labeled as collectibles, with phrases like, "Milestone" or "Collector's Item." New series were pumped out so as to create a variety of "first issues," that consumers would gobble up in the hopes that the comics would be worth a great deal of money someday, even if the "first issue" in question was simply a supporting character getting his or her own series or a character getting a new series who had been around for years (e.g., *X-Men* #1 or *Spider-Man* #1). Fancy covers became all the rage; lenticular, holographic, chromium, and so on, all added to the "collectability" of the comics. Crossover events, such as *Crisis on Infinite Earths* for DC or *Secret Wars* for Marvel, became standard during this time, another way to make comics collectible and increase sales. One big event in particular made international news headlines and sent the country into a fervor of comics sales; the *Death of Superman*. This story spanned the various *Superman* books and caused lines of people outside of comic shops, people who had not bought a comic in years or perhaps had never purchased a comic ever. The assumption was that this *Death of Superman* story would be worth a fortune someday.[21]

But there was a problem with these various collectible issues; the comic publishers published too many of them. With thousands of consumers buying thousands of comics under the impression that these issues would be rare and valuable someday, neither of these outcomes were possible. In fact, the issues were so prevalent, they were rendered nearly worthless despite their assumed value as collectibles. Comic retailers were left with too many of these issues, unable to resell them for any amount of profit and consumers were unable to resell them either. This caused the bubble to burst on the comics industry, causing some crippling effects for the publishers (Raviv 2002).[22] The collectability of 1990s comics is rarer than the comics themselves; issues that were advertised as special collector's items, such as the aforementioned *X-Men* #1 and *Spider-Man* #1, can now often be found at comic shops and book stores in the $1 bins.

While the Big Two publishers (DC and Marvel) were rolling in various crises, milestones, and other big events, the important world of independent comics began to bubble to the surface. Comix, those underground, often self-published titles that tended to lean more toward adult content, increased in popularity, allowing more voices to express themselves in comicdom and eventually spawning mainstream successes like *Teenage Mutant Ninja Turtles*. On the other side of the independent comic coin, the first major publisher to give the Big Two a run for their money in decades appeared. Image Comics was formed from former Marvel creators who wanted to own their work and use Image more akin to a traditional publisher, rather than the work for hire model at Marvel and DC. Since then, Image has seen massive success and creators who have published their work through Image have given us multimedia franchises, such as *The Walking Dead,* and works of critical acclaim like *Saga*.

The 1990s also saw another type of competition to not just Marvel and DC but to all American comics and superheroes in general explode into the fray. Manga, which means "comic" in Japan, had its first interactions with the English-speaking world as early as World War II, but the Modern Age saw its readership with English-speaking audiences expand immensely (McCarthy 2014). Manga has an incredibly rich and complex history in its native country, but for our purposes they are simply comics that are originally created in Japan, fit a particular style, and are then translated into English. This is not to be confused with anime, which is animated features that fit a similar art style and are translated or dubbed into English, though the confusion can be easy to make. After all, manga and anime share the same fanbase for the most part, and many manga titles become an anime and vice versa.

Manga filled an important gap in comics readership. One of the first manga titles to make its way to American shores, *Barefoot Gen*, was imported in 1978, and over the next two decades the style would become a dominating force in American publishing (Cornog and Perper 2009). As previously discussed, many 1990s comics were full of violence and hyper-sexualized female characters. Manga appealed to readers who were looking for something different and who were perhaps turned off by the exploitation of the female body in American comics and the overt violence.[23] Manga offered more titles featuring female leads and an array of different genres and subgenres, such as *Sailor Moon*, and the plethora of titles could appeal to girls, boys, and other demographics that American comics were missing (Cornog and Perper 2009). These included mysteries and romances, making many of these offerings more appealing to female readers, such as *Fruits Basket*. In fact, manga is mostly divided into two categories: Shonen and Shojo (see definitions earlier in this chapter).

Though American comics have finally been targeting the readership gap that manga helped to fill by including titles that are more diverse, inclusive, and appealing to female readers, manga is still going strong. *My Hero Academia* was one of the top selling comics for 2018 and a manga creator was inducted into the Will Eisner Hall of Fame (Aoki 2018). Manga continues to have high circulations in libraries, both physically and digitally (Osicki 2018). Anime and manga have their own conventions now, separate from typical comic conventions, and seem able to stand on their own two feet as an independent format, unique among comics, an already unique medium.

This leads us to another important element of comics in the Modern Age, one which is a callback to the immense social changes happening during the Silver Age; comics have had a focus on diversity. Beginning with vocal pressure from fanbases who wanted the comic publishers to know that not all their readers are straight, white males and that they would enjoy seeing themselves reflected in comics, comic publishers have made very public efforts to diversify their characters and titles.[24] Now, more than ever before in comics history, readers can find characters in comics who are female, persons of color, LGBT, and so on. The *Ms. Marvel* title for Marvel, featuring a Muslim, Pakistani American teenage girl as the titular hero has been a notable success and the Black Panther movie and recent comic run written by Ta Nehesi-Coates have been critically and financially successful.[25] Other comic publishers have embraced diversity, as well, some much earlier, like Image, whose creator-owned model lent itself very well to more diverse titles, and Archie, who made headlines in 2010 when they introduced Kevin Keller, an LGBT character.

No doubt what has had the largest effect on the comic industry has been comic book movies. Beginning with *X-Men* in the summer of 2000, Hollywood suddenly saw the potential in comic book movies.[26] *X-Men* was the first resounding success for a film based on a Marvel property, and it paved the way for what is approaching two-decades of superhero and comic dominance at the box office. True, films like the 1970s *Superman* and the late 1980s and 1990s *Batman* films were box office sensations, but those characters were already multimedia powerhouses. *X-Men* showed Hollywood that there was a vast sea of untapped intellectual property that would make for potential blockbusters, even with relatively modest budgets, by sticking to the core stories, characterizations, and themes.[27] Soon, other Marvel properties followed, such as *Spider-Man* (2002) and Hollywood started pumping out other comic book properties from other publishers as well, such as a *Batman* reboot (2005), *Hellboy* (2004), *A History of Violence* (2005), and more.

Marvel, who had once been suffering bankruptcy, managed to form their own studio thanks to these successes of their properties, allowing them to make their own movies from their own characters. The first of these Marvel Studios releases were *Iron Man* and *The Incredible Hulk* in the summer of 2008. Since then, Marvel Studios has put out dozens of movies, been purchased by media megacorporation the Walt Disney Company, and other studios have been following suit, including the assembling of DC Entertainment studios. Even comic companies like Valiant have signed agreements with Sony to bring their characters to the big screen (McNary 2018). Superheroes and other comic properties now dominate the box office and the small screen, with comic-based shows appearing on Netflix, Hulu, ABC, Fox, HBO, and most other television networks that can be named.

Of course, the important thing to discuss is the impact this has had on the comics themselves. Some of the impact is predictable; the looks, storylines, and more have all been tweaked from time to time to fit whichever movie is currently big at the box office. This includes giving characters who are normally minor in the comics but breakout hits in the movies their own comics series and any other way the publishers can create synchronicity between the two media as to boost comic sales. More recently, particularly with Marvel, there has been a trend to use the comics as proof-of-concepts for later endeavors, rather than focus on having the comics reflect the movies, allowing the comics to become more experimental and diversified (Moviebob 2017).

This massive comic movie success has some fans (and experts) worried. Big comic movies used to mean a bump in sales for the comics, but creator Michael Uslan who has worked in both comics and comic movies observes, "The biggest comic book movies now have little or zero impact on the comic sales. The movies aren't rescuing the comics; they're replacing them" (Boucher 2018). Creators like Uslan have noticed that with the enormous success of comic book adaptations and superhero properties in other media, and with comic companies becoming multimedia companies, it's the comics that are getting left behind. Comics publishers at least have other media to fall back on these days, but comics retailers are the ones who would truly lose in this scenario.

Comics sales were down 6.5% in 2017, including monthly floppies, trades, and graphic novels (Griepp 2018). Superheroes are thriving at the movie theater but are struggling in the comics pages, their original medium. For Marvel in particular, their "comics sell one-tenth the numbers Marvel expected in the 1960s and 1970s glory days when comic books were cheaper than candy bars and just as easy to find at the nation's newsstands, corner markets, and drugstores" (Boucher 2018). Rising paper and ink prices combined with the competition from other media and other formats have put comics in a bind. With comic books, now often with a price of $4–$6 that take only a half-hour or less to read, potential readers may find the value difficult to see. Meanwhile, a trade or graphic novel may cost between $25–$50 and take an hour and a half to read or less, hardly making them competitors to less expensive forms of entertainment such as a 2-hour movie on Blu-ray for $20 or a novel that entertains for weeks for the same. Comic fans worry what will happen if the comic movie bubble bursts just as the comic book bubble did, and many fear they will be left without comics or comic movies to fall back on. Jim Lee, publisher and artist at DC Comics, notes that comics are suffering from "an over saturation of saturation," which is having a negative impact on sales, similar to the 1990s, but he remains optimistic that comics will pull through (Griepp 2018). Perhaps comics will always be around because, at their core, comics are enormously simple things. "words and pictures," as Todd McFarlane said in the PBS documentary *Superheroes: A Never-Ending Battle,* echoing the sentiments of Scott McCloud and stating that, though the delivery system may change, comics will stay (Kantor 2013).

If comics are in any danger, libraries are perfectly positioned to come to their aide. Indeed, if one looked only at the success comics have had circulating at libraries through physical and digital (another change brought to us by the Modern Age) means, then one would think that comics wholesale must be wildly successful. But what's happening in libraries is not reflective of what's happening in comic stores, and this is important to note. It means that there is still an interest in comics, and, somehow, libraries may be providing that access in a way that is more conducive to the readership. Libraries must not miss this chance to be valuable. Now is the time for any librarians who may be hold-outs to embrace comics. Maximizing the success of comics can maximize the success of libraries. Throughout the rest of the book, we will talk about how to make this happen.

NOTES

1. Karen Green, interview via email by Jack Phoenix, February 18, 2019.
2. John Dudas, in-person interview by Jack Phoenix, April 3, 2019.
3. Karen Green, interview via email by Jack Phoenix, February 18, 2019.
4. Regina Shapiro, panel discussion titled, "Is 741.5 Still Helpful? Challenges and Recommendations for Making Comics and Graphic Novels More Accessible to Users," October 4, 2018.
5. Tim Hanley, email exchange, May 21, 2019.
6. Though "subgenre" is likely more accurate, as superheroes owe their origins to sci-fi and action.
7. Valentino Zullo, discussion, April 26, 2019.
8. Sheila Heinlein, OverDrive staff professional development presentation, 2018.
9. *The Walking Dead* shocked readers and media outlets by coming to a surprise end with issue #193 in July of 2019.
10. Chloe Ramos-Peterson, interview via email by Jack Phoenix, December 14, 2019.
11. Mark Waid, interview via phone by Jack Phoenix, March 3, 2019.
12. It should be noted that the beginnings and ends of the various comic "Ages" are not hard-set and are up for debate, but this is a frequently cited date range.
13. Note the comics "Ages" refer specifically to superhero comics and not the history of the medium itself.
14. Yes, yes, I see you there, fellow comic expert, shaking your head in disapproval. Yes, I am aware that comics existed before Superman; that there were comic strips and other "funnies" appearing in newspapers, dating all the way back to the Yellow Kid. I'm aware that many comics scholars would date the origin of the comic not to America, but to Europe. But, you fabulous fan, there's no denying that comics as we know them, the format of the superhero and beyond, exploded with our good ol' Supes. So, just bear with me here.
15. In his book about Dr. Wertham, Bart Beaty provides a reexamination of Wertham's complex attitudes and motivations toward his criticism of pop culture. Often assumed to be a staunch conservative, Beaty's research into Wertham's life suggests that the psychiatrist may have been far more open-minded

and progressive than he is often depicted, and his views on comics even softened later in his life. Regardless of what we think of his criticisms, Wertham still remains one of the earliest professionals to recognize comics as deserving of a critical eye and a medium to be taken seriously. Bart Beaty, *Fredric Wertham and the Critique of Mass Culture* (Jackson, MS: University Press of Mississippi, 2005).

16. But let's take a moment to talk about an important yet subtle aspect of Wonder Woman that was removed: the bondage imagery. It wouldn't be easy to have avoided the story of Wonder Woman's unique creator, William Maulton Marston, and his beliefs. Marston believed in open sexuality and that humanity would be better off if men surrendered their authority to women, allowing a matriarchy to rule in home and government. Marston frequently expressed this belief (possibly) in sexual bondage in his personal life, and a great deal of bondage imagery found its way into the Wonder Woman comics before Wertham's attacks. According to Tim Hanley, author of *Wonder Woman Unbound,* Wonder Woman was seen bound in some way, usually by villains but sometimes consensually by her fellow Amazons or the Holliday Girls, in 11% of her comic.

17. Stan Lee has been regarded as the face of Marvel for years, being actively used in promotions, appearing on panels about Marvel, and appearing in just about every movie based off a Marvel character you could name. This even persisted long after he left Marvel's employ. Lee was a staple among comics celebrities, one of the most well-known and beloved comics creators, but faced criticism over the decades as being a self-promoter who hogged the spotlight from co-creators (Van Lente and Dunlavey 2012).

18. Long before his more contemporary iterations as the defender of the "American way," Superman, in his earlier appearances, was famously using his might against corrupt and anti-union business moguls, slumlords, domestic abusers, and other politically charged ne'er-do-wells, whom he would callously fling from multistory windows with little to no care for their mortality. Superman also entered the war effort against the Nazis on more than one occasion, though he wasn't as immersed in Axis-smashing as some of his contemporaries.

19. As a personal and professional choice, I tend to shy away from the gendered term "heroine" and stick with superheroes.

20. Be sure to read about Wonder Woman's much-maligned Mod phase in Tim Hanley's book *Wonder Woman Unbound* or check out Scott Niswander's Nerdsync pop-educational video on YouTube for more details on the topic. https://www.youtube.com/watch?v=TS1L9pN9oI8.

21. The documentary *Superheroes*, which aired on PBS, provides a news clip of a woman purchasing the comic in the hopes that it would pay for her child's college education someday.

22. Marvel, which is now a company worth billions, bought by Disney, a household name, and its logo featured in all the movies dominating the box office, actually declared bankruptcy in the 1990s (Raviv 2002).

23. This is not to say, of course, that manga doesn't have its own share of sexualized females and extreme violence in some of its titles. But manga titles

were very diverse in content, and the additional offerings helped to offset the titles that could be seen as exploitative.

24. To a lesser extent, the Big Two publishers of Marvel and DC have also made at least some effort to diversify their creators as well, making it a point in the past two years to hire more people of color, LGBT persons, and female creators. Follow Tim Hanley's Gendercrunching posts on Bleeding Cool.com or his Straightened Circumstances blog to see how they're doing, as he tracks gender diversity in comics regularly. https://thanley.wordpress.com/tag/gender crunching/

25. In 2018, the first issue of Ta Nehisi-Coate's *Captain America* began, so be sure to check it out.

26. There are, of course, many who would argue that the film *Blade* was the first successful Marvel movie. Blade was undeniably a success, and no doubt helped pave the way for future Marvel movies, but *X-Men* is generally regarded by most comic experts as the beginning of the comic Hollywood boom. Unlike the X-Men, Blade was a generally unknown character before the movies and, even after the movie was a success, was not generally linked in the audience's mind to Marvel or to comics.

27. Yes, of course I realize that the *X-Men* movies and nearly all comic movies have made drastic changes from the comic, everything from costumes to accents to motivations to powersets, and so on. But you have to admit, most comic movies stick to the core of what the series and characters are about these days.

2

A Brief History of Comics in Libraries

As librarian and author Matthew Z. Wood said, "Comics and libraries are natural allies" (2018); however, this is a recent development. When the American Library Association adopted the Library Bill of Rights in 1939, which sought to establish libraries as havens for intellectual freedom, many librarians still saw themselves as guardians of the "best reading," and comics, cartoons, or most heavily illustrated materials were not fitting in their eyes (Wiegand 2015). Though the modern librarian unceremoniously vows to combat censorship as a shared professional ethic upon joining the ALA, the idea that this should mean defending comics is a relatively recent one. It has taken librarians far longer to warm up to comics than it did for them to warm up to novels or even movies. Thankfully, looking at any given public library in America today would leave no one with the impression that libraries ever stood with their heels in the ground against comics entering the building, as librarians have become mostly defenders of comics at a time when comics may need defending (see "The Modern Age" in Chapter 1). What follows is a brief history of the relationship between comics and libraries.

THE GOLDEN AGE

When comic books first hit the scene, they were rarely to be found in American public libraries. Librarian and writer about comics Martha Cornog tells us, "American Libraries must have virtually ignored comics initially—only in 1943 did the word first appear as a subheading for

'Children's Literature' and 'Children's Reading' in the venerable Wilson index, *Library Literature*" (Cornog and Perper 2009). Librarians, sadly, ignored comics at best and disdained them at worst. The idea that comics were kids' stuff, and, worse, *bad* kids' stuff, would be difficult for libraries to shake over the next several decades.

When comic books first entered the fray, they found few allies in librarians and educators, as both saw themselves in positions of control over children's reading and how that reading would develop them into intelligent adults. Comics, however, with their affordable price of five cents and their proliferation at most newsstands around the country, were beyond their control. Comics historian Amy Kiste Nyberg theorizes that comics represented, much to the ire of librarians, children choosing their own reading material, and, since they were not choosing titles selected by librarians, it seems understandable that there would be some animosity toward this upstart medium (2010). Supporting this theory is the example of a 14-year-old girl in Chicago who started her own lending library featuring comics like *Superman* and *Popeye*, which was successful for a time, since the Chicago Public Library was not carrying comics (Wiegand 2015). Librarians were practiced with books and understood books, but could not understand comics, and, rather than try, they simply vilified them or ignored them.

Besides a perceived lack of control over the medium and librarians feeling that comics were undermining their roles as intellectual gatekeepers, comics were sadly and simply seen as basic and unintelligent reading. With their colorful similarity to other heavily illustrated formats, such as early children's books, the assumption was made that anything that was heavily illustrated was not strengthening reading skills as the readers were simply looking at the pictures to get the story. No value was seen in the escapist nature of comics, just as little value had been given to other forms of speculative or sensational fiction at the time. Nyberg tells us there were three groups primarily targeting comics: religious groups and other civic-minded organizations that were concerned about the immorality they perceived comic books disseminating, librarians and educators who believed comics "diverted children away from better literature" and lowered reading comprehension, and doctors and politicians who began to link comics to juvenile delinquency (Nyberg 2010).

According to Cornog, there are a few examples in the 1950s of librarians who championed comics, truly ahead of their time. A librarian in California wrote an article defending comics for a professional publication and a New York library even featured an exhibit on comics history, which was still but roughly a decade old at the time (Cornog and Perper 2009). Sadly, far more articles that were published at this period featured titles condemning comics, calling them bad reading, and portraying them as essentially poison for the mind, something to clutter the brains of young readers so there was no room for real books. Comics simply had too many barriers and not enough allies in librarianship in order to find a home in libraries.

Then, in 1955, Dr. Wertham's book *Seduction of the Innocent* made waves, though it was more of a tsunami for comics. Any librarians, school, public, or otherwise, who may have been eager to embrace and spread the good word of comics were quickly silenced amid Wertham's shadow, and librarians who were already negatively biased against comics were given the justification they needed. If you'll recall from Chapter 1, Wertham's claim that comics were connected to juvenile delinquency had two major effects for librarians: it caused librarians (and most of the country) to focus on the key word "juvenile," causing comics to be associated with strictly kids' material for decades to come, and, more importantly, it reinforced the notion that comics were "bad" reading. Wertham even used a library publication to spread his message, the *Wilson Library Bulletin* (Cornog and Perper 2009). After this, articles about comics rarely made any appearances until the Silver Age.

THE SILVER AGE AND MODERN AGE

After the anti-comics fervor died down, the librarian's "flirtation" with comics began to see light as new articles about comics sprang up in the late 1960s, including a "list of comics in *Library Journal*'s magazine column [which] reflected a bemused disdain from both author and column editor" (Cornog and Perper 2009). By 1972, entire sections about comics were appearing in some library publications, though infrequently (Cornog and Perper 2009). The resurgence in superhero comics from readers during the Silver Age inevitably began to attract the attention of librarians, and this time the medium had just a few more allies than it did in the Golden Age.

In 1974, comic creator Will Eisner brought a new positive spotlight to comics. In an effort to make his book *A Contract with God* more palatable to booksellers, Eisner distinguished it from other comic books by referring to it as a "graphic novel," thereby popularizing the term. This helped feed the notion that comics could and should be taken seriously and that the material within them was worthy of reading and worthy of study. Eisner even wrote an article defending comics for *Library Journal*, and soon after, other articles concerning comics and collection development began to appear in library publications (Cornog and Perper 2009). Along with Eisner, scholar M. Thomas Inge's published articles were also influential in convincing more librarians and educators to explore the possibility that comics may have a home in libraries and schools as supplemental material (Nyberg 2010). Librarians were slowly and carefully talking about comics, and these were conversations that would continue to develop through professional discourse. By the end of the 1970s, the subject heading of "comics" was even expanded to "Comic books, strips, etc."

In 1983, writer James Thomas collected the aforementioned articles by Eisner and Inge and many other articles about comics and published them in a book intended for librarians and educators called *Cartoons and Comics in the Classroom* (Nyberg 2010). The 1980s and 1990s saw the term "graphic novel" catch on, especially with bookstores, and more and more comics that were "serious" works of literature began to appear, including Art Spiegelman's *Maus*. Spiegelman even wrote about *Maus* in the publication *Behavioral and Social Sciences Librarian* in 1985 (Cornog and Perper 2009). In 1985, another contribution by Eisner was published, the book *Comics and Sequential Art,* a collection of essays about comics from his time teaching college classes about the topic; it further advanced the idea that comics had merit and put yet another phrase into the lexicon.

According to Nyberg's research, though more and more articles from and for librarians and educators that looked at comics with a critical eye were published in the 1970s and 1980s, comics were still often treated with "condescension" in those very articles (Nyberg 2010). James Thomas's book, for example, was apparently full of misleading information and outright falsehoods (Nyberg 2010). Comics, sadly, despite their ever-increasing attention, were still frowned upon by most librarians, and often seen as the junk food of literature; they were good for motivation (a reward for reading a "real" book) or for purely entertainment, but rarely taken seriously as true literature or as an artform to be appreciated and which could bring any amount of enlightenment to a reader. Comics were still not seen as "real" reading and, at best, were approached by librarians as a form of gateway reading that would hopefully lead young readers into "better" books, a stigma that has not completely faded, even today. But it's important to recognize that the 1980s marked the beginning stages of the comic breaking through the stigma as being just for kids, and librarians, inch by inch, were coming on board.

In 1990, a librarian at Michigan State University and pioneering advocate for comics, Randall Scott, published *Comics Librarianship: A Handbook*, one of the first complete guides for librarians that addresses comics acquisition, classification, and preservation. Scott, the Comics Art Bibliographer of Michigan State's groundbreaking comics collection, was one of the earliest authoritative voices to publish a professional resource that took the material seriously. *Comics Librarianship's* content is based mostly on the practical: selection, organization, storage, and so on, and less on the theoretical, such as *why* libraries should concern themselves with comics (Scott 1990). However, an article published in *Library Journal* that same year by Keith R. A. DeCandido titled "Picture This: Graphic Novels in Libraries" focused more on trying to convince librarians that comics could indeed fit with their collections, providing a brief introduction to the material (Nyberg 2010).

Note the shift in terminology that began to take hold in the 1990s in library articles, as many works after the publication of *Comics Librarianship* began to instead use the term "graphic novel." In 1993, *Understanding Comics* from Scott McCloud granted even more legitimacy to the comics medium for librarians and educators, including those in higher education institutions. More and more authorities on the topic began to arise, including Steve Weiner, Robert Weiner, Mike Pawuk, David Serchay,[1] and Francisca Goldsmith. From these humble publication beginnings, there is now a wealth of published material about comics in libraries. Publications such as *Library Journal, School Library Journal, Voices of Youth Advocates, Publishers Weekly,* and more have dedicated review sections for comics on a near-monthly basis. Every year sees a new professional book published on the topic for librarians and educators, and the wealth of sources on the topic continues to grow.

Now here we are in the 21st century. With enough research and scholarship done in the 1980s and 1990s to justify their case, many librarians actively welcomed comics into their libraries. The explosion in visibility of comic book characters from feature films bled into libraries and schools, providing the perfect opportunity for champions of the materials in those fields to get them into the buildings. A slew of new materials was created featuring comic characters: not just movies, but also nonfiction books, video games, traditional novels, and comics specifically targeted toward young and beginner readers. There is now a smorgasbord of comics and comics-related materials that a library can carry. Librarians are rarely asking anymore, "Should we carry comics?" but, "What can we do to make our comics even more accessible?" In an effort to answer this very question, comics can now be found at professional development events, such as panels and booktalks, and some libraries even attend comic conventions as professional development. Conversely, comic publishers, such as First Second, Image, DC, and others now appear at library conventions.

Some libraries are even hosting their own comic conventions, large and small, bringing the joy of comics to their local communities, as well as other types of comics programming. Programs such as comic and manga clubs and comic workshops have become very popular, as well as less traditional events. Recently, the Cleveland Public Library's main branch was host to a Superman exhibit, titled "Superman: From Cleveland to Krypton," Cleveland being the "birthplace" of the Superman character. Attendees had the opportunity to see rare Superman memorabilia throughout the decades, such as the desk on which the character was drawn, learn about the history of Superman's creation, and bask in the presence of a copy of the first printing of *Action Comics* #1! There are so many ways that libraries can embrace comics, even if it means the library becomes more like a museum.

It's hard to tell from the current state of things that libraries were ever resistant to comics in the first place. Comics are in nearly every public library, have a strong presence in academic libraries and higher education, and can be found in public school libraries thanks to the use of comics in the curriculum. With monthly comic sales down and the seeming decline of comic specialty shops, it seems that libraries may be the last bastion for new readers to easily connect to comics. In the *Library Journal* article "Graphically Speaking," Josh Hayes, head of comics

FIGURE 2.1. "From Cleveland to Krypton" Superman exhibit, courtesy of the Cleveland Public Library. (Superman and all related elements are ™ & © DC Comics.)

FIGURE 2.2. Superman exhibit, courtesy of the Cleveland Public Library. (Superman and all related elements are ™ & © DC Comics.)

FIGURE 2.3. Superman exhibit, courtesy of the Cleveland Public Library. (Superman and all related elements are ™ & © DC Comics.)

FIGURE 2.4. Superman exhibit, courtesy of the Cleveland Public Library. (Superman and all related elements are ™ & © DC Comics.)

distributor Diamond, explains, "Despite a difficult 2017, libraries performed above the traditional retail channels" (Osicki 2018). Librarians are poised and positioned to introduce comics to new audiences better than just about anyone, and that's really saying a lot considering that millions of people are exposed to these characters every few months or so at their local movie theater. As long as libraries continue to champion the comic as a valid and valuable form of reading, their professional skills may be able to help the comics industry and keep new readers coming in at a time when comic shops are struggling to do so.

That's not even mentioning the other services that libraries offer besides materials that can also be useful to the comics medium. Offering a public space perfect for quiet study or meeting rooms for groups can support comics in unexpected ways, such as allowing a space for comics enthusiasts to congregate. Tim Hanley, comics historian and author of books such as *The Many Lives of Catwoman* and others,[2] benefitted greatly from libraries for his research:

I wrote the entirety of my first book in my local library, which was great. It's a quiet place to work, with few distractions, and I could really hunker down and get things done. I work more from home now, but I write at the library at least once a week. Especially now that I'm branching out into other fields and have a friend I write with, we meet at the library all the time to do work. It's convenient and welcoming. Plus, unlike Starbucks, we don't have to buy anything to hang out there![3]

THE RISE OF THE COMIC SHOP AND ITS IMPACT ON LIBRARIES

It may seem that for-profit comic shops and nonprofit public libraries would be natural adversaries. After all, libraries loan comics to the public for free, potentially cutting into a comic shop's profits. But libraries and comic shops can also have a symbiotic relationship and help each other, a trend that has been happening more and more in recent years. Later chapters will discuss the many ways that libraries and comic shops can benefit each other and the many types of partnerships that can come about. Before these benefits were discovered by both entities, comic shops had already had an impact on libraries, though indirectly. Comic shops had impacted libraries by impacting comic readers and the comics industry.

In the past, comics were sold at newsstands and other distributors of magazines and newspapers or through mail subscriptions. Grocery stores, drug stores, and toy stores all carried comics. It was hard to find a retailer that didn't carry the wonderful rags. It was in the 1970s that the first comic shops began to appear, stores dedicated to carrying only comics and comics-related merchandise that would centralize comics sales directly to the primary consumer. This model, known as "the direct market" and credited to entrepreneur Phil Seuling (Gearino 2017), quickly spread and changed the comics industry. Comic publishers and suppliers began to change how they operated in order to accommodate comic shops, such as printing two different versions of a comic, one with a barcode for newsstands and one without for comic shops who, in the time before widespread computers, would enter the price of the comic manually upon sale.

Comic shops spread across the country as newsstand editions of comics dwindled away. By the 1990s, comic shops were the primary source for comics. Some comics were still available elsewhere in the early 1990s—some Marvel, some DC, lots of Archie—on spinner racks at drug stores and in the checkout aisle at grocery stores, featuring sporadic issues. But a comic shop, with its dedicated space and shelves, became a collector's dream. It's worth noting that it was during the Bronze Age when the idea of comics as a serious collectors' item, and not just a hobby-constituting reading material, became a concept. Despite comics being collected and traded in the Golden and Silver Ages, it was in the Modern Age that comics were purchased and hoarded in the hopes that they would someday be worth monetary value.

Comic shops made serious collecting much easier; the comics were more likely to be in good shape, and the collector could count on the comic shop receiving a certain amount of each issue each month, taking away the role of luck in the process and the need to simply hope that the issue one needed was at the local grocery store. Comic shops were able to offer customer service to comic buyers that other stores that sold them passively simply could not, such as securing certain series away for customers in advance, known as a pull list, so that frequent customers would never miss an issue. These dedicated spaces and services were a benefit to comic publishers too; they were able to streamline their printing and delivery to focus on just these stores, and they were able to print even more series knowing that each store had more room for multiple titles than other retail spaces, allowing them to experiment in the hopes that every comic fan who visited the store for a current title may be tempted to try something new. It wasn't long before dedicated distributors of comics were formed, primarily to serve comic shops. These many distributors were reduced down to one in the 1990s, Diamond Distributors, which is now the leader in comic distribution (Van Lente and Dunlavey 2012).

Currently, comic shops and subscription delivery are the two best ways to purchase single-issue physical comic books. There are a few subscription services left; DC comics allows some, but not all, of its comics to be delivered monthly to your home, and so does Archie. Marvel allows subscriptions for all of its titles, but it's worth noting those are actually distributed through a comic shop, specifically Midtown Comics in New York. Bookstores like Barnes & Noble carry plenty of comics in trade editions, but they stopped carrying single issues in 2016. For collectors, comic shops are truly the only game in town, but there is mounting evidence pointing to their struggle and decline. However, comic shops are solely responsible for how comic readers shop and browse, as you will see.

The harsh reality for libraries is that comic shops beat libraries to the punch when it comes to comics. While librarians were bickering amongst themselves for decades as to whether to even carry comics, much less take them seriously, this gave comic shops the perfect opportunity to spring into being and claim the dos and don'ts of comics, writing the rules themselves, which explains why so many libraries are still having issues finding ways to get comics to fit with their methods. Had librarians jumped onto comics in the Golden or Silver Age, librarians could have made the rules of shelving, classification, and so on, with publishers tailoring some of their practices to better suit libraries and the not-far-removed bookstores. But comic shops are very different from libraries, and the publishers have tailored many of their practices to them, from the layouts of the spines to the numbering and volume systems used for trade paperbacks, to the information included on the covers and title pages.

It's not just publishers who favored comic shops in their practices; comic shops also had the opportunity to train the comic readers. As previously discussed, comic readers tend to be more knowledgeable about their reading material than even the most avid readers of traditional books. Comic readers have a tendency to browse by character, series title, or even publisher rather than by author. That's because comic shops arrange their comics in this way. Enter a comic shop and you'll likely find all the Marvel and DC and other comics separated, and often those are alphabetized by series title or by character on a wall (you may find *Spider-Man* and *Amazing Spider-Man* right next to each other), and they are organized from newest to oldest. Comic shops set this model and trained generations of comic readers to browse in this way.

By the time libraries made the decision to thoroughly embrace comics, it was too late to convince publishers to emphasize the author or convince readers to browse by author so that librarians could simply file comics with the same system they use for other books. Librarians who were around in the 1980s probably remember a similar situation with home video, allowing video stores to appear and train those customers as well. Video stores have since disappeared, however, leaving libraries as the main source in the United States for physical movies that can be borrowed. Will the same happen for comic shops, leaving libraries one of the few places left carrying comics? Let's hope not, because comic shops and libraries have been able to cooperate and benefit from each other better than libraries and video stores ever did.

As the price of comics rise, libraries can help comic shops by providing the one place where a reader can experiment with new titles at no risk, something a for-profit comic shop may not be able to offer, and hopefully, once that reader is hooked, they become a collector of that title from their local comic shop. Libraries benefit from comic shops, meanwhile, as many libraries have turned to comic shops as sources for materials. Sometimes, a library is a comic shop's best customer. This includes libraries who purchase their comics from comic shops in bulk, as opposed to ordering from traditional library suppliers such as Baker & Taylor, using comic shop staff as readers' advisory resources, and providing a resource for comic programming, such as Free Comic Book Day.

What could be an adversarial relationship between two entities, with comic shops and libraries both competing for the same readers, has instead evolved into something symbiotic that allows both entities to bolster their services to comic readers better than they could alone. Both libraries and comic shops have something to offer each other, and such partnerships may be crucial if comics as we know them are to survive. Comics must find new readership in order to continue into the future, and libraries and comic shops together can pool their resources to put comics into new hands, ensuring that generations to come won't miss out on the feel of a comic. Libraries and comic shops have something very important in common, and that's a love of the material and a desire to spread their love and passion for it to others. Such a commonality far overshadows what is separate.

THE FUTURE OF COMICS IN LIBRARIES

What does the future hold for comics in libraries? If someone had been born a merry mutant, or if someone could see through time like Dr. Manhattan, we could know for sure. But alas, all one can do is look at the current trends and ask the experts for their finest guesses. If current trends are anything to consider, then it seems mighty likely that comics will be changing, and the biggest change may be a shift away from single issues and closer to the graphic novel style as well as a greater prevalence for digital comics through libraries. We can make these determinations based on what we see currently happening.

As already discussed, single issue comic sales are decreasing, while trades and graphic novels seem to be increasing. For quite some time, after the explosion in popularity of e-books, comics were the only print medium that was actually on the rise, but those days seem to have faded. Digital comics also exploded in popularity during the e-craze, so it is likely that the future of comics rests in the graphic novel and the digital comics format. Both seem to have a convenience factor for readers that monthly comics don't have, but it's worth noting the specification of "reader" here. The increase in trades and graphic novels and digital comics is good for readers, but not so great for collectors.

As of right now, most bookstores in the United States, whether major chains or smaller local shops, carry comics, specifically trades or graphic novels. The same is true for libraries. Far more libraries choose to carry trades and graphic novels rather than single issue comic books due to the simple convenience factor; subscriptions can be a nuisance and trades and graphic novels are far closer to the traditional book that libraries are used to, making them easier to shelve, catalog, and classify than monthly issues. They are bound in a way that is more resilient and is closer to the classic codex, including clothbound hardcovers that can last a while and tolerate more punishment from readers. They are also more cost-effective; a current single-issue comic can cost anywhere from $3.99 to $6.99 and can be utterly destroyed beyond repair after just a few circulations. A nice hardcover trade, however, may be much more expensive, running around $25 to even $60, but they can be circulated multiple times and potentially last a few years, retaining their value for far longer. Housing them is also simpler, of course, since a trade or graphic novel can sit nicely on a regular bookshelf whereas most single issues will have to be kept on a spinner rack or some other type of unique structure.

Currently, DC Comics is pushing a new line of graphic novels featuring their superheroes that are aimed specifically at grade-school and tween audiences (Arrant 2019). DC also unveiled treasury-sized comic books that are available exclusively at Walmart, drawing excitement from some and ire from others who feel it is a slap in the face to comic shops. Experts have indicated this move may be DC's attempt to keep floppy comic books alive, a return to the form away from the dedicated comic shop and back into general stores where, it is hoped, new readers have a greater chance of stumbling upon them. Libraries can serve this same purpose, however, and what a shame it is that DC or some other popular comic publisher hasn't had the idea to create a unique comic featuring famous superheroes that's only available for sale to libraries. Regardless, this would indicate that comic books are in trouble, and that the graphic novel is likely where the future lies.

It's possible the future may lie with digital, though how exactly remains to be seen. Digital comics have been around since the late 1990s, but their popularity expanded tremendously in the 2000s. One of the biggest platforms for digital comics came in the form of Comixology. Comixology has a website and an app that provide digital comics for sale, redemption, and to "borrow" through their Comixology Unlimited subscription program. Reading the comics through the site or the app includes the panel-by-panel Guided View technology. Comixology began with mostly independent comics but now includes DC, Marvel, and nearly every other major comics publisher, even their own new line of original material. Comixology is now owned by Amazon and allows users to purchase most digital comics the same day as their physical counterparts, and many physical comics now come with a free digital copy that can be redeemed on Comixology through a code. Comixology helped bolster digital comics in much the way Amazon helped bolster the e-book.

Comixology, though of grand importance to digital comics as a whole, is not particularly useful for libraries, however. Comixology is designed for sales, not for lending, and to use it requires a personal account with a linked credit card. The comics on Comixology present the same issues as e-books; purchased comics are not really "owned" in the same way as physical material, but are simply licensed to the user for reading. Such a model is troublesome for libraries, who are in the business of sharing, but legally prevented from creating a Comixology account that they can share with patrons. There are examples of libraries putting Comixology to use in their favor, such as creating a staff account that they use for educational purposes. Some libraries, though it may be on ethically shaky ground, allow their staff members to access the digital comics on the staff account for product familiarization, allowing staff members to read the digital copies and freeing the physical copies to be circulated by patrons. It's worth noting, though, that this may also present issues for library fiscal officers, since it would, technically, allow staff members to have access to the library's credit card. Currently, every physical Marvel comic comes with a free digital copy of their comics, which can be redeemed on Comixology, adding the comic to the user's digital collection. Some libraries redeem these codes for a staff account, some black out the codes so that no one can use them, some use them as incentive for library programs and contests, and others simply allow patrons to redeem them, first come, first served.

Fortunately, for libraries, there are other options for digital comics, options that are designed exclusively for libraries. A few library vendors who specialize in e-material saw the need for loanable digital comics and stepped up to make this service a reality. These are primarily companies that already had experience with the Digital Rights Management (DRM) necessary to loan e-books and other digital materials to library patrons through their library cards. There are pros and cons to each of these services, and each offers different lending models of the digital materials as well as purchasing options, but all are contributing forces to keeping comics popular through libraries.

You can read more about these library vendors of digital comics in the next chapter.

ARE YOU MAXIMIZING COMIC ACCESS . . . OR INHIBITING IT?

The theme of this book is maximizing access to comics. Now that we've covered just what comics are, we will spend the rest of our time together learning how to improve and maximize the use of these materials in your library. But first, I invite you to test yourself and evaluate your library by answering these questions below. You will find the reasonings for these questions, and how and why these behaviors may be inhibiting access to your comics, throughout the book.

- Do you have all your comics shelved under Dewey?
- Do you have your comics mixed with your general fiction?
- Do you have all your comics shelved together, regardless of intended audience?
- Do you have a balance between trades, manga, and graphic novels? If one dominates your collection, do you have the statistics to show this is what your readers want?

LIBRARIANS IN COMICS

When discussing a history of comics and libraries, it would be a shame not to mention comics about libraries and librarians.[4] There are countless examples throughout the decades, but below are some of the most notable librarians in comics that you should explore.

- The cast of *Library Comics* by Gene Ambaum and Pat Coleman (librarycomic.com): The staff of *Library Comics* deal with the same patrons, sometimes nice, sometimes not, that most real library staff deal with, but they can say what they're really thinking.
- Cel Walden, *Archival Quality* by Ivy Noelle Weir and Steenz (Oni Press): Cel is a librarian who accepts an archival position at a museum where she must cope with a haunting presence.
- Suzie, *Sex Criminals* by Matt Fraction and Chip Zdarsky (Image): This very adult comic follows the exploits of a librarian with the power to stop time when she has sex.
- Lord High Librarian, *Thor* by Jason Aaron (Marvel): To seek answers, Thor visits a cosmic library that is kept by the god of librarians. Audiences will soon see this version of Thor (Jane Foster) in the upcoming movie, *Thor: Love and Thunder*.
- Rex Libris, *Rex Libris* by James Turner (SLG): Follows the adventures of the titular character, an ancient and ageless librarian who is a member of a librarian secret society, as he battles the forces of ignorance.
- Unnamed protagonist, *Six-Gun Gorilla* by Simon Spurrier and Jeff Stokely (BOOM! Studios): The librarian lead protagonist is the companion of a gun-toting, genetically-modified gorilla as they traverse a post-apocalyptic world.

FIGURE 2.5. We can see Barbara Gordon, AKA Batgirl, active in her library science graduate program, thanks to art by Christian Wildgoose. ("Batgirl" #7 © DC Comics.)

- Lucien, *Sandman* by Neil Gaiman (DC): Lucien is a companion to the character Dream of the metaphysical race of Endless, and he is the chief librarian of a library that contains all the books that have *never* been written. Quite a twist!

- Librarian, *House of X* and *Powers of X* by Jonathan Hickman (Marvel): This is a new character and, as of this writing, not much is known, as the story has yet to unfold. But this reinvigoration of Marvel's *X-Men* series gives us glimpses into alternate X-Men timelines and futures. One of these features a character referred to as "Librarian" who seeks to advance mutants and machines as rather strange bedfellows.

- Rupert Giles, *Buffy the Vampire Slayer* by Joss Whedon (Dark Horse): Based on the TV show, Giles, a school librarian, is a Watcher assigned to oversee and assist the Slayer, protagonist Buffy, as she hunts vampires and other denizens of the dark.

- Jocasta Nu, *Darth Vader* by Charles Soule (Marvel): The Jedi archivist has appeared in the film *Attack of the Clones* and throughout the Star Wars expanded universe, but this series tells us her fate.

- The cast of *Unshelved* by Bill Barnes and Gene Ambaum (unshelved .com): This plucky crew has the benefit of being comic strip characters, so real-world library problems don't phase them. Don't be too envious!

- Barbara Gordon, *Batman* and *Batgirl* comics (DC): The most famous comic book librarian, Barbara Gordon, first appeared in *Detective Comics* #359 in 1967, which coincided with her appearance on the *Batman* television show. Created by Bill Finger and Sheldon Moldoff, she is portrayed as a librarian who becomes the costumed crimefighter Batgirl. Her comics history has been tumultuous to put it lightly, but in 2016, Batgirl returned to librarianship by entering a library science graduate program in *Batgirl* #7 (2016) written by Hope Larson and illustrated by Christian Wildgoose.

Spotlight on Hope Larson, Writer of Comics and Library Supporter

You mentioned that libraries have been important to you all your life. Can you elaborate about the impact that libraries have had on you and how that may have shaped your career?

I grew up going to the library at least once a week with my parents. I'd check out the maximum number of books I was allowed, and I'd tear through them. Without libraries, I never would have been exposed to so many different kinds of stories, or had the freedom to read books that my parents might not have known about or approved of.

It is my understanding that you have partnered with libraries for such things as panel discussions, etc. What have been some of your fondest experiences partnering with libraries?

It's always encouraging to talk to children's librarians and school librarians, and hear about which books are connecting with the kids they work with. Being a writer can be isolating, and hearing from folks who interact with and champion my books once they're out in the world gives me heart.

As you may know, comics in libraries is a relatively new phenomenon, as librarians spent decades resisting comics. What would you want a librarian, who may be a hold-out and still doesn't take comics seriously, to know?

Lots of kids struggle with prose. Either it's intimidating, or they're more visual readers, or they have a hard time internalizing a character being described as happy versus seeing a character with a smile on their face. It's important to meet readers where they are so they can enjoy books and reading instead of seeing them as a chore. Maybe they'll move on to reading prose, and maybe they won't, but visual storytelling is full of intricacies that might not be clear to folks who haven't read comics extensively and is an art form in its own right.

Since getting to know libraries and librarians, have you learned anything new about librarianship that surprised you?

I didn't initially realize how much work librarians do with community members beyond the context of shelving and recommending books. Libraries are one of the few places a person from any walk of life can go and spend time without being asked to move along. That's really cool and important.

Can you talk about your experiences working more independently, such as on webcomics, vs. working for major publishers?

Working independently means more freedom, but little or no financial compensation. Working with a publisher means less freedom, but I get to make comics all day. I don't make much independent work anymore, because I have deadlines with my publishers, but I don't feel a huge creative loss. Not having to stress about money means I'm able to put more energy into making the work as good as I can.

What advice would you have for librarians who want to best support independent comic creators?

A great way for librarians to support indie and small-press cartoonists is for them to attend comic conventions or festivals, buy books directly from their creators, and spend a little time chatting with them. In addition, telling other librarians about their books is a huge help!

Some could view libraries as being in competition with publishers, comic stores, and creators such as yourself, since they loan materials to the public for free, arguably resulting in lost sales. Do you think there is truth in this or is there more to it, such as a sort of symbiosis?

It's nonsense to suggest that libraries cause an author to lose sales! Libraries buy books. Librarians champion books and help them find an audience. The more people who know about a book, the more people will buy the book.

During your run on Batgirl, *a library favorite, you returned Barbara Gordon to the realm of librarianship and even showed her taking library science courses. Can you tell us about this experience? Why did you think it was important for Batgirl to be a librarian again? Was there any pushback from this decision? What type of research did you do to prepare for the story?*

There definitely wasn't any pushback from DC about taking Barbara back to her librarian roots—my editors were totally supportive of that decision. We had just seen Barbara leave a corporate/tech environment, travel the world for some soul-searching, and decide she wanted to be more involved with her community, which fit perfectly with becoming a librarian. My research involved chatting with my friend, librarian Jack Baur, who helped me get to the core of what makes librarians so important.

Do you have anything in the works that you want librarians to know about?

I'm working on two companion books to *All Summer Long*, and Rebecca Mock and I have a new collaborative graphic novel coming out in 2020 or 2021. Beyond that, I have a few ideas, but I'm trying not to get too far ahead of myself. [5]

NOTES

1. David Serchay's books have been valuable reader's advisory resources for librarians, including: Serchay, David S. *The Librarian's Guide to Graphic Novels for Adults.* New York: Neal-Schuman Publishers, Inc., 2010.

2. Tim Hanley's next book is about Archie Comics characters Betty and Veronica and should be out sometime in 2020.

3. Tim Hanley, email exchange, May 21, 2019.

4. Steven M. Bergson compiled a fun list here: http://www.ibiblio.org/librariesfaq/combks/combks.htm

5. Hope Larson, interview via email by Jack Phoenix, November 27, 2018.

3

Acquiring Comics

Now that we've discussed why comics are important to us and to our culture, it's time to dive into the really fun stuff: how to get them into your building, and what to do with them once they're there. This chapter will cover the selection and acquisition of comics, an obviously important first step. If the previous two chapters have conveyed anything at all, hopefully it is that comics are a worthy medium and as deserving of a library's careful consideration for selection like any other material. Comic readers deserve to be represented in your library by having the materials they wish to read available to them. Conversely, comics deserve to be on your shelves so that they can be discovered by new readers who have never considered them in the past. As Francisca Goldsmith says, "Collection development continues to be a professional activity that differentiates the library's mission from the missions of other agencies that deal with graphic novels" (Goldsmith 2005). It's what separates libraries from our allies in the comics industry, such as comic shops and comic vendors. So, give it your all!

For the most part, selecting and acquiring comics is no different than selecting and acquiring other materials. You'll use the same methods; adhering to your collection development policy, vetting materials based on reviews, demand, the interests of your community, age level, and so on. The major difference will lie in the avenues you have to take. Prose books have long-standing review sources in place and their review methods are just as long-standing. Librarians are already abundantly familiar with finding these reviews and providing subject analyses on traditional books, and, though many of these review sources *now* provide reviews for comics, many of the best sources, the ones that have their fingers on the pulse of comics, come from newer, upstart, pop culture sites and publications. Utilizing both types of sources, however, is crucial to a well-rounded comics collection, since, just like regular books, comics are incredibly varied in subject, quality, and appeal. There are comics that would be considered popular materials and there are comics that would be considered literature. There are fiction comics and nonfiction comics. The medium does not fit into a neat and tidy box, and thus a critical eye is needed when one is selecting; to purchase only popular comics or literary comics would be a disservice to your patrons who are looking for either or both. Instead, you'll need a healthy balance.

Fortunately, some fantastic librarians with expertise in comics have laid out some fabulous groundwork throughout the years so we can learn from their examples. This chapter will provide some of the best practices for the selection and acquisition of comics in libraries from fellow comic-loving librarians. Francisca Goldsmith laid out these three questions any librarian should ask themselves in order to keep their collection development methods strong:

> For which members of my library's community will we be collecting graphic novels? Children? Adults? Teens? English language learners? Adult literacy students? Users of the special visual arts collection? Several of those diverse groups or another group altogether?

> What does my budget allow? Do I have seed money to purchase a sizable start-up collection? Will ongoing funds be available for additions to the collection? Is a reliable source of money available to replace lost and damaged materials?

> Does my library's collection development policy already address issues related to graphic novels, or does it need to be reworked to accommodate that particular format? (Goldsmith 2005).

With comics, you may discover more freedom to take alternative routes to collection development than you would with traditional books or even audiovisual materials. Comics, as a unique medium, lends itself to rather unorthodox collection development practices, something a librarian can have a lot of fun with if that librarian is so inclined. Exploring comics for selection has an element of fun that, in this author's completely unbiased opinion, simply cannot be matched. You'll be amazed at the doors that can open, that you didn't know possible, and the partnerships you can make along the way. Let's look at where to select and purchase your comics.

WHERE TO BUY

Local Comic Shop (LCS)

In his book *Graphic Novels: A Genre Guide to Comic Books, Manga and More,* librarian and comic genre expert Michael Pawuk first and foremost recommends selecting and purchasing comics through an LCS (Pawuk 2007). I put full support behind this strategy. If you are fortunate enough to have a comic shop within geographic proximity, pursuing the comic shop for help with acquisition can prove to be a mutually beneficial partnership that will come with some bonuses. Not only are you benefitting the LCS, the benefits that the shop can bring to your library are almost too numerous to name.

Firstly, an LCS may be able to offer the library a heavy discount on the items, as they may be able to purchase and sell them at cost. This is especially likely for comic books, as shops purchase those in bulk and may be able to offer some to the library far cheaper than the typical $3.99 cover price. Even if the LCS cannot offer the library a discount on materials, the benefits can still be great. We all know that money isn't everything, and an LCS may be able to benefit the library in other ways, perhaps even saving on time and labor. An LCS may be able to help a library boost circulation by assisting with programs, activities, promotions, and so on, using the power of their stores to send their customers through library doors. LCSs are in a unique position to assist libraries, and likewise libraries are in a perfect position to help LCSs, and you may

FIGURE 3.1. Some comic books on display at the Arlington Heights Memorial Library, supplied by the local comic shop. (Provided by Violet Jaffe.)

discover that comic retailers are eager to help simply due to their passion for the medium.

An LCS may be able and willing to help a library save on labor by assisting with selection, rather than just playing the role of a typical vendor. Many collection development librarians are busy enough with traditional books, audiovisual media, and more, so an LCS employee may be willing to lend their expertise and make recommendations for what the library should purchase that month. An LCS is already tracking sales projections, hype, and trends of titles, so it can be easy enough for a shop employee to simply put a collection together for purchase by the library within a specified budget. Even if a library prohibits selections of library materials by anyone outside of library staff, an LCS is likely still useful for recommendations and their own brand of readers' advisory.

If you're of a more cynical nature and you find yourself reluctant to engage with an LCS because it is a for-profit business, remember that LCSs are struggling. Rare is the LCS owner who is immensely wealthy, and most did not break into the comic retail business with the expectation of being so. Most comic retailers became comic retailers because they love comics, and it's as simple as that. Most are fans first and retailers second, and as fans they have a passion for the medium and want to see it succeed. Partnering with libraries can help them see this mission through. The LCS knows that a library can help fill the gaps between the shop's current offerings. A reader may discover a new title at the library and love it so much they decide to buy it from the LCS. A reader who needs the next entry in a series can turn to either the comic shop or the library if either one lacks it, keeping the reader engaged with the product, which benefits both the library and the shop. So, if you want to add a comic collection to your library or if you already have one and want to enhance it, please consider contacting your LCS by using the Comic Shop Locator tool (comicshoplocator.com) and introduce yourself. You'll be surprised at the kind of opportunities that can arise when heroes team up.

Spotlight on John Dudas, Comic Shop Owner and Library Partner

Tell us about yourself and your store.

My name is John Dudas, and I live here in Cleveland, Ohio, where my mom and I co-own Carol and John's Comic Shop. My great grandfather was a Polish immigrant, and he bought and read comics to help him learn English. He left me a pile of comics that no one else in the family really cared about, but I came to love them. I started going to newsstands, then found a copy of the *Overstreet Guide to Comics* at the library, which had an ad, which led me to my first local comic shop. I eventually got a job at a store that sold comics, North Coast Nostalgia, and he hired my mom, too. Unfortunately, we were both laid off from that store, but then we decided to open a shop of our own. I put my whole comic collection into the shop, and mom and I launched our store as a 50/50 partnership. The store opened in 1990, and, at that time, having a woman's name attached to a comic shop was unusual, but in our modern times it's an instant win for our customers. I'm also a member of Comics Pro, a not-for-profit trade association that has over 250 comic shops as members. I ran for board of directors and now I'm the treasurer.

It would seem that comic retailers and libraries would be natural adversaries. Why do you think the two entities can instead help each other?

Ultimately if two entities care about stories, care about sharing stories, care about literacy, then that's more common ground than anything else and all that really matters. Any library system is a representation of its city, just like any comic shop is. Both libraries and comic shops tend to rally communities and become community hubs. Besides, the modern library is more of a community resource center and a place to get things done. You have working adults or maybe adults applying for jobs at the library, and it's nice to know that they can leave children with a library comics collection while the parents be productive. If libraries are willing to support the medium and take it seriously, then that elevates the entire comics industry. We have always had very strong advocates in libraries, especially CPL (Cleveland Public Library), and so we will strongly advocate for them.

In what ways have you partnered with libraries to provide them with comics? Which libraries?

We are a selection partner for Cleveland Public Library and Cuyahoga County Public Library (CCPL) and all their branches, Rocky River, Cleveland Heights, University Heights, and even

Pickaway libraries, which are not local. We also partner with the Westlake Library for Free Comic Book Day (FCBD). What I've learned is that if you give the library the tools to have an event, they'll do it, so sometimes that's all they need from us. We are a partner for some but a resource for all. We help with selection by providing them lists of suggestions. We try to promote diversity by suggesting comics that match the library's demographic. We let the libraries know what's coming in and what's going out. We only order periodicals, monthly comic issues, for libraries, and not graphic novels, but we are still happy to answer questions or make recommendations for graphic novels if a library asks. We handle distribution of the comics and ensure that they are in good condition, and we deal with Diamond Distributors on the library's behalf.

In what ways have you partnered with libraries for programming?

We've partnered with CPL for the Wonder Woman Symposium, the Superman exhibit, the Coffee and Comics program, and more. For other libraries we'll usually host after-parties with any comic-related event, plus we've hosted a class series on the history of comics for CCPL. For most libraries we partner with them for FCBD, providing them with comics and swag and any assistance we can. The core of FCBD is giving away free books, but the real event is everything happening around it. FCBD is by far the most successful event we help libraries with, and we support about 40 of them at different library locations each year. There is a reciprocal nature to all of it, as we are allowed to put our store stamp on each comic that is given away, so each one becomes an ad for our store, hopefully leading library patrons to us as customers.

What would you say to comic shops who see libraries as competition?

Anything that pushes the medium forward is worth exploring. Even other shops who are competitors can lift each other up. Sometimes, you just have to benefit the hobby.

Since reports say the comics industry is struggling, what do you think the future holds for comics and comic shops?

I think the concern is slightly unwarranted. Even if monthly comic book sales are down, change is part of the business. The industry looks very different than it was 20 years ago, and it will look very different in another 20 years as comics and comic shops adapt to what's going on. When one of the best ways to move a business like a comic shop forward is to put yourself into your community and the best way to do that is through schools and libraries. Because our customers know how much we support schools and libraries, and are then supporting our community, it makes the customers want to support us by buying here. We've had to adapt in these changing times and we have changed many times. We've had this shop in different locations in the past, and the last move we decided that instead of adding more square footage we would expand our presence in the community, and that's one way we have adapted. Are there things the publishers can do to improve the industry and attract new readers? Of course. But there's a responsibility on comic shops to find new readers, too.

Is there something more you would like to see libraries do for the comics industry?

I would like to see libraries refer more and more patrons to us as resource. We not only sell comics, but we're also experts. Don't be afraid to send patrons to us with comic questions or to help them find the next book in a series if the library doesn't have it.

There's been a lot of discussion in libraries as how to best organize their comics and graphic novels. Since comic shops have more or less "trained" the consumers on how to expect comics to be organized, do you have any input for libraries?

Educating your customers about how to get what they want from you is key. We don't have a lot of signage, but people know how to find stuff, because we give good customer service and try to show them the ropes when they walk in for the first time. I definitely recommend separating comics by age group, but that can mean different things between libraries and retail. Our partner libraries ask us to distinguish the comics we order for them between all-ages and teen. We do the best we can, but sometimes the books don't turn out like you would think, and may be a bit questionable for the intended age group. For example, the imprints DC Zoom, which is for grade-schoolers, and DC Ink,[1] which is for teens, just launched, and one of the teen titles had content that some may not consider teen-friendly in a library setting. Comic shops are more aware of where things go age-bracket wise, and I care about where things are racked because it's my problem as a small-business. It's good to rely on our expertise but also to rely on a comics champion on staff. How to rack (shelve) your comics is another good reason to partner with your local shop, because together you can come up with a good system that works for the community.

Is there something more you would like to see the comics industry do for libraries and comic shops?

Returnability is key. The pressure goes to us to order the right amount of a comic book. "Customer service" are two important words for a comic shop, but "inventory control" are really the two most important words. If the publishers can take a bit more of that risk for unsold items, it makes things easier for us and therefore for our partner libraries.[2]

Diamond

If you are not fortunate enough to have an LCS in proximity or there is any other obstacle making partnering with an LCS impossible, then you can go straight to the source. Diamond Distributors is the country's dominant comics distributor, and most, if not all, comic shops order their comics through them. Diamond has been dealing directly with comic shops since the mid-1990s and has since become undeniably expert at delivering comics to retailers, as well nearly the only game in town when it comes to the distribution of monthly comic books.

Lately, Diamond has been reaching out beyond retailers with their Diamond BookShelf platform, "The Graphic Novel Resource for Educators & Librarians" (diamondbookshelf.com). This is truly a well-rounded, wonderful resource for librarians, as it offers the latest updates in comics news, helping librarians keep up with the trends. It also provides a list of bestsellers, upcoming releases, digital versions of the *BookShelf Magazine,* and many other resources. The site also has the Comic Shop Locator tool embedded, so that you can search for your nearest comic shop more accurately than using Google. These efforts on behalf of Diamond to reach out to librarians and educators are worth your time exploring, even if they aren't as practiced at dealing with libraries as some of the other vendors on this list.

The other big plus of using Diamond as your library's comic supplier is the availability of nearly every comic currently being published, as well as improved odds that they can find more obscure and older titles. Diamond has partnerships with nearly every comic publisher, so you're unlikely to hit snags in what you can offer your patrons. Diamond also has every print format of comics you could want: monthly comic books, trade paperbacks, hardcovers, graphic novels, and so on. They also offer promotional materials, such as posters, that are sometimes free with a purchase of comics. Diamond publishes the *Previews* catalog, a comprehensive look of upcoming titles that any selector will find invaluable. Outside of a partnership with a comics retailer and expert, Diamond may be the next best option, especially for larger libraries.

Baker & Taylor

Most library staff who are at all involved in collection development are familiar with Baker & Taylor (B&T), a long-standing library vendor. You can count on B&T to have most current trade paperbacks, hardcovers, and graphic novels that you could desire, but you'll find it difficult to obtain older titles and they don't carry monthly comic books at all. There are certainly benefits that come from ordering comics through B&T, though, and they are the same benefits the vendor offers with traditional books. For instance, sometimes library pricing on a comic from B&T is less expensive than the retail price. For a fee, B&T will also process comics with protective wrap and call numbers to prepare them for library circulation. B&T also offers standing orders on titles, allowing a library to automatically receive all *X-Men* or *Batman* books, for instance. The upside to standing orders of this fashion is obvious. The downside, however, is that it throws off careful, individual selection of such items. After all, it's possible that not every *X-Men*-related trade released each month is of equal quality, but with standing orders, the library has likely already paid for the item. This can be very useful with a title like *Saga*, which doesn't have nearly the same output of publications. B&T does offer returns on some materials.

Rachel Bild, Teen Librarian at the Oak Park Public Library in Illinois who orders both adult and teen comics, describes her B&T process:

> Ordering and selecting graphic novels takes a lot of work, it really does . . . The way that I order, I get this one cart that is the Diamond Bestsellers that my rep from B&T puts together, and she's B&T's comics expert on staff. And then I have a cart of things that have been reviewed, so everything that B&T has reviews from, such as Library

Journal and Foreword, and that helps cast a wider net. And then I have series carts, but I don't include superheroes. I don't do any standing orders, because then I wind up with titles that I don't really need, especially older stuff. The problem with the series cart is I need to count on B&T to have accurately tagged each series and not deviate, they have to make sure each time that a new volume comes out that they are cataloging it correctly. I also have publisher carts where I get everything from that publisher in a date range; 147 items that are YA, primarily Marvel and DC, but also Valiant and some other stuff, and I have to look and see if it's something that we would want.[3]

Ingram

Ingram is another traditional library vendor and they offer most of the benefits, such as preparing materials for circulation for a fee. Ingram also offers standing orders and returns of unwanted items as well as library pricing. But Ingram comes with the same drawbacks as B&T, such as limited availability on older titles and monthly comic books are not really an option. Still, if your library is concentrating mostly on trades and graphic novels, as they are much closer in physical structure to traditional books and fit easily on shelves, then Ingram is a good choice. Their customer service department is used to dealing with libraries and their needs. You may find traditional library vendors like Ingram and B&T to be rather flexible and willing to go the extra mile to help libraries fill their comic needs.

Small Distributors

Smaller distributors have popped up over the years attempting to break Diamond's monopoly on comics distribution, but few have lasted. Some of these are regional, such as Emerald City Distribution in Seattle or Iron Circus Comics in Pittsburgh (Wood 2018). Matthew Wood tells us, "Many smaller comics presses also work with book distributors such as Consortium Book Sales, W. W. Norton, Macmillan, and others" (2018). Don't forget to also check sources for self-published works, such as Lulu, iUniverse, Blurb, and more who may have some self-published comics that could be of interest, as well as scoping local comic cons and small press conventions to look for independently published comics.

Amazon

Some may find Amazon's suggestions based off of browsing and purchasing histories helpful, and Amazon's user interface is certainly one of the finest and easiest to use for shopping. However, Amazon isn't always the most convenient to use for tax-exempt businesses like public libraries, and you're likely not going to get much of a discount. I would recommend only using Amazon if you have a dedicated comics expert doing selection and would, therefore, already know what they are looking for. Otherwise, Amazon can also be useful for supplementing your purchases from other vendors, since they will carry most trades and graphic novels as well as monthly comic books from third-party sellers.

Subscriptions

Marvel, DC, and other comic publishers offer by-mail subscriptions of their monthly issues, but there are definite limitations. For starters, though Marvel allows all of their monthly series issues to be delivered by mail, DC only offers a few. Naturally, there is no guarantee that the comics will come in pristine shape, since they are travelling by postal service. And, of course, this is only an option for monthly comic books, not trades. If you are interested in creating a ready stream of comic books flowing through your library, this option can be a very inexpensive one (Marvel offers most of their subscriptions for around $25–$30 a year and they provide a discount for renewals and multiple titles). This can be a good option if you want single issues to circulate, since they certainly won't survive too many circulations anyway, at least you may assume. Violet Jaffe, collection supervisor for the Arlington Heights Memorial Library, claims that her library's comic books last "77–80 circulations before they are completely destroyed and have to be discarded."[4] If your comic book collection is so fortunate, that's a lot of bang for a little buck!

At the London Public Library in London, Ohio, the staff tried comic subscriptions for a while. Each month, they received single issues of some Marvel titles such as *The Amazing Spider-Man* and *Avengers,* DC titles such as *Superman* and *Batman,* and they even had a subscription for *Sonic the Hedgehog* from Archie Comics. The comics were kept in bags and boards to keep them in as best shape as possible, but they would still get roughed up rather quickly. The library learned that the single-issue comics would typically only last an average of seven circulations, which went by pretty quickly considering how quickly these items can be read, and that's if they were returned at all. Any comic that had a #1 on the cover, such as the 2012 relaunch of *Avengers,* never came back, likely because patrons assumed, incorrectly, that, despite the library stamps and labels plastered on it, it would be worth something someday.

DIGITAL COMICS

OverDrive[5]

The largest supplier of e-books and digital audiobooks is OverDrive, hands down, providing digital materials to roughly 90% of public libraries as well as many school libraries. OverDrive boasts many thousands of titles available for libraries to purchase that they can then loan to patrons through their digital platforms, specifically the library OverDrive-supported website, the OverDrive app, or the Libby app. OverDrive has thousands of comics available to libraries from many major comics publishers, including Image, First Second, Viz Media, IDW, Dark Horse, and more. Many DC Comics are available through OverDrive, but, unfortunately, their selections are inconsistent, with some delays and some missing volumes when it comes to newer materials. In 2018, Marvel Comics finally partnered with OverDrive to allow most of their newer content to be available. Currently, Fantagraphics does not have their newer materials available through OverDrive, creating a very noticeable gap in their offerings.

OverDrive sells these comics in mostly two lending models, depending on publisher. These models are One Copy/One User, which means the library pays one price, usually on the higher end, and the library can keep the title with no expiration, and Metered Access, a model that expires after so many circulations or time frame, which the library has to repurchase at a generally cheaper price in order to keep the title available. Each of these copies can only be checked out one at a time, like a physical book, and patrons have to place copies that are "checked out" on hold. Recently, OverDrive offered a third model, in which, notably, many comics from DC and Marvel are now available. This model is Cost Per Circ (CPC), which allows multiple users to read the same copy at the same time, and the library pays a small amount for each circulation instead of a larger amount regardless if the copy checks out or not.

OverDrive also offers many of their comics in a variety of formats, including EPUB, PDF, Kindle, and OverDrive's proprietary and browser-based format OverDrive Read. Many of the comics OverDrive makes available are in "Fixed Layout," which is a good way to read comics, picture books, and any other heavily illustrated materials. Fixed Layout allows the user to magnify and minimize the illustrations with ease on the screen, useful for comics fans who may be reading from a phone-sized screen or a smaller tablet. In December of 2019, it was announced that investment firm KKR had purchased OverDrive, which means that OverDrive and its chief competitor RBdigital will now share an owner (Enis 2019).

Hoopla

Chomping at OverDrive's heels is Hoopla, a digital vendor owned by Midwest Tape. Hoopla has used Midwest Tape's long-standing relationships with publishers and movie studios to its advantage, offering a wide variety of popular materials including e-books, audiobooks, videos, and music in digital format. These materials are borrowed through the Hoopla app on smartphones and tablets. Hoopla also has thousands of comics available from major publishers, and, importantly, they have focused on the reading experience of comics.

Hoopla has comics from Archie, Image, Dark Horse, and many of the same publishers as OverDrive. But, importantly, unlike OverDrive, Hoopla has had deals with DC and Marvel to carry their comics for some time now, including an exclusive deal from 2016 to carry most DC digital trades and graphic novels on the same day they are available in print. Hoopla is a library patron's best option to read the most popular and newest digital comics, though they still lack many of the independent publishers' titles as well as Scholastic Graphix titles.

Hoopla's major drawback would be their pricing models. Hoopla's comics, like all their other materials, are only available in a CPC model, so the library must pay for each circulation, something that can be troublesome for the most popular materials. Hoopla does allow monetary caps on their CPC models, but this can cause customer service problems, permitting inconsistency in availability to patrons. On the plus side, there is no need for holds for their titles, so they all appear as constantly available. Hoopla sells their titles as packages, another drawback since it may prevent librarians from hand-selecting individual titles to best suit their collection development needs. The library can also set circulation caps on their patrons, allowing their patrons to check out only a certain number of titles each month. There are pros and cons to the CPC model, and it's up to each library to decide what is best for their patrons.

When it comes to the reading experience of comics, however, Hoopla is hard to beat. Hoopla offers its comics with Action View technology, a similar technology to Comixology's Guided View. The reader can turn this technology on and off with just a tap. This allows the reader to read a comic panel-by-panel, perfect for smaller screens, and is a similar digital experience to how the human eye reads physical comics, focusing on each panel individually. This makes the comic experience of Hoopla unique among library vendors and makes Hoopla one of the more patron-friendly platforms, even if it is not the kindest to the library itself.

Hoopla as a vendor has a lot going against it, but it's hard to deny that, at least when it comes to comics, the experience they can offer library patrons is a great one and will leave readers satisfied. Their incredible selection combined with their Action View reading technology makes them a leader in comics for libraries. Many libraries offer both OverDrive and Hoopla to their patrons in an attempt to fill any service gaps between the two, but both platforms offer competitive options for libraries and patrons to choose from. For selection and experience, Hoopla is fantastic, but OverDrive is still the leader when it comes to most e-materials, making them a sure bet as well.

RBdigital

RBdigital is the digital arm for libraries from Recorded Books, offering a plethora of e-media options, including comics. They offer a variety of pricing models, similar to OverDrive. RBdigital does not have a fixed layout method like Hoopla, but they do allow the user to zoom into panels easily with their fingertips. In 2018, RBdigital added comics from Marvel to its digital repertoire, plus they had an overhaul of their app to make it a more seamless experience. With their efforts to boost their offerings and platform, plus sharing an owner with OverDrive, this is a service to keep your eyes on.

Comics Plus: Library Edition

Comics Plus is the only library app that is dedicated strictly to comics. The service, which is owned by RBDigital (Recorded Books) and powered by iversemedia, boasts over 90 publishers, including Disney, Archie, IDW, Valiant, Dark Horse, Boom! Studios, Dynamite Entertainment, and more, including over 16,000 comics. Comics Plus also carries *Bone* from Cartoon Books, something the other two services cannot boast, though as of this writing it is missing the two biggest names in comics, DC and Marvel.

Like Hoopla, Comics Plus comics are only available in the CPC model, and so a library must pay every time a comic checks out. The lack of holds is a boon for Comics Plus, since multiple users can read the same comic simultaneously, and libraries can host a wealth of comics on digital display for their patrons without paying for them until they circulate, but libraries are then, of course, forced to apply caps on the spending. Popular titles, such as *Bone*, can get very expensive very quickly if they circulate a great deal.

Digital comics may be the future for libraries, or they may just be another option for library users to access their comics. Will digital comics eventually fade? After all, like e-books, digital comics did level off after their peak in the mid-2000s. There's really no way to tell for sure. But what is for sure is that, here and now, digital comics provide a portal to a new world of reading, with the 24-hour, often instant convenience that e-media has to offer. Digital comics can be a fantastic way to introduce new readers to comics or to provide the best possible service to seasoned comics fans, who have multiple options of searching and reading comics from the comfort of their homes without having to set foot in a library. That's not even mentioning the benefits that digital comics can provide readers with low vision. There are even digital graphic audiobooks now for the those with low vision.[6] As with most library services, being a member of a library consortium is the best way to provide one or more of these digital services to patrons and keep it affordable.

WHAT TO BUY

Subject analysis is one of the most important components of collection development. That not only includes reviewing potential subject headings and areas of the collection that may be filled by a particular title but also vetting the titles against reputable review sources. It's a given that comics are quite numerous. The monthly output of new series, trades, and graphic novels is huge. No one, no matter how much of an expert they may be, no matter how gloriously nerdy and consumed by comic fandom, can possibly be familiar with them all. This makes reviews so invaluable to what librarians do, since purchasing only comics with which one is already familiar is very unwise collection development indeed and would likely leave many of your comic readers in the lurch. Just because you've never read *Phoebe and Her Unicorn* by Dana Simpson, doesn't mean it's not important to someone. Your patrons deserve the best comics you can buy. As we've already covered, a proper balance between popular and literary, fiction and nonfiction, demographic representation, and so on, are all crucial to having a strong comics collection, just like any other collection in a library.

Graphic novels can be very tricky because the book jobbers, the publishers, and librarians don't necessarily agree on what is age-appropriate. Some of our adult graphic novels, such as *Saga, Sex Criminals*, and so on, definitely cross boundaries for a visual medium. There's the access for teens angle and we want to make sure that teens have access to materials that they are ready for (some of them) and that are interesting to them (many of them). Other titles that are for adults may not necessarily break some kind of rule, content-wise, for being teen appropriate, but they are still intended for adults, interest-wise, so we have to make sure we are placing those appropriately, too. I've been pretty loosey-goosey following comics ratings in the past. If YALSA says that something belongs in the teen section, I was doing it, but I also have to be mindful of titles that are maybe better for the tween crowd than the teen and vice versa.[7]

Something that is important to keep in mind as you search for comic reviews is that comics are still suffering from the remnants of stigma and still sometimes struggle to be accepted as valuable. What you will find is that many review resources will either focus on comics deemed to have literary merit or are pop culture fare like superhero titles but rare is the resource that reviews both. Some of the publications that librarians rely on have become better about this, such as *Library Journal* and *School Library Journal,* but a publication like *Kirkus* is more likely to only feature graphic novels and graphic memoirs, for example, but probably not trades of superhero titles. Meanwhile, online resources such as *Newsarama* or *The Mary Sue* that review any and all comics may lack the authority that librarians usually prefer. If your collection development policy requires a review from a reputable source, you may have to advocate adjusting the policy for comics to allow reviews from some "pop" sources. It's also important to remember that collection development isn't just about the reviews, but also the trends, and many of the internet pop culture sites are the best places to keep abreast of the latest comics fads. Here are some sources for reviews, some you may know, some may be new, that will be able to help you achieve said balance.

Awards Lists: Comics are commonly winning literary and book industry awards these days across the country, such as the National Book Award. Keep your eye out for the comics that are nominated, and, of course, don't forget to check the annual awards that are just for comics (see Chapter 1).

Bestseller Lists: You are probably reviewing these lists already, either for the purposes of selection or readers' advisory, so just be sure to keep an eye out for comics in bestseller lists for *The New York Times, USA Today,* and others.

Booklist: A common review source for librarians, *Booklist* is generally published twice a month, and it includes reviews on comics for adults, children, and teens as a staple. *Booklist* also releases an annual publication specifically about comics.

Comic Book Resources (CBR): This website does offer the occasional review, mostly for single issues, but it's more beneficial for keeping up with news, hype, and upcoming releases (www.cbr.com). The writing and journalism from the site can sometimes leave much to be desired, and it's not written with librarians in mind, but it's still a simple resource to follow to learn what the readership is excited about.[8]

Comics Worth Reading: Priding itself on being an independent review source, this site reviews comics and comics-related media of all kinds, dutifully maintained by expert Johanna Draper Carlson who also writes for *School Library Journal*. (https://comicsworthreading.com)

Good Comics for Kids: This *School Library Journal* blog is a handy supplement to their other offerings, focusing strictly on comics for juvenile audiences. (http://blogs.slj.com/goodcomicsforkids)

Kirkus: *Kirkus* is renowned for their reviews and their "Graphic Novels & Comic Books" Book Reviews column follows in this grand tradition. *Kirkus* typically only reviews comics that are deemed to have literary quality, and very rarely reviews trades and superhero fare.

Library Journal: Published twice a month, this trusted source has a regular column for comics and is uber-reliable because the reviews are written *for* librarians.

No Flying, No Tights: Speaking of sources for librarians, this website was also created *by* a librarian (http://www.noflyingnotights.com). This is a fantastic resource for non-superhero comics, so you'll find lots of graphic novels, manga, and plenty of comics that may otherwise fly under the radar.

NoveList: *NoveList* has been a reliable source of reviews, useful for readers' advisory and selection, since 1994. *NoveList* now has comics in the repertoire of reviews. *NoveList* is owned by EBSCO. This service is available through most library and consortium database packages.

Otaku USA Magazine: This is a great resource for all things manga, covering news, upcoming events, as well as reviews, that may otherwise fall through the cracks of some other sources. Along with manga, you'll also find news and reviews for anime and J-pop.

Publishers Weekly: Published weekly as its name suggests, *Publishers Weekly* provides solid reviews with librarians, educators, and others in the book world in mind, as well as regular articles about what's trending with comics.

School Library Journal: With comics reviews and articles galore, if you are selecting comics for children or teens, then this monthly publication will be just as invaluable to you as it has been for other children's formats such as picture books and chapter books.

Voice of Youth Advocates: If you are selecting comics for teens, this monthly publication is the best place to look. You'll find a review column dedicated to YA comics reviews, articles about the trends and benefits of comics for librarians and educators, and occasional recommendations for adult comics that are appropriate for teens.

BUDGETING AND SELECTORS

Like budgeting for any other material, how you budget for comics will entirely depend upon your library, its staff and collection structure, and its financial situation, but there are a few different approaches to consider. We will begin with the most ideal situation, but remember: what's most ideal for many libraries, may not be ideal for *your* library. When budgeting for comics, it's important to have cooperation from the library's fiscal authorities, because comics are expensive. You'll need to have your arguments in tow as to why said money should be set aside for comics and the benefits that comics will bring to your library and its users. Though comics (particularly full-color comics) are more expensive than many other forms of print materials, library discounts through vendors should help tremendously. Wood suggests, that by ordering paperback comics that likely run at a discounted rate of about $10 a book, "a library can fill 24 feet of comics shelving (total) for about $2,500," and this is a solid place to start (Wood 2018). And that is, of course, not including any comics that are likely already currently in your collection. Expand this by a few dozen books a year, depending on the size of your library, and you'll likely have a strong collection. Rachel Bild continues:

> They come with unique problems . . . [such as] having items fall apart easily but still be very popular. For instance, Marvel has the *World War Hulk Omnibus*, which is $75 but for us is closer to $50 (library pricing). The thing only lasted two circs. You don't necessarily know when you're reading the physical description on the vendors' sites what you're getting. It may not sound that different from any other hefty illustrated book, but surprise, it's giant and doesn't fit well on the shelf.[9]

The most ideal situation for comics budgets would be for comics to have their own discrete budget. This could be a line item in the overall collection development budget, but not shared by any other medium or format. Even more ideally, you will have a single comics expert on staff as the selector for the medium who would propose and spend from this budget. This comics selector would be in charge of all collection development for comics and would select comics for adult, young adult, and juvenile. Centralizing collection development of comics under a single decision maker can maximize the collection, since a single, dedicated staff member can provide the care and attention that the best comics collection requires. If this is a possibility for your library, make it happen. If not, don't despair. There are plenty of other options to make the most of your comics. A specialist overseeing it all is not a requirement, it is simply the best option if it is within the realm of possibility.

If you cannot have a single comics specialist overseeing a dedicated comics budget, then the next best thing is to ensure that each age group gets some comics money secured from the other print materials budgets. Selectors for juvenile, YA, and adult print materials should purchase comics for their respective age groups out of their individual budgets, and each should be proportionate (for instance, YA and juvenile would likely have a higher percentage of their budgets going to comics than adult). These selectors can set aside a certain amount annually for comics if they wish, but truly these individuals should be familiar enough with comics to make selection and review analyses part of their everyday process (if they aren't familiar, books like this one in your hands can hopefully help!). The point is that if staff members are selecting comics and paying for them from their print materials budgets, they should be sure to give comics just as much of a thorough and thoughtful selection process as any other print items.

The option that is least preferable, and one that many libraries implement, is to have all comics be purchased from the budget assigned to an age group, such as a children's or YA print materials budgets. This also often means, unsurprisingly, that only a children's or YA selector is acquiring all the comics for the library, which may mean the exclusion of adult materials. If all the comics are coming out of the adult budget, then sometimes it's children's or YA that suffers. Many libraries take this route primarily for two reasons: it's the path of least resistance or it's based on the still-present stigma that comics are only for one particular age group, usually juvenile or teen. This can be troublesome for having a maximized comics collection, since the individual purchasing the comics will undoubtedly spend 90% of the rest of their collection development time and effort focusing on one age group.

This is, of course, not a complete disaster if the individual is qualified. Someone who is a comics fan and specialist but happens to be a children's librarian may be perfectly suited to also purchase comics for teens and adults, for example. And there is always the possibility that just because someone is not a comics expert *now* that they couldn't become wonderfully fluent in the medium with a little time, research, and a willingness to learn and adapt. It would be a true shame to only carry comics for a single age group in your library. This would be a great disservice to the rest of your patrons who may or may not realize what they're missing. As long as this does not happen, it doesn't really matter where the money for the comics comes from, just as long as all of your community's comics needs are being served to the best of your library's ability. A dedicated budget nor a specialist selector are absolutely necessary to have a brilliant comics collection, just as long as the money is put to its maximum use by a selection process that is just as thorough as it is for other materials, ethical and lacking bias, is well-researched and thoughtful, serves the community well, and is an otherwise wise way to spend public funds. The only reason you should have no comics in your library at all is if you have evidence to suggest your community would not be served by them, and, especially if you work in a public library, this is very, very unlikely.

COLLECTION DEVELOPMENT POLICIES

Like any materials your library carries, a strong collection development policy is crucial. It is crucial for determining selection practices, it is crucial to ensure you are spending money wisely, and, most importantly, it is crucial as a safeguard against patron challenges. Comics, being still relatively new to libraries and still battling the Golden Age stigmas of being low art, are highly susceptible to challenges from patrons, especially due to their highly visual nature. Hence, a tightly worded collection development policy can be your best defense and a way to reassure patrons that the library should have something for everyone. There is little worse than getting caught off guard by a patron's complaint about material and having nothing in writing to back up the library's position. A patron should never have to just take you at your word.

A good collection development policy will do much more than protect you from angry patrons, though. It's a guide for selection, a justification for the material's presence in the library to begin with, and a sort of covenant between the library and the patron that this item is not here on a whim; it was a thoughtful, meticulously chosen purchase that has the library's mission and dedication to the community in mind. There are a couple of common ways that libraries include comics in their collection

Library Comic by Gene Ambaum and Pat Coleman   librarycomic.com © 2018 Ambauminable LLC

FIGURE 3.2. Unlike the librarian in this Library Comic, you probably can't be this blunt with concerned patrons. (©2018 Ambauminable LLC, used with permission.)

development policies. The first and most common is to have a policy that is broad enough to allow a multitude of materials in a multitude of formats with an overarching justification and process for them all, so that the policy does not necessarily need to be altered every time a new

Graphic Novels

Graphic novels have gained literary acceptance as a new medium through which a combination of text and sequential art are used to tell a story. The Willoughby Eastlake Public Library graphic novel collection is made up of core and popular titles that serve informational and recreational reading interests of children, young adults, and adults.

The library will collect graphic novels in English, based on popular demand, reviews, author and publisher reputation, literary and artistic merit. Patron requests will also be taken into consideration when purchasing graphic novels. In selecting adult titles, graphic novels that are primarily erotica will not be purchased.

The library strives to select graphic novels that serve the children, young adult, and adult readers. It remains the parents or adult care-givers responsibility to determine which materials are appropriate for their children.

Graphic novels are retained as long as they are in good condition to circulate. If a publisher produces books with bindings that do not stand up to typical library use, these books are not purchased or replaced.

FIGURE 3.3. An example of a graphic-specific policy under the collection development policy. (Courtesy of the Willoughby-Eastlake Public Library.)

format is introduced. The other is to specifically list comics in its own section in the policy or subsection under print materials. There are pros and cons to both. A broad policy may come across a bit wishy-washy and leave lots of room for interpretation for you *and* your patrons, practically begging for arguments. But a format-specific policy regarding comics will need to be very detailed and carefully worded, and in effect, it may feel too limiting and smothering as you work with the material.

Weeding

A good policy should guide a library on its comics purchasing, but it should also provide efficient weeding practices. Weeding comics can be tricky and frustrating. Comics can be more expensive than the average book, but sometimes (hopefully due to frequent circulation), they won't even last you a full year before they become too tattered to circulate. As Shivon, librarian at Reedley College says, "I get excited when the comics are literally falling apart. That means they're being read!"[10] Since comics tend to have higher circulations, especially superhero titles, regardless of actual quality or content of story, it may be difficult to discern whether or not it should be reordered. You'll need to ask yourself, "If I reorder this comic that has circulated very well, will it continue to circulate just as well in the upcoming years?" It's possible that it might not, and it is fine to simply weed the item and not reorder it. But then again, maybe the title is destined to pick up even more momentum.

This is where the hype sites like Comic Book Resources can come in handy. If you pay attention to the big news and big trends, you may gain some industry knowledge that will give you a better instinct as to whether or not a title should be weeded. Sites like that can tell you things like:

- Is the series to which this title belongs still going strong or is it due for cancellation? Perhaps it's already cancelled?
- Is there a sequel series, follow-up event, or tie-in event coming that may make this comic still relevant?
- If the series is cancelled, is it being relaunched? If it is being relaunched, is it a complete reboot or will the new, relaunched series rely heavily on the stories that took place in the older series?
- Is there an adaptation of this comic on the horizon, such as a film or video game, that may give it the spotlight in the near future?
- Has a creator of this comic, perhaps writer or illustrator, recently achieved acclaim? If so, would people be interested in reading their earlier works?

Here is an example of the type of situation you may run into when weeding comics. In 2014, Marvel published *Spider-Verse,* which was written by Dan Slott, and a crossover event that ran throughout the *Spider-Man* titles. This was published as a trade paperback. Let's say in 2014, you purchased this comic for your library and in 2017 you see that it is very beaten up. It must be weeded, but the book is over $30, even at library pricing, so you're not sure if you should reorder it. It was clearly loved, and you could use that $30 for something new! But you hop onto Comic Book Resources and you see some news: not only is there a sequel series coming out in 2018 called *Spider-Geddon* that readers may not understand if they don't read *Spider-Verse* but there's also an animated film called *Into the Spider-Verse* coming out, too. If you weed the title and don't reorder it, you may be missing some upcoming demand, but the story is 4 years old. What do you do?

Just like when this situation happens with traditional books, you will have a lot to consider. If your library is made of money, reordering it may be a no-brainer, but if it is not, is it better to have something new on the shelves to keep your readers interested? Perhaps your library can inter-loan the older title for anyone who asks for it? These are all questions that practice, familiarity with the product, and, most importantly, a strong collection development policy, can help you determine. Comics, like any other materials you may work with, deserve your thoughtful, professional approach and deserve to be included in your collection development policy in some fashion, as long as that fashion serves the needs of your community.

NOTES

1. The DC Zoom and DC Ink imprints were short-lived, as DC announced in June 2019 that they were rebranding their lines to DC Kids, DC, and DC Black Label.

2. John Dudas, in-person interview by Jack Phoenix, April 3, 2019.

3. Rachel Bild, interview via email by Jack Phoenix, April 17, 2019.

4. Violet Jaffe, interview via email by Jack Phoenix, April 25, 2019.

5. Full disclosure: I was employed by OverDrive as a Content Specialist from June of 2017 through September of 2018.

6. Check out graphicaudio.net and you can find plenty of audio comics from Marvel and DC.

7. Rachel Bild, interview via email by Jack Phoenix, April 17, 2019.

8. Similar sites, *Newsarama, Superherohype,* and *comicbook.com* can also be helpful for following comic book news; but be warned—you may have to tolerate clickbait headlines, misspellings, and improper grammar. Comic Book Resources has, in my opinion, the most journalistic integrity of its kind, though that still leaves a bit to be desired.

9. Rachel Bild, interview via email by Jack Phoenix, April 17, 2019.

10. Shivon, email exchange, June 10, 2019.

4

Making Comics Accessible

The Ohio Library Council (OLC) once hosted a presentation at the OLC Convention and Expo titled "Comics Aren't Books, and That's Okay!"[1] The room was full. The presentation expressed the idea that our libraries are designed for traditional books; our classification systems, our shelving, our systems, our methods . . . all of it, and our libraries are often woefully inadequate at organizing comics in a way that benefits them or their readers. Presentations just like it, dealing with comics organization, have been popping up at professional development events all over the country, so this is clearly an issue yearning to be addressed on a national scale. Hopefully, this book has (if you didn't know already) demonstrated to you that comics are unique. They are not traditional books, and, perhaps, shoe-horning them into systems designed for traditional books is doing them and their audience a disservice. Our usual cataloging and shelving practices are not conducive to comics, and the amount of discussion happening on the topic demonstrates that librarians are concerned about it.

If you need further evidence that this is a topic worth addressing, the 2018 New York Comic Con's day for librarians and educators (called NYCC @ NYPL 2018), held in the Stephen A. Schwarzman Building of the New York Public Library, held a panel discussion with librarians/ comics experts called "Is 741.5 Still Helpful? Challenges and Recommendations for Making Comics and Graphic Novels More Accessible to Users." This panel of seasoned experts discussed the same issues as the OLC presentation but with librarians from all over the country. It was another packed house. During the ALA Graphic Novel Interest Group

Meet-Up at C2E2 2018 one of the hosts asked what the most important issue was they wanted to see a future ALA Comics and Graphic Novels Round Table to address. The room, almost in unison, resoundingly agreed that it must be cataloging standards. Following this, a panel presentation was held at C2E2 called "Get It Sorted: Keeping Collections Browse-able @ Your Library." Librarians everywhere are eager for these conversations.

If you too are feeling the frustration over those pesky comics not fitting into our beloved cataloging and classification schemes, just know that you're not alone, and maybe, hopefully, this book can help. Since no authoritative body has decided on hard-set cataloging rules, let's explore recommendations and alternatives put forth by other libraries. Perhaps together, dear reader, we can discover what could be or should be best practices to maximizing comics access for your patrons and boosting circulations for your library. This chapter will discuss what the issues are and, rather than clear-cut solutions, some possibilities you can pursue, tinker with, and ponder as you work with comics in your own library setting. Please note, these are not definitive, concrete answers to the challenges, nor will you find any one-size-fits-all solutions, since every library may be dealing with different issues when it comes to providing access to comics. Librarians who love comics sometimes wish our superpowers included altering reality just enough to allow for a comics cataloging and classification standard, because *that's* how you solve the universe's problems, Thanos! But perhaps seeing the problems articulated and then being presented with possible solutions may inspire you to think outside the long box with comics and come up with creative solutions of your own. Let's get started!

CATALOGING

Cataloging comics has been a frustration for catalogers, reference librarians, and patrons for years. The cataloging standards we use as librarians were simply not created with comics in mind. Many of the problems that arise when cataloging comics are the same problems that come from cataloging other serials, which is an imperfect method at best, having each individual issue share a common bibliographic record. Though this is simpler on the cataloger, it can be a disaster when it comes to comics as this medium, unlike most other serial publications such as magazines that libraries carry, are usually telling a single story from issue-to-issue, volume to volume. Even if such a cataloging method can work for single issues, cataloging trades is where the confusion really comes in.

What exactly are the problems then? Basically, the bibliographic records for comics don't prioritize the information that comics seekers are looking for when they search for their comics, causing catalogs to be cumbersome and confusing. To most comic seekers, three pieces of information are most important: series title, volume/issue number, and publisher (Phoenix 2015). There are, of course, exceptions that happen all the time, such as a comics seeker desiring works by a particular creator, but in general, these are pieces of information comic readers use when looking for their next title, making library bibliographic standards inconducive. A comic fan is very likely to know the name of the series they are looking for and who publishes it, whether that's Marvel, DC, Image, and so on. Books from smaller publishers are another exception, since most comic seekers won't know those company names, but considering Marvel, DC, and Image dominate the comics industry, more of their titles are likely to be sought. If a comic reader is looking for a particular story, they may look by creators, but they are even more likely to look for a particular issue or the trade volume in which the issue is reprinted. Librarian Laurel Tarulli says, "The fact that many fans of graphic novels want their graphic novels separated by publisher, rather than series, poses further challenges for catalogers. While catalogers might appreciate that separating DC from Marvel is indeed useful because of the browsing trends of graphic novel fans, catalogers struggle to balance serving the needs of our patrons, with the need for uniformity of cataloging practices" (2010).

So, as it turns out, our bibliographic records are simply not conducive to how comic seekers look for their comics. This stems from applying the same FRBR MARC record standards for regular books to comics (Fee 2008), resulting in inadequate bibliographic records. As Fee states, "Comic books have a number of characteristics that differentiate them from other formats" (Fee 2008). This includes the integral illustrations, their (often) serial nature, the chance for irregularities in their publications (such as series being cancelled and then relaunched years later with the continued numbering or starting over with new numbering as a new "volume"), as well as "frequent changes in title, character, creator and even publisher" (Fee 2008). Often comics are created by a team of at least three people; writer, artist, colorist/cover artist (Fee 2008). Many of the typical standard cataloging practices that librarians use simply don't fit comics perfectly, leaving gaps in the bibliographic records or creating misleading author responsibility statements or main entries.

THE "VOLUME" PROBLEM

The term "Volume" is a tricky one when it comes to comics, and you have trades to thank. As discussed in Chapter 1, when talking about true graphic novels, like *My Favorite Thing Is Monsters*, Vol. 1 and Vol. 2 simply indicate that one entry follows the other. Simple.

The same is mostly true for trades. But remember, trades are a collection of serial comic books. The word "volume" applies differently to serial publications like journals, magazines, and comic books. Every time a comic book relaunches at issue #1, a new volume of that title begins. A particular volume, for example, volume 1 or volume 2 of a comic book, indicates a particular series when there are two different series with the same name, same publisher, and same character(s).

For instance, *The Amazing Spider-Man* series, which began in 1963, had its last issue before it was relaunched in 1999. So, that is *The Amazing Spider-Man Volume 1* and the relaunched series began *Volume 2* with a new issue #1. There have been three relaunches since, with the most recent one happening in 2018. In July of 2018, *The Amazing Spider-Man #1* (which would be *Volume 5*) was released. So, yes, there are multiple issues of *The Amazing Spider-Man* that have been printed that are known as *The Amazing Spider-Man #1*. But that issue would be *The Amazing Spider-Man* (Volume 5) #1.

Now, keep in mind that every time a comic book series is relaunched, the issues are then collected into trades, and those trades then start over with their numbering, as well, using a different sense of the word "volume." So, the first several *The Amazing Spider-Man (Volume 5)* comic books will be collected as a trade titled *The Amazing Spider-Man, Volume 1*. Considering that *The Amazing Spider-Man* has relaunched a few times in the past decade alone, this means (take a deep breath), that currently on any given library shelf there may be three different trades called *The Amazing Spider-Man, Volume 1* (and the real kicker is they may share the same writer).

All of this relaunching and renumbering is difficult for comic enthusiasts to track, so imagine being a new reader who wants to jump on board. This is just one of the reasons why comics are such a nightmare for librarians to classify, catalog, and overall organize on the shelves in any way that is friendly and easy to follow for staff and patrons. The Grand Comics Database (comics.org) and Comixology can be very useful tools for navigating the "volume" problem, and hopefully you can find some ideas in this chapter that can help from some clever libraries' in-house classification systems.

Speaking of main entry, one of the ways our bibliographic standards and comics seekers don't mesh is how our bibliographic records prioritize author and title as the main access points for an item's metadata. This works just fine for graphic novels, for the most part. After all, the graphic novel *RASL* is a self-contained story, a self-contained volume if in hardcover, and it lists Jeff Smith as its main creator. That, then, would not be difficult to find via a public catalog and most seekers of the title would find it. But when it comes to trades, "author" gets confusing. As Fee pointed out earlier, the "author" of the work may or not be important to the reader. The reader may not know nor care who wrote the comic. The reader may be more interested in the artist, or the reader may not care about any member of the creative team at all. Comic fans who are very in the know, those seasoned comic readers, are very likely to know and appreciate the names of the creative team behind a certain work, but the casual fans may not. But the problem truly lies in the title.

Bibliographic record standards, whether AACR2 or RDA, say that a trade's subtitle, not series title, should be placed in the prime slot so it shows up dominantly in the catalog. The problem is, with comics, the subtitle is rarely the most important element. There are exceptions of course, such as seminal storylines like "The Phoenix Saga," but the most important piece of information for most comic readers and most comics is the series title. Unfortunately, the standard bibliographic record relegates the series title to the bottom of the record and in very small print on the catalog display. Fee discusses the importance of providing a proper "Title Statement" to a comic's bibliographic record that may not fit the standard. "The issue here, of course, is that according to AACR2R 12.0B.2 the cover title is to be preferred over the masthead [indicia]" (Fee 2008). Referencing the work of Randall Scott, Fee argues that favoring the title page or the cover title of a comic is not the best option, for comics "editors are given a great deal of freedom in the cover title" (Fee 2008). Fee argues, instead, that the indicia, the fine and very small print that comics and trades have in their first few pages, is a constant and will always provide the most reliable title to use as the Title Statement in the bibliographic record. This is the actual publication title of the work, the title the very publisher will record it under for its own records.

Here is an example of typical AACR2 or RDA MARC record standards not fitting very well with comics. Most monthly comic book series have two titles they are known by, the series title such as *The Amazing Spider-Man* and the story arc title (which could also be called a subtitle), such as "The Death of Gwen Stacey," which is the title of that particular story within that series, which often takes multiple issues to tell. Some story arc titles are very well-known, such as the aforementioned, but most are not. When comics are collected in trades, it is not uncommon for the publisher to print only the story arc title (subtitle) on the title page, while having the series title on the cover and spine and everywhere else on the book. So, when a cataloger, following AACR2 or RDA cataloging standards, makes a MARC record of this title, they may include the lesser-known story arc title as the main entry in the bibliographic record rather than the series title. This practice can infringe convenient access to the item for the user. An example of this within the Central Library Consortium (CLC) in Ohio catalog is *Cable and X-Force. Vol 1. Wanted*, which showed as simply "Wanted" in the title field.

CLC addressed the cataloging problem and created a consortium-wide standard for cataloging comics amongst its member libraries. This standard, however, calls for actually breaking *traditional* cataloging standards, such as using what is on the title page as the 245 field main title entry. This is an example of a very strong library consortium using unorthodox means to make the cataloging best suit the item and the user, not the other way around, which is precisely what I urge you to do. Cataloging standards are very useful, as standards are important for consistency and consistency is vital for organization. But with comics, there may be a way to be consistent, by allowing comic bibliographic records to have their own unique standards that break from traditional books. Gasp! Is this book actually suggesting you ignore cataloging training and authorities by creating your *own* standards for comics in your libraries? Yes. Yes, it is. Being part of a consortium like CLC, though, makes it easier, if you can get them on board. If you can't, well, that's another story.

Table 4.1 is an example of some of the confusion and inconsistency that can befall comic bibliographic records when they are shoe-horned into MARC record standards.[2] Under the aforementioned CLC guidelines, catalogers know to include additional information in the title field of any comic that passes their workstation. The standard 245 field for a trade paperback or hardcover is $aSeries title.$nVolume number.$pSubtitle.

TABLE 4.1. A recreation of a solid comic (specifically a trade) bibliographic record. (Courtesy of the Central Library Consortium and the Grandview Public Library.)

100	1	$aBennett, Marguerite,$eauthor.
245	10	$aBombshells.$nVolume 3,$pUprising /$cwritten by Marguerite Bennett; art by Mirka Andolfo, Laura Braga [and others]; color by Wendy Broome, J. Nanjan, Kelly Fitzpatrick; letters, Wes Abbott.
246	30	$aDC Comics Bombshells. Volume 3, Uprising
246	30	$aUprising
264	1	$aBurbank, CA:$bDC Comics,$c[2016]
300		$a1 Volume (unpaged):$billustrations (chiefly color);$c26 cm.

To see how this can improve access in comparison to using orthodox cataloging rules, let's look at the *Cable and X-Force* comic mentioned earlier.

Figure 4.1 is from the CLC catalog, and these are the first two entries that would appear if a user typed in the search terms "Cable and X-Force" into the search box. Both of these items were cataloged before CLC implemented their comic cataloging standards. As you can see, both are missing immediately available information that would be helpful to any seeker of this comic series. The first entry tells us the subtitle and the volume number, but not the series title. True, the series title is available on the thumbnail image and in fine print in the "Series" entry, or if the user clicked full display, but why should a library patron be forced to squint and examine this entry to get such vital information? Would librarians find this acceptable for any other medium? The series title is the most important piece of information, yet it is not treated as a main entry.

In Figure 4.2, we have the improvement of the series title being immediately visible in the main entry, as well as the subtitle. But nowhere in this entry are we given another crucial piece of information, which is the volume number. The seeker of this series has no way of knowing if this is volume 2 or volume 5 to the volume 1 shown. Such inconsistencies in cataloging are usually considered unacceptable for cataloging librarians, but, as the literature makes apparent, inconsistencies are a frequent problem for comics in libraries.

Figure 4.3 is another entry for this series from the same search. The difference compared to the top two is obvious, and this item was cataloged after the CLC standards were put in place. Here, instantly, the

2013

1. Wanted : Volume 1
   by *Hopeless, Dennis.*

... Wanted : Volume 1 ;/ [by] *Dennis Hopeless* , writer ; artist, Salvador Larroca, Gabriel Hernandez Walta. ... Where has Colossus been since the Avengers battled the *X* -Men, *and* what's wrong with his powers? What will happen when *Cable* faces his foster daughter, Hope, Earth's "savior"? *And* most important, why has the new *X - Force* targeted a civilian company? Caught red-handed at the scene ...

Publisher, Date: New York : Marvel, 2013.

Description: 1 v. (unpaged) ; chiefly color ill. ; 26 cm.
Series: *Cable and X-Force* ; v. 1.

Local Availability: 0 (of 0)
System Availability: 0 (of 1)

WHERE IS IT?

FULL DISPLAY

PLACE REQUEST

FIGURE 4.1. The results of a search for Cable and X-Force would originally display inconsistently thanks to a lack of cataloging standards for comics. This is a Cable and X-Force trade, but it displays differently than Figure 4.2. (From London Public Library catalog, part of the Central Library Consortium.)

2014

3. *Cable and X-Force*. This won't end well
   by *Hopeless, Dennis*, author.

... *Cable and X - Force* . This won't end well / writer, *Dennis Hopeless* with Cullen Bunn (script, #12-13) ; artist, Salvador Larroca ...

Publisher, Date: New York, NY : Marvel Worldwide, Inc., [2014]

Description: 1 volume (unpaged) ; color illustrations ; 26 cm
Series: Marvel now!

Local Availability: 0 (of 0)
System Availability: 3 (of 3)

WHERE IS IT?

FULL DISPLAY

PLACE REQUEST

FIGURE 4.2. The results of a search for Cable and X-Force would originally display inconsistently thanks to a lack of cataloging standards for comics. This is a Cable and X-Force trade, but it displays differently than Figure 4.1. (From London Public Library catalog, part of the Central Library Consortium.)

searcher is provided with all the important information. In bold and in the main entry, easily visible, they are given the series title, the volume number, and the subtitle. However, even this entry is not perfect and is one that fell through the cracks of the CLC standards. Figure 4.4 is an example of an item that does fit the standard perfectly. This is how a comic does and should appear in the CLC catalog, and other library systems would be wise to make this a priority.

FIGURE 4.3. A much better search result with series title displayed prominently. (From London Public Library catalog, part of the Central Library Consortium.)

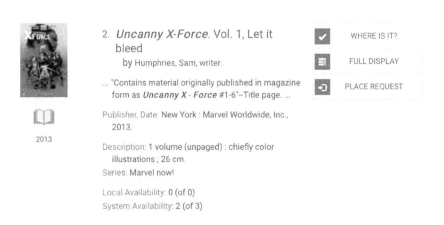

FIGURE 4.4. A perfect display for a comic search, thanks to an adopted bibliographic standard for the medium. (From London Public Library catalog, part of the Central Library Consortium.)

To summarize, when patrons search for comics in your online public access catalogs, they are most likely to search by series title, since most comics in your library will be issues of a series that are collected as trades, and from there they may look for volume number, subtitle, or creator. Therefore, it is essential to have the series title, volume number, and subtitle in the 245 main title field of a bibliographic record. Even though this is breaking MARC record standards, it provides all of the information your comic-loving patrons will need in full and in easy-to-read text displayed on the screen. If you're not a cataloger, your catalogers' heads may implode if you tell them to break the standard. If you are a cataloger, just remember that it's not about breaking the standard; it's about creating a new standard for a unique medium. Most importantly, it's what's best for the patron, and why are we here if not to do what's best for the patron? Making the comics as easy to find in the catalog is just one more step to maximizing their circulation and maximizing your service to comic readers.

Common Problems, Simple Solutions

That was a lot of information. Let's take a simpler look at some of the common practices within libraries that can create problems with library comics cataloging as well as some solutions that libraries across the country have used.

CLASSIFICATION AND SHELVING

"One of the most common complications librarians struggle with is the classification and collocation of graphic novels" (Fee 2013). Integral to the cataloging problem is the question of how to classify comics. As far as Dewey is concerned, comics have their place in the scheme of Dewey Decimal Classification (DDC) nestled under its 741.5 number. But just because something has a Dewey number, that doesn't mean we are obligated to use it, despite common feelings. Librarians have been ignoring Dewey for decades. Look for a library in the United States that interfiles its fiction books or its DVD movies under DDC with nonfiction materials, and I dare say you'll be hard-pressed to find one, and I just might have to buy you a cookie if you do. Librarians decided long ago that it was acceptable to separate certain materials, particularly certain formats, into their own special collections, ignoring Dewey for these collections completely. Yet comics, so frequently, are filed under Dewey in libraries along with nonfiction titles, due, no doubt, to library staff not recognizing comics as a format worthy of exclusion. I imagine the thought

TABLE 4.2. Here are some common library practices, why they may not work for comics, and simple solutions

Practice	Problem	Solution
Treat all comics as serials and attach multiple items to a single bibliographic record.	This does not easily allow for the inclusion of story arc titles and differing creators without the bibliographic record becoming unwieldly, nor does it accurately display in a public access catalog.	Be selective as to which comics are treated as serials. Comic books and most manga titles can more easily share a bibliographic record. Trades and graphic novels should be given monographic bibliographic records.
Using the title page as the main source of information for the bibliographic record.	This is just fine for prose books, but not for comic trades. Comic publishers tend to shift what information is included on the title page. For instance, the volume number may not be included on the title page, but it is visible on the spine.	Catalogers must be willing to look at the entirety of the item for information, not just the title page. If this is a problem at your library, it would help to create a document telling the catalogers for which pieces of information they need to look and where they are likely to be found on the item.
The series to which an individual title belongs goes in the 490 field in a MARC record.	For prose books, the series title is often not as important as it is for comics. *A Clash of Kings,* the second book in *A Song of Ice and Fire* will display just fine in a catalog with traditional standards. However, the series title takes more priority for a comic, not only in the structure of how the works are published but also in how users look for them.	Because the series title is so important, and there are so many series out there that are similar (e.g., *Captain Marvel, The Mighty Captain Marvel),* the series title should be included in the main title field, 245. See Figure 4.1 for a good example.

(continued)

TABLE 4.2. Here are some common library practices, why they may not work for comics, and simple solutions (*continued*)

Practice	Problem	Solution
Including the subject heading of "Comic books, strips, etc." in the MARC record.	This is actually correct, since this should be included with the subject heading of any comic bibliographic record. Unfortunately, it is slightly inaccurate at the Library of Congress level, since comics is a format and not fully a subject. Sometimes, catalogers will include this subject heading and stop, without looking any further at the work.	Catalogers need to be sure they are being thorough with their subject analysis of a comic, just as they would be with any other work. Is the comic a memoir? Is it journalism? Is it about science or history? All such appropriate subject headings must also be included. In the case of a superhero comic, it doesn't hurt to include the character's name along with the "Fictitious characters" subject heading.

process goes something like, *This resembles a book, but it can't go in Fiction where it would sit next to popular titles and literature, because would you just* look *at all those pictures!* Hopefully, you realize by now that comics deserve more thoughtfulness in how your library chooses to classify them.

In 2004, the Online Computer Library Center (OCLC) proposed some slight modifications to DDC to allow comics to fit better and in more specified classifications for the different types of comics. This allowed for comics, works about comics, instructional works, and so on, to remain under the same first, second, and third summary, but to then be divided by classification distinction via decimal numbers, allowing the items to remain within proximity but still have their own areas. If you work in a public library, you surely know how this works. The proposed alterations from OCLC were:

1. Cartoons, caricatures, comics, graphic novels all together in 741.5 . . . Our proposal is to improve the development at 741.5 rather than to relocate graphic novels to another set of numbers.[3]

2. Adaptations of works of literature, film, television, stage production . . . Graphic novels that are versions of works of literature, film, television, or stage production are treated as adaptations and classed as graphic novels in 741.5 and its subdivisions, not in the numbers appropriate for the original works.

3. Single works and collections of cartoons, caricatures, comics, graphic novels in 741.59 . . . We propose to class single works and collections of cartoons, caricatures, comics, graphic novels alike in 741.59.

4. Works in 741.59 subarranged by country of artist or writer . . . For example, a work by a French artist or writer is classed in 741.5944, a work by a Belgian artist or writer in 741.59493 . . .

5. History and criticism; biographies and critical appraisal . . . We plan to keep general history and criticism of cartoons, caricatures, comics, and graphic novels (not limited geographically) in 741.509.

6. New subdivisions of 741.5 for techniques, for genres, special qualities and themes . . . we propose to provide a general techniques subdivision of 741.5 for works on how to draw cartoons, caricatures, comics, graphic novels.

7. Cartoons, caricatures, comics, graphic novels whose purpose is to inform or persuade . . . unlike nonfiction graphic novels, we have classed political cartoons with the subject, without worrying about artistic license in either the text or the graphics; we have regarded political cartoons as primarily intended to persuade, not to give factual accounts of actual people and events.

8. Fotonovelas (photo novels) . . . We propose that fotonovelas, which are based on photographs, be relocated to the photography portion of the Dewey schedule (OCLC 2014).

These proposals were intended to clarify things, but, despite OCLC's best efforts, it still doesn't address the core question that troubles so many library staffs; do comics really belong in 741.5 with "art"? Is Dewey useful to comics at all? The trouble lies in Dewey being inadequately able to address the uniqueness of comics. They are, undoubtedly, art, yes. Comics are heavily, graphically illustrated, otherwise they wouldn't be comics. But they also tell a narrative, sometimes long, sometimes short, but always a narrative, even when providing factual information. Otherwise, they wouldn't still be comics. Though OCLC absolutely acknowledges above that comics are narratives, we still have the DDC essentially deciding that the art overshadows the narrative, despite what would surely be protests from comic fans and writers, that the art *is* the narrative and the narrative *is* the art. To label comics strictly as art is a disservice to the often-superb writing that can be contained within, and vice versa to label them exclusively as literature. So, what are comics? The DDC doesn't really have an answer (Dewey 2006).

"So," you ask, "what's the solution, then? If comics shouldn't be classified under Dewey with nonfiction, then I suppose it's off to the fiction shelves." Heavens to Murgatroyd, no! Most libraries organize their fiction sections by author, and the classification is actually just the name of the collection. But interfiling trades, graphic novels, and manga with fiction under the authors' names will create just as much as chaos for your comic seekers as filing them under 741.5, perhaps even more. If you'll recall in Chapter 1, many, if not most, comics have multiple creators, and it's common for a single trade, to have multiple writers, not to mention different writers on a single series between sequential volumes. Splitting up volumes of the same series and placing them in different locations on a shelf is hardly improving access.

> Classification by author can separate the physical collection for this title into widely different locations, even if the graphic novel collection is only 2 or 3 shelving units. In like fashion, if a title is shelved by subtitle, the sequence of a title can be vastly disordered, as illustrated when *Justice League: American Dreams* (volume 8) is filed before *Justice League: New World Order* (volume 1) (Fee 2013).

"Well, we can fix that," you say, "we'll make sure that all the comics will be filed in the fiction section under title instead of author. That way they all stay together." It's better, but not exactly great. You see, one of the many tricky things about comics, especially trades, is that the titles are not always consistent either. It's not uncommon for a series to change its title, sometimes only temporarily, but continuing the same story (such as *The Amazing Spider-Man* becoming *The Superior Spider-Man* and then back to *The Amazing Spider-Man*). Not to mention that if a graphic novel gets a proper sequel, it may have a title that is unrelated, and then those will be physically separated on the shelf, as well. Interfiling comics in a fiction section by author or title will create problems either way. Not to mention the other crucial detail that not all comics are fiction. There are plenty of nonfiction comics, including memoirs.

"Fine then," you shout in frustration, "I'll just file the fiction comics in fiction and figure it out, and, since you say 741.5 isn't good enough, I'll just file all the nonfiction comics under their subject along with all the other books, so that graphic memoirs go under biographies." This is an option that could work for some libraries. In this scenario, you are ignoring the idea that comics are a format, which may not be such a bad thing, as you are acknowledging their literary and informative value, by filing them with other books. You are allowing people who would not normally read comics to perhaps find one serendipitously by placing comics with the other books and subjects they are already browsing. Unfortunately, while you may be opening a door to invite someone new to discover comics, you may be punishing the seasoned comics-faithful readers by separating them throughout your holdings.

If you choose to go the route of filing comics with traditional books with the subjects they represent, you are on the right path to maximizing their impact. Expert Gail Dickinson says, "Your catalog should reflect classification number by content for nonfiction, and author for fiction, but a special display will highlight the most popular" (2007). The special display here is key, and it exemplifies something I want to point out about this entire discussion. If you choose this method, you are choosing to break DDC standards, you are choosing an unorthodox route, and one could argue you are choosing to break tradition . . . but you are doing it for the sake of your patron. This is the key to maximizing comics in your library. You must be patron-focused. You must be willing to see the library and its collection through your patrons' eyes, and meet them where they are, rather than make things more difficult for them simply because it's "how we've always done it." This is truly the crux of the problem with comics classification. If you are a comic fan who enters your library for the first time looking for a new comic, where would you think to look? Do you truly believe that your patrons will think to look in the nonfiction section for a story about a modern-day sorcerer who protects Earth from otherworldly threats? Would you think to look in fiction for a graphic memoir about a Holocaust survivor?[4] The point is that if being beholden to Dewey or to Library of Congress (LCC) means making things more difficult for the patron, then maybe it's time to consider alternatives.

This is the right path, but we are not quite there yet. What libraries are finding is that the best way to classify comics is with an in-house classification system. Read on to learn more.

SOLUTIONS AND ALTERNATIVES

If DDC and LCC are not providing the optimum access to comics, then what is a library to do? Libraries actually have plenty of options, but you have to be willing to break the rules, as it were. Or at least go against the standards. The idea of such a thing is enough to make some librarians, who, if I may stereotype, tend to be perfectionists by nature, get a little tense. But many librarians are also service-oriented people, and, upon realizing that the practices they have in place are not providing the best service, they are usually willing to experiment. So, here are some ideas that you may find useful and that you can tinker with at your own libraries, tweaking as you see fit to best suit your public. These are, as previously stated, not one-size-fits all solutions. My hope would be that you read about some ideas and what other libraries have done, and it ignites a spark allowing you to come up with your own creative solutions for maximizing your comics. Let's look at some of the ways you can improve access to your comics on the physical shelves.

If your comics are interfiled with traditional books, then one obvious but still sure-fire way to draw attention to them is to highlight them with stickers, shelf-talkers, and facing them out for display. These simple, common, but very effective methods can easily boost circulation of your comic titles, and this allows them to remain shelved with the other materials of like topics, making the much-desired serendipitous discovery possible, particularly with nonfiction. This, in fact, may be the most effective way to attract new comic readers, as it improves the odds of a patron taking a risk on a comic since the patron was theoretically already browsing the particular subject area. Having comics such as *Persepolis* and *My Friend Dahmer* in your biography section improves the odds they'll be found by biography fans, as opposed to strictly comic fans. Parents who are looking for a good science book for their young readers may be thrilled to discover the award-winning *Science Comics* series amidst the other science books, allowing comics to leave your library with people who had no idea they even existed. Comics can be a real treasure to the parents of reluctant readers, to say nothing of the readers themselves.

All of the major vendors who sell practical products to libraries, like Brodart and Demco, carry stickers that can be placed on the spine or front of a book indicating it's a comic, though most of these stickers say "graphic novel," so they will be a bit misleading to add to a nonfiction title. These same major vendors carry some style of shelf-talker or shelf labels, as well, or it's easy to make them yourself if you're the crafty sort. These can be a lot of fun, and you can even take some cues from bookstores by allowing staff to write reviews of the books that they believe deserve a patron's attention. Some options that I've seen say things as simple as "GRAPHIC NOVEL!," "COMIC!," or "Perfect for reluctant readers!" I've seen other libraries use shelf-talkers to highlight comics on the shelf that have an upcoming movie or TV show, such as a flashy, little sign that says "DEADPOOL" under the shelf location of the Deadpool comics when the movie *Deadpool 2* was approaching release. I know, I know, this is simple, and libraries do it all the time, but it works.

Any way you can draw attention to comics, the better their circulations will be.

Never underestimate the power of a good display. Whether you're simply using a bookstand to prop up a particular title so that it faces out from the end of a shelf or you're decorating a dedicated display space, displays and merchandising are a must to improve circulation and enthusiasm for all library materials, and comics are no exception. A solid comic display boasting your library's collection can truly work wonders, catching the eye of all who enter, sounding the alarm to any who were unaware that this library has comics. Like the aforementioned shelf-talkers, displaying titles that have hype surrounding them, such as an upcoming movie or TV show, is a fun way to invite new readers to the medium and give the experienced ones a chance to refresh. Comic book movies are making billions at the box office, so libraries shouldn't waste any opportunity to capitalize on the hype and boost circulation. You never know who might be willing to pick up the latest *Venom* trade at the library after having enjoyed the *Venom* movie in the theater.

Again, I'm aware that this is pretty basic stuff. Using stickers and displays is likely the type of thing you are already doing in your libraries, and my intention is not to condescend. But I have encountered many libraries who are stickering and displaying their traditional books, but not their comics for whatever reason. Some libraries who are on board and carrying comics, still have a tendency to ignore them and not treat them with as much care and attention as the traditional books in their collections. But as I have argued, not only are comics deserving of equal care, but they are also deserving of their own unique care. Since we've established that DDC and LCC are not the best equipped to classify and organize comics, then giving comics their own classification is the best way to maximize your users access to them. The aforementioned methods are things that nearly every library can do for their comics to at least some capacity. What we will discuss now is what you can best do for your comics if you have the time, the labor, and the space to spare. Even if you don't have such luxuries, perhaps you'll be inspired and come up with an idea that you can work with within your means.

For maximizing comics, you can't beat an in-house classification system. For those of you who work in libraries where you are using BISAC or an alternative classification other than DDC or LCC, this won't be that much of a stretch for you to accomplish. For those of you who do work in libraries using DDC or LCC, just remember that, if you need justification, you likely already have collections in your library, such as DVDs, fiction, or biographies, that are classified outside of DDC or LCC. Not only can an in-house classification system be fun to create, it gives you the opportunity to look at your entire collection of comics, take your user's point of view and staff's point of view into account, and create a system that caters to the needs of both. You'll need to get lots of buy-in—your director, your catalogers, your pages—and, of course, you need to make sure that it really is the right thing to do for your patrons, so be sure to do some research, like looking at circulation stats and maybe providing a survey.

An in-house classification system will allow you to organize your comics on the shelves in a comic shop style, therefore organizing them in a way that prioritizes just how your comic fans will go looking for them. The best method would be to organize by publisher, which is especially important for the Big Two of Marvel and DC, as both of those publishers tend to generate reader loyalty. Next you can prioritize Image or manga, but some libraries simply organize the titles by "DC," "Marvel," and "Other," though I do recommend keeping manga separate. Plenty of other libraries, though, throw all of their comics together and organize them by author or title, and that's still better than nothing. It all depends on the space you have to work with.

Next, you should classify your superhero titles by hero (or franchise), not by series title. Comic shops do this all the time, and it requires some more-than-general knowledge of comics sometimes, but it's what is best for your patrons. Your patrons who are looking for Spider-Man titles will typically not care if it's *The Amazing Spider-Man* or *Peter Parker: The Spectacular Spider-Man* or *Spider-Man 2099*. Comics in the Spider-Man family of titles are likely to be of more interest to Spider-Man fans. It's a simple concept, but an important one to keep in mind. The reason why some knowledge of comics would be important in this scenario, though, is because it isn't always as obvious as having "Spider" in the title. For instance, if you're going to keep all of your Batman titles together, you'll need to know that *Nightwing* and *Red-Hood and the Outlaws* are Batman titles. If you want to keep X-Men titles together, you'll need to know that *Jean Grey* and *Iceman* are X-Men titles, and so on. And what about non-superhero titles? You can either organize those by author or title. It's something that could be seen as inconsistent and could drive a cataloger nuts because it's subjective, but it's how your patrons look for comics, and that's what should matter.

You'll then want your comics to be organized by volume number or book number. This sounds easy but watch out. Remember the complications we talked about in earlier chapters with comics. Comics, especially superhero titles, get rebooted frequently, restarting a series at #1 even though it shares the same title with its previous incarnation. Hence, you may have three different *Captain Marvel* trades that each say volume one. They are all connected serially but are still different series. You'll want to check the date and indicia information to make sure that you align all the entries for the right series. This is where a handy call number can come in. You have the chance to really include all the information you'll need to keep these things organized for you and your patrons.

With an in-house classification system, you have the opportunity to create in-house call numbers. Some libraries use "GN," which no doubt stands for "Graphic Novel" sometimes, but it can also stand for "Graphic Narrative" to encompass all comics. Hopefully, you'll be organizing your comics by publisher, so you'll want to include that information, as well as the main character, franchise, or series title. If you don't have a label maker that can print the hero's entire name, like Captain Marvel, then you can try unique abbreviations for each hero, so Captain Marvel could be CMR. Then, very importantly, you'll want to include which volume of the series and which volume of the trade (remember that "volume" has two different definitions within the realm of comics). So, for instance, a call number for the first trade of the second volume of the *Captain Marvel* series should look like "GN MAR CMR 2.1." If that's too much information for a single call number and doesn't fit your library's style, then you can always leave a less crucial piece of information off that is a bit more obvious, like the GN.

If you want to keep titles in the same "family" together (e.g., Batman family, including *Nightwing* and *Catwoman)*, then you'll need to dedicate additional space on the book somewhere for a small label indicating its franchise. Obviously, you'll want to be careful of overcrowding your spines with labels and stickers, but this information will be useful to your shelving staff, and your patrons will appreciate having titles in the same franchise together. I must reiterate, though, this is the optimal organization, it all depends on what your library can and cannot do. If you don't have the resources to organize your comics in this way one hundred percent, you should consider organizing them by series title, which is the next best thing.

To recap, the best classification system will organize comics in this way:

- By overall franchise name (hero/team/main character)
- Then by series title
- Then by volume number
- For true graphic novels, organize by title or author
- Also consider organizing by publisher and separating manga

In 2008, one of librarianship's foremost experts on comics in libraries, Robert Weiner, published an article and an essay in his book, *Graphic Novels and Comics in Libraries and Archives,* about his efforts and successes in creating an in-house classification system for the comics in his library's collection. One of the first to be published about this topic, Weiner created a unique system of organizing comics, which was a tremendous success for improving circulation and being user friendly (Weiner 2008, 2010), and the next section will provide details of how that went about. Laurel references this in-house classification system in her essay in the same book (Tarulli 2010). She assesses and critiques the ways that libraries catalog comics and her observations reinforce many of the problems that Weiner sought to address in his in-house classification system. She discusses the gap that exists between front-line and technical staff at the library, highlighting why you'll need to get lots of staff buy-in before you can create your own classification system and reorganize your comics collection. But you'll likely find that, as long as you can make a strong case for it, most library staff members will care deeply about making items in your collections as browser-friendly as possible (Tarulli 2010).

CPL, "The People's University," uses LCC in its stacks, and Christina Pyles discussed quite a few suggestions on how to improve access to the comics (2012). She explained that studies have shown that circulation statistics go up when comics are added to a collection, a message to any library out there that may still be a hold out. She then echoed what Weiner had said and the reasonings he used for his in-house classification; cataloging, classification, and shelving are important for access and should be unorthodox in order to improve access to comics. Whether your library is Dewey or LCC, comics and comic readers are better served by a dedicated classification system.

In her article, Pyles tells us of CPL's main branch, which, at the time the article was written, had their comics scattered throughout three genre collections—popular library, literature, and young adult—making these items difficult for patrons to find by browsing or specifically searching. The "lack of library classification for graphic novels" is a problem (Pyles 2012), and proclaims that librarians who shelve the items by LCC or DDC call numbers are doing their users a disservice.

> Because the graphic novels are not sorted by author, publisher, character, or in any way that is appealing to the user or makes them easy to find. The inability to classify comics and graphic novels in a logical and visible way affects the way that users access this information . . . Suggested methods of improvement include the development of a formal

and in-depth classification system, the maintenance of an online comic database . . . Libraries have to come up with a universal and encompassing classification system. (Pyles 2012)

This suggestion is one that mirrors the actions that Weiner took at his library by creating the specified indexes for the "graphic novel" collection, and I also used her suggestions as a framework for my own in-house classification at the London Public Library. Her suggested method is to classify the items by publisher, then, under publisher, by character, and then for them to be arranged chronologically by story arc. She quotes Ryan Searles, "Comic book fans are the most informed group of readers. If a reader is aware of the story arc, he is aware of the author. If the books are arranged chronologically, there is no need to organize by author" (Phoenix 2015). Comics, it seems, require a library to be creative and a bit suggestive in order for them to be handled appropriately.

EXAMPLES OF IN-HOUSE CLASSIFICATION SYSTEMS

Below you can see some examples of in-house classification systems that may inspire you. Each one comes with advantages and disadvantages, as there is simply no perfect system yet. You can decide for yourself which one sounds best for your library, if any at all, but perhaps you can learn a few tips that will help in crafting your own organizational system for comics to best suit your community.

Lubbock Public Library

Notable traits: Organized by major publishers first; includes non-comic materials that are comic-related; mixed age levels.

Weiner created the in-house system at his library by combining all comics (i.e., all sequential art; comic books, trades, graphic novels, comic strips, etc.), regardless of age level with a mixed and subjective treatment of content and format. For not only were all the comics in one section, but they were joined by all other print materials related to comics, perhaps inspiring readers to pick up prose books, as well.

I did not put them in Dewey order . . . I separated DC from Marvel books, and I divided all the Spider-Man, Batman, Superman, X-Men, and Calvin and Hobbs books into separate groups. Then, I noticed that the X-Men and Batman prose novels, which were classified under science fiction, really were not circulating in that area. Therefore, we put them with the graphic novels; and after they moved, circulation of the Batman, Superman, Spider-Man, etc. prose novels improved. (Weiner 2008)

Rather than rely on the DDC, Weiner partnered with his technical services director to invent an organizational and classification system specifically designed for their new "graphic novels" section. They worked together to create a shelf index and an alphabetic index and created a system that they hoped would be browser-friendly and easy for all readers and staff members to find specific titles (Weiner 2008). This unorthodox method created a high-circulating collection, one that draws in a diverse readership, and fuels the desire for the items as well as fulfill it (Phoenix 2015). "We absolutely note that this system is not perfect, and it is subjective," he says. "It is designed to be adaptable and easy to change" (Weiner 2008). By thinking outside the box, Weiner showed a willingness to challenge cataloging standards for the sake of better accommodating his library's comics fans' browsing habits. He put ease of use for his patrons first and foremost, therefore maximizing access.

This system was written up as a policy to make it easier for other branches and other libraries to follow. He explains that his system "is designed to be both general and specific" and "it is primarily a browsing collection" with the collection organized in a "'loosely' coherent way" (Weiner 2010). He included call numbers that organized the comics by publisher and hero/main character. This is from Weiner's essay in the 2010 book *Graphic Novels and Comics in Libraries and Archives: Essays on Readers, Research, History and Cataloging:*

Graphic novel call numbers are composed of two or three lines. The first line of the call number is always "GN," clarifying the collection (Graphic Novels) in which the title belongs. The second line is generally a four-letter abbreviation for the category in which we are placing the title. DC is the only exception to the four-character abbreviation rule. Here is an example of a basic call number for an Elfquest Graphic Novel.

GN

ELFQ

Occasionally there are three lines in call number. Since we decided to keep all of the DC and Marvel comic books together, in these particular circumstances, the second line of the call number represents the publisher (DC or Marvel). Here are some examples of DC and Marvel call numbers.

GN   GN

DC   MARV

SUPE   XMEN

Nonfiction [comics] are another exception. The first line of the call number will be "GN." The second will be the Dewey Decimal number for the book. The third line will be the first four letters of the author's last name. Here is an example:

GN

940. 5315

SPIE

What makes Weiner's system so desirable is his inclusion of nonfiction titles and the acknowledgment that perhaps they deserve their own unique treatment among the greater comics umbrella. By including the DDC call numbers in the comics classification system, the nonfiction titles can maintain their DDC subject classifications and remain ordered rather than be mixed in with superhero titles and other works of fiction. With this system, comics could be organized thusly: Marvel, DC, Indie/Other, Manga, Nonfiction. Weiner's system actually has much more specific categories, seventeen in total, ranging from Marvel and DC to Star Wars and Movies and Television (Weiner 2010).

London Public Library (LPL)

Notable traits: Organized by major publisher first; teen and adult titles combined; good for small collections

In 2015, LPL, a stand-alone library, conducted a survey of its comic readers, and used that survey to determine how to improve the organization of the comics section.[5] Originally, this library's teen and adult comics and graphic novels had been placed on a simple rack, with no organization, in the teen area, and were later placed on separate shelving and alphabetized by author. This changed after the results of the survey (see Appendix A) and after taking notes from an LCS.

LPL began with an in-house classification. It was decided to ensure that all the teen and adult comics' bibliographic records[6] had series title, then volume number, then story arc title within the 245 field, but that the items would be shelved according to three major categories (Marvel, DC, and Indie), then by hero or franchise. Then a call number was crafted corresponding to each shelf, which indicated the items format, publisher, and franchise title. With much effort from Kim Michener, the technical services specialist on staff, all the comics in the collection were given these new call numbers, and she was careful not to cover up the volume number on the spine with labels. Examples of these call numbers are:

For *Batman: Detective Comics, Volume 1: The Court of Owls* (DC)

GN

DC

BAT

For *The Uncanny X-Men, Volume 1: Disassembled* (Marvel)

GN

MAR

XME

For *Saga, Book One* (Image)

GN

IND

SAG

This system would allow all like titles in a franchise to remain together, so all Batman titles would be shelved together, and so on. Pages were instructed to shelve alphabetically by series title under the overall franchise and by volume number.

LPL had three wooden bookshelves dedicated to teen and adult comics, and, when they were organized by author, this led to one Spider-Man title being shelved on the upper-right shelf, while the next volume in the series was shelved in the lower left, and so on. When the reorganization began, Shelf 1 became the Marvel shelf, Shelf 2 the DC shelf, and Shelf 3 the Independent shelf, while manga was kept on the spinner rack. It was decided to leave the top and bottom shelves of each unit dedicated to display space, allowing newer titles to be identified more easily by patrons.

Once LPL's comic collection was reorganized, a library staff member spent the next three months tracking circulations and making note of any comments, positive or negative, made by users of the collection. The new organization was met with very positive responses based on user comments, staff comments, and circulation statistics. Circulation of the collection increased roughly 10% within the first month with the Marvel titles circulating the most. There was not a single complaint reported for the new organization, but there were at least fifteen positive comments reported, with users expressing gratitude that their favorite comics were now together on the shelf, that the independent titles were separated from the Big Two, and that the collection as a whole was much easier to navigate and much more browsable. Staff members who needed to find items from the collection for various reasons admired the collection's new aesthetic and also claimed that items were easier to find. It also became much easier to point a seeker who came in looking for "Spider-Man comics" to a specific spot.

Oak Park Public Library (OPPL)

Notable traits: Year of publication is on call number; crossover events are shelved together; age levels separated

In 2014, Rachael Bild, high school services librarian at OPPL, took over ordering teen and adult graphic novels for her collection. "Right away I looked at the shelves and thought, as a reader, this cannot stand . . . stuff was constantly going missing, being mis-shelved, the holds list was using the volume title [subtitle or story arc], and just overall preventing items from being checked out . . . we were wasting the time of the reader."[7] A major change was in the works already, relabeling the "YA" section to "teen," so, seeing the opportunity, Rachael partnered with catalogers, volunteers, and other library staff, and got to work crafting an in-house classification system. One system was attempted, but staff realized that the items were still difficult to shelve and find, so OPPL decided to return to the drawing board and conducted a survey among their patrons.

Once they had their results, they decided their comics would be organized by age level, then franchise, then year of publication to distinguish different series[8] within that franchise with the same title, and then volume number. In the case of a large crossover event that didn't quite fit

FIGURE 4.5. Oak Park Public Library graphic novel call numbers. (From C2E2 PowerPoint presentation. Provided by Rachael Bild.)

FIGURE 4.6. Oak Park Public Library graphic novel shelf. (From C2E2 PowerPoint presentation. Provided by Rachael Bild.)

under any particular franchise or superhero, it, and all of its tie-in titles, would be classified under publisher.

This system ensures that all titles in a series, such as all volumes of Scott Snyder's run on *Batman,* wind up at least within physical proximity of each other on a shelf, thanks to the inclusion of the year. This makes items easier to find via call number for both library staff and patrons. "Whatever changes we made," says Rachael, "we also had to remember that we were part of a consortium, so titles still needed to show properly in the consortium catalog. It was important to me to create a system that someone who does not understand comics, like someone after my time here, could still understand and follow."[9]

When designing this system, Rachael looked for inspiration from other libraries, including other libraries in the SWAN consortium and even the Michigan State University which has done innovative things with their comics classifications under Randall Scott, though many of her colleagues explained they were also suffering the "Batman problem." Since the reorganization of the teen graphic novels was successful, the OPPL has now extended the process to the adult section as well.

Arlington Heights Memorial Library (AHML)

Notable traits: Comics are divided into multiple categories; each category has own shelf unit; divided by age level; good system for a library with lots of shelf space

Violet Jaffe is the collection supervisor for AHML, and she has worked in collection development for over 6 years. In her role, she supervises all adult and teen graphic novel purchases. In the past, all the library's comics were filed under DDC in the 741s, and the patrons didn't realize they were there, so they did not circulate. The adult nonfiction selector at the time started a committee to solve the problem, and one solution was to visit a comic shop for ideas. The committee decided to break down the adult comics collection into categories including superheroes, fiction, manga, nonfiction, and comic strips. "We did that for adult about 8 years ago," says Violet. "After there was a huge increase in circs, people loved it. We did the same thing for teen."[10]

Referring to the entire overall comic collection as graphic novels, each of these categories has its own shelving unit, signage, and call number. This allows for superheroes to be segregated for the superhero fans on the Graphic Novel—Superhero shelves and true graphic novels to have a cozy home on the Graphic Novel—Fiction shelves. From these initial categories, items are organized by franchise, except for the Graphic

FIGURE 4.7. The Fiction section of the Arlington Heights Memorial Library's Graphic Novels collection. (Provided by Violet Jaffe.)

Novel—Nonfiction and the Graphic Novel—Fiction sections, which are both arranged by author. These shelves each have a corresponding call number that is then used for their respective items, such as SUPERHERO for the superhero shelf, COMIC STRIP for the comic strip shelf, and so on. For example:

For *The Complete Chester Gould's Dick Tracy,*
Volume 24 (Library of American Comics)

GN

COMIC STRIP

DICK TRACY

Teen call numbers simply have TEEN added above GN. The teen shelving layout is similar, with the inclusion of special sliding shelves that reveal the manga collection. "Manga has its own secret little hiding spot,"

FIGURE 4.8. The Superheroes section of the Arlington Memorial Library's Graphic Novels collection. (Provided by Violet Jaffe.)

FIGURE 4.9. Spine labels of the Nonfiction section of the Arlington Heights Memorial Library's Graphic Novels collection. (Provided by Violet Jaffe.)

FIGURE 4.10. Spine labels of the Superheroes section of the Arlington Heights Memorial Library's Graphic Novels collection. (Provided by Violet Jaffe.)

TABLE 4.3. A snapshot of Arlington Memorial Library's Graphic Novels collection's circulations. (Provided by Violet Jaffe.)

Graphic Novel Circulation for March 2019		
Location	Total Items	Total Circulations
Adult	1416	451
Teen	1638	471
Kids	3340	2197
Total	6394	3119

Violet explains. "Teens love it because it feels like a secret. Our kids' graphic novels are already Cuttered [as in Cutter number] by character, but they haven't had this same type of organization." This system also allows for a great deal of display space for items to face out and to be more of an aesthetic lure for patrons. At the time of this writing, Violet reported their graphic novels circulations remained respectable and provided documentation. This system works very well for this library.

Elmwood Park Public Library (EPPL)

Notable traits: Entries in a series[11] can remain together, even if the series is relaunched; divided by age level; simple spine labels with maximized information

When teen librarian Sean Gilmartin first came into his position at EPPL, he noticed that the graphic novels were a problem area. "It was confusing for me and, no doubt, confusing for the patrons," he says. "Once I began interacting with people browsing the section I became more familiar with their needs . . . so I was excited to completely restructure and streamline the collection."[12] So, Sean sought help from other library staff to prioritize reorganizing graphic novels. After an inventory and having staff weed the comics collections, they got to work. With teamwork, their library created a marvelous in-house classification system.

Lucas McKeever, head of technical services who had very little knowledge of comics at the time the project began, describes how he sought ideas for how an in-house classification system should work, "I grabbed all of the materials for Batman in January 2018. I sorted through all of the materials based on series and tried to get a feel for a system that could possibly work to make sure all like-things sat on the shelf together . . . For the most part, a series title would be used, then the first word of the title, and then a volume number."[13] What they decided on was a system that respected what Lucas calls a subseries, which can be a story arc, a series relaunch,[14] an event like *The New 52!*, or anything else that would distinguish one series from another series with the same title. By emphasizing the importance of this, all volumes within a series stay together on a shelf, making them easier for readers to keep reading and for staff to locate. Once a subseries is identified, it is assigned a number that goes in the call number. "What I realized was if we could replace that subseries word or first word of title with something static that is artificially assigned regardless of what the item itself contains," says Lucas, "we can create a system that is no longer reliant on the publisher to make their product work in our system. Assigning each subseries a number gave us just that."[15]

What results is a very efficient system that addresses the frustrations that so many librarians have with organizing comics. The comics are in collections divided by age level. They are organized first by franchise (or "overarching series"), then by subseries, so all titles related to Captain America, for instance, may be organized by "CAPTAIN." Then a subseries is identified, something that distinguishes that particular Captain

America comic, whether that is a series relaunch, a story arc, and so on, and that particular subseries is assigned a number. For instance, the series *Captain America* written by Rick Remender, which ran from 2012–2014, the series *Captain America* written by Mark Waid, which ran from 2017–2018, and the series *Captain America: Steve Rogers* written by Nick Spencer, which ran from 2016–2017, can all be distinguished from each other by assigning the numbers 1, 2, and 3 respectively. So, their call numbers would reflect CAPTAIN 1, CAPTAIN 2, and CAPTAIN 3. So, the trade *Captain America vol. 1*, written by Rick Remender would be labeled CAPTAIN 1 / VOL 1 and all other volumes of that series will be shelved together. Meanwhile, true graphic novels are alphabetized by author. That may have sounded confusing at first, but this is truly a simple and efficient system.

So far, EPPL's teen and children's graphic novel collections have been reorganized with this system, and the adult collection will be reorganized

Overarching Series	Story Arc Title	Call Number Line 2	Call Number Line 3
CAPTAIN AMERICA	N/A (monographs)	CAPTAIN	
	Mashups, vs., ect. (other heroes like x-men, superman, etc.)	CAPTAIN 1	
	CAPTAIN AMERICA MARVEL NOW! (VOL. 1 IS 9780785168263)	CAPTAIN 2	VOL
	CAPTAIN AMERICA (ED BRUBAKER) (VOL. 1 IS 9780785157083)	CAPTAIN 3	VOL
	DEATH OF CAPTAIN AMERICA (VOL. 1 IS 9780785124238)	CAPTAIN 4	VOL
	CAPTAIN AMERICA MARVEL KNIGHTS (VOL. 1 IS 0785111018)	CAPTAIN 5	VOL
	CAPTAIN AMERICA SAM WILSON (VOL. 1 IS 9780785196402)	CAPTAIN 6	VOL
	CAPTAIN AMERICA STEVE ROGERS (VOL. 1 IS 9781302901127)	CAPTAIN 7	VOL
	CAPTAIN AMERICA DAN JURGENS (VOL. 1 IS 9780785135171)	CAPTAIN 8	VOL

FIGURE 4.11. Call Number Rules Document for Elmwood Park Public Library's graphic novels collection. (Provided by Lucas McKeever.)

Call number	Title
T GN CAPTAIN	Captain America. Prisoner of war / writers, Ed Brubaker ... [and others] ; artists, Tr...
T GN CAPTAIN	Captain America & Bucky. The life story of Bucky Barnes / writers, Ed Brubaker & M...
T GN CAPTAIN	Captain America & Bucky. Old wounds / James Asmus & Ed Brubaker, story ; James...
T GN CAPTAIN	Captain America. Land of the free / Mark Waid, Tom Defalco, Andy Kubert ; with Jay...
T GN CAPTAIN	Captain America. White / Jeph Loeb, Tim Sale, storytellers ; Richard Starkings of Co...
T GN CAPTAIN	Captain America. Volume 22, Man without a country / writers: Mark Waid, William M...
T GN CAPTAIN	Captain America : to serve and protect / Ron Garney ... [and others].
T GN CAPTAIN 1	Captain America and Black Widow / writer, Cullen Bunn ; artist, Francesco Francavilla.
T GN CAPTAIN 1	Captain America and the Falcon : the complete collection / Christopher Priest, writer...
T GN CAPTAIN 2 VOL. 1	Captain America. Castaway in Dimension Z. Book 1 / Rick Remender, writer ; John ...
T GN CAPTAIN 2 VOL. 2	Captain America. Castaway in Dimension Z. Book 2 / Rick Remender, writer ; John ...
T GN CAPTAIN 2 VOL. 3	Captain America. Loose nuke / writer, Rick Remender ; penciler, Carlos Pacheco (#...
T GN CAPTAIN 2 VOL. 4	Captain America. Vol. 4, The iron nail / writer, Rick Remender ; Issue #16, penciler,...
T GN CAPTAIN 2 VOL. 5	Captain America. 5, The tomorrow soldier / Rick Remender, writer ; Carlos Pacheco...
T GN CAPTAIN 3 VOL. 1	Captain America. [vol.1] / Ed Brubaker, writer ; Steve McNiven, Giuseppe Camuncol...
T GN CAPTAIN 3 VOL. 2	Captain America. [Volume 2] / Ed Brubaker, writer ; Alan Davis, penciler ; Mark Far...
T GN CAPTAIN 3 VOL. 3	Captain America. [Volume 3] / Ed Brubaker, writer ; Patch Zircher, Mike Deodato (#...
T GN CAPTAIN 3 VOL. 4	Captain America. [Volume 4] / by Ed Brubaker.
T GN CAPTAIN 4	The death of Captain America : ultimate collection / writer: Ed Brubaker ; art: Mike ...
T GN CAPTAIN 4 VOL. 1	The death of Captain America. [Vol. 1], The death of the dream / writer, Ed Brubake...
T GN CAPTAIN 5 VOL. 3	The man who bought America / writer, Ed Brubaker ; artists, Steve Epting, Butch Gu...
T GN CAPTAIN 5 VOL. 1	Captain America / writer, John Ney Rieber ; artist, John Cassaday ; colors, Dave St...
T GN CAPTAIN 5 VOL. 3	Ice / Writers, Chuck Austen, John Ney Rieber ; artist, Jae Lee.
T GN CAPTAIN 5 VOL. 5	Captain America : homeland / writer, Robert Morales.
T GN CAPTAIN 6 VOL. 1	Captain America : Sam Wilson. 1, Not my Captain America / writer, Nick Spencer ; ...
T GN CAPTAIN 6 VOL. 2	Captain America, Sam Wilson. vol. 2, Standoff / writer, Nick Spencer.
T GN CAPTAIN 7 VOL. 1	Captain America, Steve Rogers. [1], Hail Hydra! / writer, Nick Spencer ; artists, Jes...
T GN CAPTAIN 8 VOL. 1	Captain America. [Vol.1] / by Dan Jurgens ; [pencilers, Andy Kubert ... [and others]...
T GN CAPTAIN 8 VOL. 2	Captain America by Dan Jurgens. [Vol. 2] / [writers, Dan Jurgens & Bill Rosemann ; ...

FIGURE 4.12. How Elmwood Park Public Library's graphic novels appear in the catalog. (Provided by Lucas McKeever.)

FIGURE 4.13. Elmwood Park Public Library's graphic novel spine labels. (From C2E2 PowerPoint presentation. Provided by Lucas McKeever.)

FIGURE 4.14. All the various Captain America trades on Elmwood Park Public Library's shelves wind up together and in proper order. (From C2E2 PowerPoint presentation. Provided by Lucas McKeever.)

soon. Staff and patrons have been happy with the new system, including shelving staff, and Sean reports that the collection is seeing a lot of use. "In the Kids & Teens department we have a return shelf for items that are pulled from the shelf and need to be put back . . . I can say that I have seen more titles pulled from the same series. For example, multiple Batman volumes have been pulled so this could give us some indication that patrons are finding additional volumes with more ease."[16]

GETTING BUY-IN

If you want to develop your own in-house classification system and reorganize your comics, you'll need lots of buy-in from lots of staff, from the top down. You'll need permission from your director and managers to make such a drastic change, and you'll find the task much easier if you have the support of support staff, especially pages and other shelvers. "We added it to our 2016–2019 strategic plan," says Lucas, which involved weeding the collections and collecting information from all staff involved to decide what would work best. You'll need to develop a plan, and you'll need to know what's involved.

You may want to start with conducting a survey to find out exactly what can be changed about your collection to best suit user needs, like LPL and OPPL did. You should gather as much information from patrons and staff as you can about the need and the time it will take. "When I include my time, catalogers' time, library students', volunteer hours, it's a lot of labor hours we used to accomplish this," says Rachael. When asked how many labor hours he estimated EPPL staff spent on the reorganization, Lucas had to consider other priorities that his department had at the time, and said, "This is not a straight-forward answer . . . I finished the Teen section in August and began the Kids in September and finished in December . . . I would say it would be safe to guess around 5–7 hours a week. That would be about 140–196 hours for Teen?" He also stated, "Once the system is created, it gets a lot easier and faster to apply it to other collections/materials."

As you can see, it may be difficult to determine just how much labor and time will be needed for a project, depending on your collection's size, so it may be best to err on a liberal scale. If your comics collections are divided by age level, then you should consider beginning the process with one before implementing it for the others. If you have plenty of input from patrons and staff as to why a reorganization is needed, as well as solid examples from other libraries who have been through such a process, then you should put together a proposal for your library authorities. You can find an example of a proposal for reclassifying comics in the Appendix B.

NOTES

1. Okay, okay, it was me. It was my presentation.

2. This example is originally from my Master's Research Paper, "Comics Are Not Books, and That's Okay: Exploring Common Problems and Solutions to User Access to Comics and Graphic Novels."

3. This is in response to recommendations from librarians to move graphic novels into the 800s along with other forms of literature and away from the 700s where they reside with graphic arts and other comics.

4. Though, as pointed out in the graphic novel discussion in Chapter 1, what is fiction and nonfiction in comics can be a bit different than in traditional books, just one more way the medium is unique.

5. Full disclosure, this was my project when I worked at this library. This reclassification project was part of my master's project for obtaining my MLIS.

6. This would later become less of a chore once the Central Library Consortium, which London Public Library joined, adopted its own bibliographic standards for comics and graphic novels.

7. Rachael Bild, interview via phone by Jack Phoenix, April 17, 2019.

8. See the discussion about "Volume" earlier in the chapter.

9. Rachael Bild, interview via phone by Jack Phoenix, April 17, 2019.

10. Violet Jaffe, interview via email by Jack Phoenix, April 25, 2019.

11. See the discussion about "Volume" earlier in the chapter.

12. Sean Gilmartin, interview via email by Jack Phoenix, April 19, 2019.

13. Lucas McKeever, interview via FaceTime by Jack Phoenix, April 5, 2019.

14. See the discussion about "Volume" earlier in the chapter, yet again!

15. Lucas McKeever, interview via FaceTime by Jack Phoenix, April 5, 2019.

16. Sean Gilmartin, interview via email by Jack Phoenix, April 19, 2019.

5

Comic Programs

So, your library has its comic collection. You've enhanced the access as best you can through unique classification, flashy organization on the shelves, and superb bibliographic records so the titles really pop out of the catalog. But now what? You check the circulations, and you see that, sufferin' Sappho, they're not circulating as well as you'd hoped. The circulations are certainly better, but maybe not worth the amount of effort you gave. But you did your research and followed all the advice from the comics librarians before you. You are so disappointed in the results, and you're worried that you've wasted all the time and resources. Well, just remember that comics, as unique as they are, are just like any other collection in your library. They won't sell themselves.

As any collection development librarian knows, access is important, including organization and merchandising, but in this age, with libraries facing greater competition from apps, streaming services, video games, and more, access isn't enough. What good is access if people aren't coming into the library? More importantly, who is going to check out your comics if the comic fans don't even know you have them? No, friends and colleagues, your job isn't over. You'll need your comics to look attractive and be noticed and easily findable when patrons are in the building, but you'll need to put in the extra effort to get the patrons into the building first. This is where programming comes in, and never forget how vital programming can be to your library and its collections. The next few chapters will cover promoting your comics through various ways, but this chapter will deal with providing comic programs for your community. Programs are currently a focus for libraries as they continue to evolve to better serve their communities beyond books, but programs aren't new. Libraries have been hosting educational and entertaining programs for literally centuries. Programs, as it happens, are another way a library can fulfill its mission; a mission to connect people to information.

As you know, librarians define "information" fairly liberally, as this also includes entertainment. Programs are a source of information just like any of your collections, and should be treated with just as much professional consideration. While it's true that hosting a comics program can bring people into your building, promote your comics collection, and enable their circulation, this should not be the sole reason you provide comics programs. Library programs bring your community together and so they must fulfill a need in your community, be of interest to your public, and provide enrichment, enlightenment, education, or entertainment. A program should not be provided just as a supplement to your collection, but should fit the needs of your community in much the same way an item in your collection would. Programs are important, have been important, and will continue to be important for libraries.

Let's discuss some of the ways that your patrons, your library, and your comics will benefit from programs, and the variety of programs that you can provide. Since libraries embraced comics, a plethora of comics-related program ideas have spread through library publications and conferences. Some programs are very small, very simple, and inexpensive. Other programs require months of planning, are grand in scale, lasting an entire season, and can be very expensive. You will have to do what is best for your community and work with the resources you have, just as you have to do with your comics collection. And just as with your comics collection, you'll need buy-in from your staff, your superiors, and your public.

It's likely that your library has a programming budget. Your comics programs should be proportionate to your comics collection, depending upon your goal for the collection or your departmental goals. If your goal is to show the world that you have a comics collection, then you may want to consider programs of greater proportion. You may also want to consider a great deal of programs if your comics collection is vast and very popular in your community. But keep all these factors in mind, as it won't do to have a grand, successful comics collection with little programming when it's clearly popular, nor would it be wise to host a great deal of meticulously-planned comics programs if you don't have the collection to reinforce the interest. Your hope would be, after all, that after any comics program, a patron will have an interest sparked and would want to read the material.

Programs can be a daunting thing. It can make any library staff member feel intimidated, facing the pressure to come up with creative ideas. There is always the anxiety that no one will show up to a program or that too many people will show up to a program, causing stressful chaos. But if you apply the same knowledge and care to programs that you do to your collection, you'll be able to handle any programs that will fit your community. Regardless, you can always take advantage of the practice that is at the very foundation of librarianship: sharing. This chapter will present some of the ideas from library programming staff that have come before, and hopefully you can find some inspiration and direction for your own programming endeavors. Why waste time reinventing the wheel, when your colleagues have already come up with such fabulous ideas for you?

Librarian and author Steven Miller breaks down programs into three kinds:

- **Active participation:** These are often structured programs in which the audience must be physically or verbally involved in the activity. Some examples would be book discussions, or an evening of tabletop miniature golf.
- **Passive participation:** These structured programs generally involve less action on the part of the audience.
- **Independent participation:** These programs allow patrons to participate at their own pace and do not often require active participation of library staff beyond the planning stage. Independent programs generally allow patrons a longer time frame for participation (Miller 2005).

Now, many of you may recognize that these days we define "passive programming" as being closer to what Miller calls "independent participation," but this just shows how much the librarian view of programming has been evolving over just the past decade. Programs are going from something *extra* the library provides, a sort of bonus if there's time and resources, to being a library staple, necessity, and priority, something that has time and resources being redirected into. At first thought, the idea of limiting programs to just the topic of comics may seem horribly constrained, but the truth is it's a surprisingly broad topic, able to encompass a variety of subjects, just like comics themselves. Comics programs won't pigeonhole you, as long as you're willing to do some research, keep abreast of the current trends, and let your creativity flow.

TRADITIONAL PROGRAMS

Book Clubs

Book clubs are a staple among library programs, and even libraries that don't make programs much of a priority will still often have some kind of book discussion group. This can be an after-school program for teens or a program for adults; both groups can benefit from the comradery of discussing a shared reading experience. There are even libraries out there that offer a comic book club as a sort of intergenerational program, allowing teens and adults to converse. A book club can get your patrons interacting with a title in a way that little else can provide. It can lead to thoughtfulness about the content and expose them to a variety of opinions and points of view, providing insight as to how a particular work can affect different people in different ways. Book clubs can make comics truly an immersive experience.

The Get Graphic book club series CPL has been a fun-filled romp for everyone involved. It draws in a small, intimate group of participants, who are very diverse in age and background. Some are longtime comic fans, others are still learning the medium, having only begun reading comics thanks to the book club. The reading selections are just as diverse, as the group reads everything from superhero trades like *Ultimate Spider-Man* to literary graphic novels like Octavia Butler's *Kindred*. One idea you could steal from this book club is their use of themes. The group meets twice a month, and they will often have themes that will last four sessions, such as "Black Lives in Comics."

Comic book clubs have a lot to offer your patrons, because many readers may find comics more easily accessible than the standard book club fare. They are more pop culture, even when they are considered literary, and that can make them more appealing to some members of the public. As part of pop culture, there's a chance you'll lead new members into your circle since you may very well read a comic featuring a character from the latest hit movie. And, of course, many may find comics simply easier to read and less intimidating. They are also far less of a time commitment, which can be very attractive to working adults and busy teenagers, and this may allow your club to read more books more often, hence why Get Graphic meets twice a month. Meeting more can mean more fun and it means your members will be in your building more often, bonding with you, your building, the comics, and each other. Finally, book clubs cost, well, nothing! They are one of the most reliably inexpensive programs you can put on.

Book Talks

Here is another extremely simple program you can do, which is especially perfect for school visits. Just pick some stellar comics and provide your audience with a catching, in-person synopsis and maybe a review if you've read it. You can tailor the review to fit your audience, so be sure to do some research about your audience and about the title, so you can mention anything that might hit that demographic right in the fancy. And even though this is a perfect program for school visits, it can be great for adult audiences, too. Don't forget your senior centers; it's true that comics don't typically appeal to that demographic, but if you're clever with your readers' advisory skills, you may find that senior citizens can be open to trying all kinds of things. Plus, it could lead to some lively discussions about what's happened with comics in their lifetimes, since many people of a certain age may have read comics when they were children in the Golden or Silver Ages.

Trivia

Let your comic fans test their mettle in a friendly trivia match, complete with prizes. Comicdom is vast, though, so you'll want to offer some sort of specificity, with Marvel trivia or DC trivia always being popular bets. You can find plenty of trivia questions online, or you can always just use the handy Marvel and DC Encyclopedias published by DK. You can go outside of the source material and have a trivia session on the Marvel Cinematic Universe or get even more specific and limit it to Teenage Mutant Ninja Turtles trivia. The options are endless and it's a fairly simple program to conduct. You just need a timer and some candy as prizes.

Superhero Story Time

Find a fun superhero-centric picture book and invite a costume enthusiasts group or some local cosplayers to come read it to the little ones. Don't forget to set up a spot for photo ops so the parents can have a memento to last forever.

Comic Book Game Night

This one will require the acquisition of some games, but once you have them, the program basically runs itself. Just about anything and everything comic related right now is being licensed for games of all kinds; card games, board games, role playing games, you name it. A quick trip to the local game shop or a hop onto Amazon and you can find comic-related versions of Monopoly, Clue, Code Names, and more, as well as many comic properties with their own, unique game, like *Chew*.

Munchkin, a popular game that is sort of a lite version of Dungeons and Dragons, has many comic-related versions that are fun to play, such as X-Men and The Walking Dead. Don't forget about games like HeroClix, which are made specifically for comic fans. HeroClix is a role-playing game that uses small figurines of licensed superheroes, such as Marvel, DC, and Image. The biggest challenge with hosting this game at your library is that HeroClix can become expensive, but if you have the budget, it will likely be a hit.

Comic Book Movie Night

Playing movies based off of comics is another simple program that's likely to please. You'll need the appropriate license to publicly play movies and, obviously, the movie itself. You could always add the software MuV Chat to enhance the experience. MuV Chat allows the audience to text messages that appear on the screen while the movie is playing, so it becomes live commentary. It's a great way to make the movie watching experience more interactive.

Comic Swap

Resurrect a piece of the Golden Age with this activity. Invite comic book collectors to meet up and trade comics to read. If it's in your budget, it would be a good idea to buy a collection of comic books off the bat to initiate the swapping. Keep in mind, most serious comic collectors, mainly adults, may not take the idea of parting with their comics all that fondly. But younger patrons may love it and you'll be tapping into a rich history of kids trading comic books and sharing their enthusiasm.

Comic Creator Visit

This may not be possible for every library. It's dependent upon your library's budget or whether you have a comic creator within geographic proximity. If you're not sure if you have a comic creator near your library, ask your local comic shop. Chances are the staff there will have had encounters with any local comic creators or at least be aware of them. Another valuable resource is Chloe Ramos at Image Comics. She invites libraries to contact her and she can help find comic creators that have worked with Image Comics that are in your area. You can find more information about Chloe in Chapter 1.

Spotlight on Tony Isabella, Legendary Creator, and Library Supporter

Tony you've been in comics for a long time. Can you tell the readers about you and your career?

I learned how to read comic books before I was four years old. Adults would read to me, but I wanted to cut out the middle man. I paid very close attention and, essentially, taught myself how to read. I taught myself to write in pretty much the same manner before I was five. I have worked in comics for 46 years, starting my career at Marvel.

You created one of the most prominent black superheroes. Can you tell us about why you created Black Lightning? Was there any pushback?

I grew up in Cleveland, a very segregated city. My first black friends were comic book fans who traveled from the east side of Cleveland to my comic book club meetings on the west side of Cleveland. "Diversity" wasn't part of my language at that point, but it seemed unfair that my black friends didn't have any super-heroes of their own. There were rarely any people of color appearing in comics, and I promised myself that if I ever broke into the industry, I would try to work on and create characters of color. At Marvel I worked on characters like Luke Cage, Fal-con, and I turned the character Bill Foster into Black Goliath (later called Giant Man). When I was working at DC, the com-pany was planning on launching their own black superhero called Black Bomber. The black bomber character, however, was unfortunately a white racist. I talked DC out of publishing that, and I was given a short time to create a new character. This led to the creation of Black Lightning. I made Jefferson Pierce (Black Lightning's alter ego) a teacher to make him relatable to young people, and it was about 4 hours before the pitch meeting before I even came up with his superpowers. I had no name or powers but then I saw a sketch for an upcoming Wonder Woman cover. Wonder Woman was lassoing a lightning bolt and referred to it as "black lightning," and I thought that sounded very catchy. A few years ago, I was given a sketch of that cover by a different artist. I have written the Black Lightning character in the '70s,

'90s, and a recent reboot, titled "Cold Dead Hands." I've been involved unofficially in the *Black Lightning* TV show from before there was one. DC Comics asked me to write a core values paper as a guide. I had conference calls with the show runners and spent a day with the show's writers. I corresponded with many of the cast members and still do.

Every week, viewers get to see your name flash across television. Did you ever imagine that you would see a Black Lightning TV show?

Yes, from the moment I created the character I thought it could be a great TV series. I knew we were telling more down-to-earth stories, and I knew it could be translated into a good TV series. This is just confirmation.

What are some of the other characters or stories you have worked on that you want librarians to know about?

Black Lightning is far and away my favorite, but I also created the Champions for Marvel. I've also worked on Daredevil and Ghost Rider. In *Ghost Rider,* I tried to inject an opposing point of view by adding a character who was a Jesus figure instead of a demonic one. Unfortunately, an editor didn't agree and altered the character, which did not sit well with me. I created the character Tigra. I created Misty Knight and she appears in the shows *Luke Cage* and *Iron Fist* on Netflix. Bill Foster's character got me a special recognition in the credits for the film *Ant-Man and the Wasp.* I am proud of all that work. I did some pretty cool Dracula stories, some Star Trek stories, and I did a weird book called *Satan's Six.* It's a book about souls who weren't good enough to get into Heaven and not bad enough to get into Hell so they decide to try to get into Hell by doing bad deeds, but they accidentally end up doing good in each of the stories I wrote. I wrote a book called *1000 Comics You Must Read.* I co-wrote one Captain America novel and one Star Trek novel with Bob Ingersoll. Currently, I'm writing a book called *Black Lightning and My Road to Diversity,* and what I think diversity in comics means. Whether you're black, white, gay, straight, atheist ... people should see themselves in comics. Whenever I get the opportunity in my career, I try to diversify comics.

Do you believe comics can be a source for social change?

Of course! They've always been progressive within the limits of the decade, so there have been some insensitive stories and racial caricatures for sure. Despite this, Superman in his earliest appearances took out wife beaters, ran corrupt businessmen out of town, and laughed at corrupt politicians. Captain America punched a Nazi on the cover of his first issue. The Justice Society brought food to starving Europeans. The tide of history will always move toward more inclusion. "He-men, women-hating comic readers" are dinosaurs waiting for the comet to hit. We now have great comics coming from Japan and all over the world. Writers and artists of color, gays, women . . . diversity is here. Now is the best time to be a comic reader.

Having been in the industry a long time, you have no doubt seen a lot of change in comics. Which of these changes make you happy, and which of these changes are you perhaps not so fond of?

I'm very proud of the increased diversity in comics. I'm proud of the diversity of stories being told in the format, too, since comics aren't just superheroes anymore. I'm very pleased about the success comics have had in movies and TV (especially since I get to go to a lot of TV and movie premiers). I'm very pleased about the increased presence of comics in libraries. It's good for the industry. *Scooby-Doo Team-Up* is one of my favorite comics right now, and I discovered this comic at the library. People will discover comics and graphic novels at the library and then buy them or others like them at their local comics shop and elsewhere. Things that I'm not so fond of would be the reliance on crossovers and stunts in comics. Continuity shouldn't be such a big deal, since it's more important to tell stories that are true to the core values of the characters.

I understand you are an avid library supporter. Have you participated in any library events?

I did a Coffee and Comics workshop for the Cleveland Public Library last year, and I'll be doing another one soon. I've spoken at library events about diversity and comics and about my career. When there were forces trying to suppress library funding, I was a very vocal supporter of the library. I wrote opinion pieces in newspapers and other news outlets, because the library is far more important than a certain person's individual religion or politics. A library is a depository of knowledge, and knowledge doesn't take sides.

How have libraries had an impact on your life and career?

Before the internet, I used to frequent the library to do research for my stories. In one story, Black Lightning's civilian identity had been shot, and I knew nothing about gunshot trauma. The library staff were delighted to put that research together for me. These days, I try to do research online, but I know I can turn to the library for more extended research.

As you may know or may not know, libraries resisted carrying comics for decades. As a library patron and a comic creator, what would you say to librarians who are still reluctant to support comics?

I would say get over it. Comics are an American art form that has spread throughout the world. There are so many important stories and subjects for all ages being told in comic form. If a library really wants to support their community, they need to include comics in what they offer. It's a different way of telling stories and providing information. There's no reason not to embrace comics if you're embracing computers.

Is there something more you would like to see libraries do for the comics industry?

I think every library should carry more of everything I write (laughs). They should do more comic programs. Most libraries have local creators in the area and they should bring these creators in for workshops, presentations, and historical information. Comics have always been my favorite artform, and I think the more the public is exposed to them, the more they will get into it. When libraries buy comics, it simply increases the sales and increases the royalties to the comics creators. Also, be aware of diversity in comics. Dearborn, Michigan, a city with a high population of Muslims, for example, should have multiple copies of *Ms. Marvel,* a character created by and written by a Muslim American woman. If your library is in a mostly black community, carry black titles like *Black Panther, Black Lightning,* the graphic biography of Frederick Douglas, and so on. Look at the community and see which comics match your community.

Is there something more you would like to see the comics industry do for libraries?

I certainly think it would behoove companies to send information packets to libraries to let them know what's available. Very often, comic book companies will decide that a collection has finished its shelf-life, and I know that some companies provide these to comic shops. I would like to see them donate them to libraries. They should provide information to libraries about local creators, as well, so that libraries can reach out to these creators and ask for their assistance with programs.

What do you think the future holds for comics?

The future for print comics is a little shaky right now because comic shops are closing. Potential readers now can get the same kind of fix from movies and TV. The future of comics will be brighter if we can find a way to connect to the movies and TV fans. We are basically R&D for movies and TV, and we need to find a way for print comics to benefit from this relationship. What's going to revive the comics is to convince the people who are watching these television shows and movies to check out comics.[1]

Comic Expert Visit

A visit doesn't have to be from a comic creator in order to be enriching and fun for the community. Consider, too, hosting an expert in comics, such as an historian, podcaster, writer, critic, or educator. People in these roles and more study and care deeply for comics and can present wonderful presentations for your public, sometimes for free. Author Tim Hanley, who is often asked to present about gender and comics, speaks about his experience:

One particularly fun one was a book fair at the public library in the town around Penn State. They do a summer event that focuses on comics and graphic novels, and they invited me to come one year, set up a table, and do a talk. It was a blast, and a great mix of people, too. The con aspect of it brings out comic fans, as you'd expect, but the library did a great job of getting the community involved so all sorts of folks came through who weren't necessarily hardcore comic fans, or really fans at all, but were interested in hearing about the history of feminism through this unusual lens. It was fantastic. Libraries have such a broad reach, and it's wonderful when they use that to introduce the community to new and different art forms and experiences.[2]

MAKERSPACE AND STEAM PROGRAMS

Create Your Own Comic

This can take all kinds of forms. You can easily create a passive program by printing off some blank comic templates (you can find plenty online). Provide your patrons with some colored pencils, markers, or crayons and let them create their own comics at their leisure, which you can post in a special place in the library. Or, for older audiences, you can host a more serious comic-creation session, providing books about creating comics and hosting a contest. You can even have these comics inexpensively published for the winner through Lulu or another self-publishing service, or even submit the winner to Comixology for digital publication. Or if you want to keep this out of the digital realm, combine a create-your-own-comic event with DIY bookbinding to give your patrons a real treat.

Comic Mod Podge

Get your hands on some throw-away comics, either from weeding, by donation, at garage sales, or from your local comic retailer. Let your patrons tear out the pages and Mod Podge those pages all over bird-houses, mailboxes, rocking chairs, Little Free Libraries, and even jewelry. Comic pages give any Mod Podge project a vibrant splash.

Button Making

You can also use old comic pages to create fabulous buttons. The easiest way to do this is to use a circle cutter along with an actual button maker device, but you can find some alternative methods on the internet, including using Mod Podge or lamination, or your local craft store may have some swell ideas. Just have your young patrons pick an interesting illustration or word bubble from an old comic page, cut it out, and use the button maker to turn it into a fun, bubbly accessory. You can similarly create magnets with old comic pages, too.

Superhero Ornaments

DIY ornaments are always a hit during the holiday season, and there are a couple of fun and simple options for comics fans. First, simple bulb ornament decorating with paints and glitter is always a sure bet. Invite your patrons to paint their favorite superhero logo on a glass bulb ornament and then let them take it home to find a place on the tree. Next, wooden peg ornaments are colorful, easy, and adorable. Just head to a craft store and buy some wooden pegs or wooden clothes pins, both of which are vaguely human-shaped. Have your patrons decorate them with acrylic paint into their favorite superheroes, stylized and smooth. Add a hook to the top using a screw hook or hot glue, and this becomes a splendid crossroad craft between folksy and nerdy.

Cosplay Workshop

Though at this point it could be argued that cosplay has split into its own pop culture hobby away from comics, comics and cosplay are still closely linked. Find out if there are any local cosplayers or if your nearest metropolitan area has a cosplay organization and invite a cosplay enthusiast to teach your teen patrons all about the craft. This could involve an introduction to cosplay basics and be a single session or a series that becomes more involved. Along with learning about plaster and crafty things, this could be an opportunity for your young patrons to learn additional life skills, such as ironing, sewing, and even welding, as some cosplay warrants very advanced techniques. This can be a prime opportunity to implement the use of makerspace technology, like 3D printers, if your library has one or can borrow one.

BIG PROGRAMS

Free Comic Book Day

In 2002, a new nerd holiday emerged. It was called Free Comic Book Day (FCBD), and it started with humble beginnings, simply an idea from a comic professional that went viral. The idea was to attract new readers to comics by giving out free comics during the release of a big comic book movie to take advantage of the heightened interest. Every year since, hundreds of comic shops have participated and thousands upon thousands of free comics have found their way into the hands of readers. FCBD is always the first Saturday of May,[3] which means it usually coincides with the opening of a comic book movie in theaters and the start of the summer movie season.

As of this writing, every major comic publisher and most small publishers participate in FCBD by releasing special-edition comics printed specifically for the event. These comics tend to be shorter than the average monthly comic book, sometimes featuring multiple short stories that will lead into grander storylines to come, hence the FCBD comics often function as advertisements for the publisher's other offerings. Occasionally, these comics are also reprints of previously published stories that may tie-in to some other cultural event. Some publishers release a single special comic for a particular FCBD and other publishers, such as Marvel and DC, may release multiple options, with some being more sought after by readers than others. FCBD comics tend to be lighter as far as language, violence, and sexual content. FCBD comics are ordered through Diamond Distributors and often cost between 12 to 50 cents each. Though they are free to the public, they are not free for the retailer.

If you hadn't guessed by now, FCBD is not only for comic shops. Over the past few years, libraries have also joined in on the fun. A library can be a perfectly positioned place to host a FCBD event, especially if your library is located in a comic book desert where there is no LCS within 50 miles or so. Along with giving away free comics, you can provide crafts, games, and other activities, as well as invite comic creators, speakers, even food vendors. Libraries can obtain FCBD comics in one of three ways. Two involve contacting Diamond Distributors and the other involves partnering with an LCS. There are advantages to either option but relying on a comic shop will likely be the best bet depending on your library's budget.

Partnering with an LCS is an especially nice choice if your library doesn't actually have an LCS nearby. If the nearest comic shop is far away, then you may have to pay more for shipping and handling of the comics, but you'll be sure that you aren't stepping on the comic shop's toes, since the shop will no doubt be hosting a FCBD event of its own. If your library is in a large, metropolitan area then both entities can still host FCBD without competing with each other. Simply contact a comic shop early in the year (since FCBD offerings often begin appearing in catalogs in January and February) and explain that you would like to host a FCBD. The comic shop may be willing to place the order for you with Diamond and the library can simply pay the comic shop for the price of the comics. You may be able to tell the comic shop the exact amount of which comics you want to order, the library will reimburse the comic shop for the price of the comics and, hopefully, shipping and handling if the comic shop is also willing to mail them to the library.

If the comic shop is willing to mail the comics to your library rather than make a library employee pick them up, then distance is no longer a factor. Your library can partner with a comic shop that is in another city or another county. If the library offers to give "sponsored by" acknowledgment on behalf of the comic shop in its FCBD promotions, the comic shop may be even more willing to help out, as they may jump at the chance for promotion of their business in another city for the effort of ordering and shipping. The vast majority of libraries that participate in FCBD do so through a partnership with a comic shop, even larger libraries that could easily order the comics directly from Diamond themselves. Ordering from Diamond directly is the second of our three options, but there is an upside and a downside to doing so.

A library can cut out the so-called middle man by ordering from Diamond directly, and this can be a very stress-free option. If a library cannot find a comic shop with whom to partner, this will be the only route available, after all, but there are things to consider. Ordering through Diamond directly will require a library to open an account with Diamond, which likely means you'll need to have your library's chief fiscal officer or business manager's involvement, as they will likely have to control the account. By ordering through a comic shop, it's entirely possible, depending on your library's policies, that you may only need to have your fiscal officer's approval of an invoice to the comic shop, but dealing with Diamond directly may turn your fiscal officer into the middle man instead of the comic shop, and the fiscal officer will likely place the order for you. If you're not a comic expert, taking the direct route can be challenging, because you won't have the expertise of the comic retailer, who will have a finger on the pulse of which FCBD books will be hot or not, to help guide your selections. If you are a comics expert and confident in your selections, however, then ordering directly can be a time-saving boon, one that prevents you from having to play phone or email tag with an LCS.

If your circumstances are not ideal for your library to host a FCBD due to budget or geographic limitations, there is still an option for you. If your library contacts Diamond early in the year, you may be able to get some FCBD comics for free, compliments of Diamond, and without having to create a billing account. If you contact Diamond early enough, inform them of your budget constraints, and as long as you don't have an LCS within 50 miles, they may send you comics free of charge, which will likely arrive a week before FCBD. Despite how charitable this is, there are many drawbacks; you won't have a say in which comics you receive; you're not likely to receive any comics from the major publishers; you won't know until nearly last-minute exactly which comics you'll have to offer or how many quantities of each, a question that your patrons may ask. But, as it's never a good idea to look a gift horse in the mouth, this is a wonderful option if your library's circumstances aren't ideal, and your patrons may be exceedingly grateful to have a completely free comic to take home.

FCBD has become an important holiday for the pop culture and nerd communities. It attracts the long-standing comic collectors as well as those who are brand new to the medium. It's too great an opportunity for a library to miss. Patrons of all backgrounds and ages love free things, that's no great revelation. But meeting nerds or budding nerds where they are and showing them that your library is not only aware of their nerd needs but aware of FCBD and the importance it has to the nerd community will put your library in a very positive spotlight. FCBD is a relatively simple and inexpensive way to host a big comic event, so don't miss the chance to bring this coveted demographic, multi-generational appeal into your library. Let them come in for the free comics, but convince them to come back showing them all the other wonderful (and still free) things your library has to offer.

Comics Symposium

A symposium is the type of event that is a bit more on the erudite side of things. Though it can be a nice way to counterbalance the pop culture effect of comics by displaying their more literary and academic qualities, a symposium is still essentially a celebration and can be (should be) a lot of fun. All that's needed to host a symposium is a topic and a speaker or two about that topic (or even multiple panels of speakers) or to speak about different elements of that topic, similar to what a librarian would find at a library convention or conference. The best symposia are centered around something specific, though, so you may want to avoid simply doing a symposium on comics in general and instead pick a specific topic within comicdom, such as a particular character.

CPL hosted a Wonder Woman symposium in 2016 for the character's 75th anniversary, which included speakers such as Wonder Woman artist, writer, and enthusiast Phil Jimenez. There was also a tie-in discussion about women in comics, including a discussion about Lois Lane from Laura Siegel, the daughter of Superman co-creator Jerry Siegel, plus many more. The entire event was held in partnership with Kent State University, the Ohio Center for the Book, the Ohio Humanities Council, Carol and John's Comic Shop, and others, so, as this is a way to show off the more serious, literary side of comics, your library should seek help from like-minded organizations so you can afford the most interesting speakers who will be a draw.

Spotlight on Valentino Zullo, Comics Scholar, Library Advocate, and Former Scholar-in-Residence at the Cleveland Public Library

Valentino, tell us about yourself. What makes you an expert on comics?

My name is Valentino Zullo, I am currently a PhD candidate at Kent State University, I am a maternal depression therapist at OhioGuidestone, and I am the former Scholar-in-Residence at Cleveland Public Library where I continue to lead the Get Graphic Program. The program includes biweekly book discussions, which have been ongoing since 2014, a speaker series, a workshop series, Free Comic Book Day events, and more. I am also the American editor of one of the longest running peer-reviewed journals on comics, the *Journal of Graphic Novels and Comics*. I have studied comics for years now, and I have published several articles on the topic.

How long were you the Scholar-in-Residence for Cleveland Public Library (CPL)? How did you get that position?

I was the Scholar-in-Residence from January 2016 through August 2018. I got the position because I had been leading the comics programming at CPL as a volunteer and Amy Dawson, the then manager of the Literature Department, wanted to give me a more specific title to describe my role. The purpose was to honor the research that can be done in the public library and to create an opportunity for others to do the same with the intention of bringing in future scholars-in-residence.

Will the scholar position always be comics focused?

The current Scholar, Whitney Porter, is comics focused, but it won't be a requisite for the position (though I do hope it would be!).

What did that position entail?

My goal was to create programs that would share academic thought in the community following CPL's motto "the People's University." This included an ongoing seminar series (or book club), speaker series, comics-making workshops called "Coffee and Comics" at the Rising Star Coffee Roastery (a local coffee company), Free Comic Book Day, the Wonder Woman Symposium in partnership with Kent State University, etc. I helped a little with collection development, since staff would seek my recommendations to build the collection. I would pick a theme such as "Memoirs of the Middle East," for one of our series, and that meant the library would add those books to the collection. I like to believe I helped diversify the collection. Additionally, the fliers created to advertise my programs also helped with readers' advisory, acting as a recommended reading list.

What programs stand out as your favorites or the ones that make you most proud?

In March through May of 2015, our Get Graphic series had the theme Women Warriors. It was all about intersectionality, and we read titles such as *Ms. Marvel,* which allowed us to discuss how race and gender intersect. I loved the Memoirs of the Middle East theme, too, that was particularly fun, because I'm Middle Eastern myself, Persian to be exact. I'm very proud of the Wonder Woman Symposium, which I worked on as coordinator with my dissertation advisor, Vera J. Camden (Director of the Wonder Woman Symposium, also a comics scholar and American editor of the *Journal of Graphic Novels and Comics*!) after she won a grant from the Ohio Humanities Council. The event brought together nearly 30 departments, nonprofits, and other community organizations, including the English Department at Kent State University, the Mandel School of Applied Social Sciences at Case Western Reserve University, the Cleveland Psychoanalytic Center, Carol and John's Comic Book Shop, CPL (of course), and even the Kent State University College of Architecture and Environmental Design. That event overall had an attendance of roughly a thousand people. You can find all the presentations from that event printed in issue 9.6 (December 2018) of the *Journal of Graphic Novels and Comics,* which was edited by Vera Camden and myself.

Can you tell us about your early experiences with comics and why you chose comics as a field of study?

I read comics as a kid partly because my mother was interested in comics and gave them to me. English was not my first language and so comics made learning English easier, since the visuals helped with word association. Later in life, during my sophomore year of college, one of my professors, Vera Camden (you'll recognize at this point that she has had a defining impact on my life), asked what we like to read. I gave traditional answers, knowing that was expected of me, and then finally admitted "I really like comics." She simply said, "Why don't you study comics?" Then she said that I reminded her of a student she had years ago named Peter Coogan, who had gone to become one of the most prominent comics scholars in academia and is co-chair of the Comics Art Conference at San Diego Comic-Con. Professor Camden's simple question, which she also asked Peter Coogan, "Why don't you study comics?" became the most important five words of my life. She essentially gave me permission to study comics and I held onto that conviction that this was what I needed to do. I believe that the last 10 years of my life have all spun out from that singular question. I cannot stress enough how important it was that she gave me permission. I would not be a therapist, nor would I be studying comics today, if it was not for her, nor would I be as intimately connected with Wonder Woman!

What is your focus in your comics studies?

I find myself landing on two topics: mental health and comics, and queer comics. The topic I am asked to speak on the most is queer comics or queer theory and comics. I recently wrote an article for the book *More Critical Approaches to Comics* published by Routledge on the topic of queer theory and comics. Regarding my focus in mental health, unlike some comic scholars, my work is not merely theoretical. I have a major investment in the topic as both a critic and practitioner since I am a practicing therapist. I can speak to comics use in therapy based on my training and ongoing therapeutic practice. I am one of the only comics scholars trained dually in the humanities (with a soon to be PhD in English) and also trained and licensed to practice in healthcare.

How did CPL benefit your study of comics? What benefit did you provide CPL enhancing their comics?

I read comics differently now because of the library. I absolutely believe that. I think about the uses of comics differently, the way they can help us, not just in academic settings, but practically, to think about community and forming community, building bridges. I also believe I would not have been as adamant about the connection between mental health and comics, if I had been strictly teaching in an academic setting, I would not look at them the same way. Comics act as a bridge between disciplines and communities. The library reminded me that though comics have found new life in the academy, they come from the city and are intended for people to read individually (and together), and it's important to remind the world of that. Libraries can help us as academics remember where narrative comes from. Comics is a lived form, used and explored daily, and how do I negotiate the rigorous investigation of these comics vs. supporting their life in the public? Libraries are perfectly suited to help with both. As far as how I helped CPL, I facilitated public/private partnerships, and I expanded CPL's reach with comics programming. So, it was definitely beneficial for both entities involved.

What are the comics that you think should be in every library?

Persepolis by Marjane Satrapi, *Fun Home* by Alison Bechdel, *Maus* by Art Spiegelman, *100 Demons* by Lynda Barry, *My Favorite Thing Is Monsters* by Emil Ferris, *Palestine* by Joe Sacco, *Batwoman: Elegy* by Greg Rucka and J. H. Williams III, and *Iceman* by Sina Grace. I would also recommend the trades of *The New Mutants* by Chris Claremont coupled with the book by Ramzi Fawaz *New Mutants: Superheroes and the Radical Imagination of American Comics. The New Mutants* comic was so radical and inestimably brilliant. It advocated for this queer utopian world and imagined what the creative possibilities of multiculturalism can actually look like. Professor Marston, the creator of Wonder Woman, asked in his stories, if we weren't putting our mental energy into war, what could we create? I think New Mutants asks a similar question as it thinks about the future. Other books about comics I would recommend, especially for libraries with an academic slant, are *Disaster Drawn: Visual Witness, Comics, and Documentary Form* and *Graphic Women: Life Narrative and Contemporary Comics* both by Hillary Chute, *Projections: Comics and the History of Twenty-First Century Storytelling* by Jared Gardner, *Understanding Comics: The Invisible Art* by Scott McCloud, and *Arresting Development: Comics at the Boundaries of Literature* by Christopher Pizzino. Also, comics scholar Nick Sousanis is also a comics creator, and he created a comic called *Unflattening* as part of his studies. It should also be in every library.

After working closely with a library, was there anything that surprised you about library services, maybe something you learned about libraries that you did not know before?

At some level, I knew . . . how integral to community success a library is, but now I believe more than ever that the public library is a pillar that holds up American democracy. I use the library system as the best example of democratic socialism that we have; when we pull our resources together, we shore up the publishing industry to the benefit of us all. There is a return on investment and it all comes together because we are pooling our money together.

Is there something more you would like to see libraries doing to benefit comics?

I would like to see libraries supporting local creators. Whether giving them an opportunity to present, or host a workshop, comics is such a varied medium, there are so many ways to build with it, and there are many different ways to go about that. Artistic endeavor or critical one, give local creators the opportunity to learn and share their knowledge in the library.

Is there something more you think the comic industry could be doing to benefit libraries?

Comics scholars need to partner with libraries more often to disseminate knowledge, programming, etc. Leave the walls of the university and engage with the public more through public libraries. That is a powerful way to support the humanities, which is often the mission of scholars. I would love comic publishers to create comics that are original to libraries. DC is currently doing this for Walmart, but let's see some comic companies create some books that the public can *only* obtain through their libraries.

What do you think every librarian should know about comics?

IT'S A MEDIUM [emphasis his]. Not just a format, not fully a genre, but a *medium*. And please stop calling them graphic novels!!! [emphasis also his] Not all comics are graphic novels.

What are some of the current trends in comics (academic, social justice, and so on) that you think librarians should know?

Graphic medicine is an important one that has a lot of buzz around it now. There is also the growing interest in queers and comics. Comics is ideally suited to understanding gender, gender identities, and sexualities, and it's a fluid form that can stand as an introduction to many other topics.

What are you reading now?

I am reading *Unstoppable Wasp* by Jeremy Whitley and Elsa Charretier. I actually wrote an article on it! Also, *On a Sunbeam* by Tillie Walden and *Lumberjanes* by Noelle Stevenson. I am also reading *Ironheart* by Eve Ewing, *Snagglepuss* by Mark Russell, and *Black Panther* and *Captain America,* both by Ta-Nehisi Coates.[4]

The best symposium to have would be one of local interest. Find out if there are any comics or characters created in your area or in your state. There are likely a few. Perhaps there is a comic creator who is from your state or perhaps there is a popular comic that takes place in your state. Find out what nerd history exists around you and plan from there. Even though it is similar to a conference, there is no need for it to be dry, and you can host multiple mini-events or activities to tie-in for various age-groups just like you would FCBD. To reiterate, there's no reason why your symposium can't be both fun and classy, with elements of a party and a conference. You're bringing together people of like-interest, so it's a swell time to throw distinctions between high art and low art out the window.

Comic Convention

Wondering why this wasn't mentioned sooner? That's because hosting a comic convention at a library has become such a big topic, it deserves its own chapter. Head to the next chapter to learn all about it!

NOTES

1. Tony Isabella, interview via phone by Jack Phoenix, February 28, 2019.

2. Tim Hanley, email exchange, May 21, 2019.

3. The one exception to this so far was in 2004 when FCBD was held in July to coincide with the release of the film *Spider-Man 2*. Every FCBD since then has been the first weekend of May.

4. Valentino Zullo, in-person interview by Jack Phoenix, January 29, 2019.

6

Hosting a Comic Convention

Want to a host a really big comics or fandom event? There's nothing bigger than a comic convention, AKA comic con.[1] In fact, you could wrap up all of the programs discussed in the previous chapter under one big comic convention at your library. Comic conventions have existed for decades, but they have morphed over the past 20 years into events with more widespread appeal, becoming focal points of pop culture as a whole, beyond just comics. Whether this is a good thing or a bad thing is up for debate, but comic conventions are undeniably appealing to a wider range of people than just the comic collectors these days, as they have become a celebration of film and speculative fiction and have given rise to the hobby of cosplay. The most famous of these comic conventions, and also the largest, is the San Diego Comic-Con (AKA Comic-Con International), which has become the pinnacle of pop culture happenings and has come to represent the full immersion of comicdom into the mainstream. Let's not forget the appeal of conventions that are more focused on a particular type of fandom, rather than comics or pop culture in general. These fandom conventions have also become extraordinarily popular.

Cons are no longer exclusively for big cities like San Diego and New York, as the past few years have seen a boom in libraries hosting their own con events. These library cons range from smaller, half-day romps in geekdom to multiday affairs. Hundreds of libraries across the United States and Canada now host or participate in a convention in some fashion, and some of those events have become anticipated, annual staples of the convention season for the communities involved, such as the Boise Library Comic Con "which draws nearly 10,000 Idahoans with artists tables, panels, and cosplay" (Baume 2017) Just as carrying comics for

COMIC-CON IS A REGISTERED TRADEMARK OF SAN DIEGO COMIC CONVENTION. USED WITH PERMISSION.

FIGURE 6.1. The logo for the Brown County Library Comic-Con (Designed by local graphic designer Carolyn Paplham.)

circulation and hosting other comic-related events, throwing a library con is a sure way to bring a whole new audience into your library, and likely a multigenerational one to boot. Libraries of all sizes, from the Willoughby-Eastlake Public Library (OH) to the Meadowvale Public Library (VA) to the grand Toronto Public Library, have reported resounding success with their library cons (MacDonald 2014b).

Just as what exactly you can do in regards to materials and programs, the capacity that a library can participate in a con will depend upon the resources available to your library. Big or small, you may be surprised to learn of the different avenues a library can take to become part of the con phenomenon. Larger libraries with seemingly unlimited budgets will have more freedom to do what they want, while the smaller libraries may have to get creative and resourceful. Either way, community partnerships will be key. There are three major ways that a library can participate in a con, and any library, big or small, will rely on other organizations in the community for it to be a success. No library, no matter how big, is likely to be able to offer everything that a con-goer

BASIC FANDOM TERMINOLOGY

AU (Alternative Universe): A story or art that places characters in another life than they are originally. For example, Thor works in a coffee shop

Canon: The actual facts given in a work, or confirmed by the creator

Cosplay: Dressing up as a character from a fandom

Fanart/Fanfiction: Art or stories created by fans using the characters or settings from another work. For instance, "Fifty Shades of Gray" was a Twilight AU fanfic that then had the names changed

Fanon/Headcanon: The facts that vary from a work that are either generally accepted by the fandom community or that you believe

Gender Swap: A character portrayed as a gender differing from the one they have in canon

OTP (One True Pairing): This is the character couple that brings you ultimate happiness in seeing together, whether together or not in canon

Shipping: To have an affinity for a romantic relationship between two fictional characters. Example: "I totally ship Mystique and Destiny as a couple." Or as a noun: "I am here for the Mystique and Destiny ship."

Slash/Femslash: Like shipping, but specifically wanting two male or two female characters to hook-up. Often seen in fanfiction or fanart

Stan: An obsessive fan, can be of varying degrees. Originally applied to obsessive-stalkerish fans of celebrities (Dawson et al. 2019)

would want without inviting some community support. Your library may discover that a con can open far more doors and networking opportunities in the community than just those in the comics industry world.

The three key ways in which a library can participate in a con are for a library to host its own, a library to provide space for another organization's con, or for a library to participate in an already-existing con. There are benefits to each option and each option offers opportunities for libraries of various sizes and budgets. Whichever course a library chooses to pursue, any option can have a beneficial impact on your community and for comics as a medium, and also library attendance. Whether your library is in a major metropolitan area or on a remote island, there are possibilities to explore when it comes to cons, and your community will be all the better for it. Sometimes, it may require some outside-of-the-box thinking to make your event a success. Let's explore the three options in reverse order and discuss the different routes you can take for success, but first, let's talk about the "why."

Why a comic or fandom convention? It's a question that will need answering. You may have to answer the question to your direct supervisor, your direct supervisor to the director, the director to the board and fiscal officer, and the library as a whole will have to answer the question to the community. Just like your justifications for carrying comics in the first place or throwing any other comics-related program, your answer cannot be because *you* like comics. Throwing a comic or fandom convention can be an expensive, time-consuming, and labor-intensive project, so your reasons for doing so must be solid and you must be able to provide reasons how it would benefit your library's service community. Some common questions to consider will be:

- *Is my community interested in comics? If so, is it interested enough in comics to warrant a comic convention?* Some simple ways to find evidence of this interest is to look at the circulations of comics in your library, attendance for other library programs that are comics-related, and even how well-attended and how much "hype" surrounds comics-related events elsewhere in the community, such as the premier of comic book movies at local theaters. If your community doesn't seem interested in comics, would a fandom convention, focusing on a particular genre, franchise, and so on, be better, like a video game con or a Star Wars con?
- *What is the scope of the convention?* How much money, time, and staff will need to be dedicated to this event? Is a grand affair necessary or will a smaller, half-day event do?
- *How will the convention benefit the library?* How will collections or other library services be promoted during the event? How will the event's success be determined?
- *Which demographic will benefit from the convention?* Will your convention target an older audience, a younger audience, or will it be a wide range?

PARTICIPATING IN AN ALREADY-EXISTING CON

This may seem like the simplest way for a library to join in on some comic or fandom con fun, and it may be, but it depends on how much involvement your library is seeking. Participating in an already-existing con can range from simply having a booth at a convention along with other vendors to engaging in a full-on partnership with the convention authorities. This can be easy, but it can also be almost as complicated as a library hosting a convention itself. There are many factors to consider when deciding what type of arrangement would work best for which library.

A large library in a major metropolitan area may find that its city already has a large comic convention, so hosting one's own would create competition and ultimately not benefit the library. In these situations, some of these libraries have sought to partner up with the convention rather than compete, and the library becomes host to special events that are officially part of the convention and legally labeled as such. Two major cities with major conventions come to mind where we see this kind of partnership take place: San Diego and New York. I think you can see how it would be a rather silly idea for San Diego and New York libraries to throw their own comic conventions, considering that their cities are hosts to the first and second-largest comic conventions in the country, respectively. San Diego Comic-Con (SDCC) and New York Comic Con (NYCC) each host a sort of "librarian and educator day" on the first day of the convention, which is held at one of the libraries' buildings and has special events for library professionals[2] and patrons.

Even if a library cannot pursue an official partnership with a local comic convention, the library still has an opportunity to capitalize on the event. It's a simple matter of throwing some comic-related events and programs that tie-in to the convention scene. Ideas could range from throwing an after-hours library event, hosting a cosplay contest to incentivize convention-going cosplayers to come into the library, providing a comic convention scavenger hunt and inviting patrons to turn it in at the library for a prize, or hosting multiple events in the week or month leading up to the convention. There is nothing stopping a library from celebrating a community event in its own way and creating tie-in programs can be a simple and inexpensive way for a library to tap into the excitement without dedicating an unusual amount of labor hours.

At many comic conventions, one can find library booths amongst the other vendors. This is a more prevalent way to participate in a convention, though it can be expensive and labor intensive, so you'll need the budget to pay for the booth and the labor hours to spare for someone to work it. If your library wants to be present at a convention, it would behoove you to contact convention officials very early, as they may have a separate policy for nonprofit vendors and they may be willing to cut your library a deal. Some conventions have been known to allow libraries to set up booths for free, offer prime booth real estate, or allow a library a full booth for the price of a half-booth. Wizard World is a brand of convention that has cons in many major cities across the United States. They are not what one would consider library friendly, but many libraries will still be present in booths, advocating and advertising library services.

Library booths can be lots of fun for con-goers and library staff alike. One can find library con booths with a variety of activities. There are crafts, such as a giant "community comic," which involves a large roll of paper with comic panels that the public is invited to contribute to or simple coloring sheets. There can be games and contests, such as a spinning wheel or comic trivia for prizes. At NYCC and C2E2, the ALA GNCRT had a booth, a Collaborative Pop-Up Library, that saw between 1,500 and 1,600 visitors in 2018.[3] The booth often consists of a readers' advisory activity (where visitors are invited to write down three comics or subjects they like and are given three title recommendations by on-site librarians), various crafts for little ones (like decorating a superhero mask and gluing it to a popsicle stick), and even a collection of comics, plus a pup tent under which visitors can relax and read quietly, taking a break from the convention commotion.

Obtaining a booth at a comic convention can, of course, come with budgetary and staffing stresses. But overall, it is a simple and effective way for a library to make its presence known to the geek world and perhaps encounter members of the public it otherwise wouldn't. A library's presence at a convention can be a perfect promotional opportunity, as the library can hand out fliers and pamphlets of library services and upcoming programs. Though most vendors with booths at conventions hand out such materials, sometimes to the chagrin of con-goers, members of the public are more likely to accept and actually keep items from a library because a library isn't trying to sell them anything. In a place as capitalistic as a comic convention, with every vendor trying to make money at every booth, having a library simply making their presence known to offer free services to the community can be a bright and shining star.

PROVIDE SPACE FOR ANOTHER ORGANIZATION'S CON

In 2015, Columbus, Ohio, was descended upon by massive geekery and artistic spirits. This was the first Cartoon Crossroads Columbus (CXC), an event celebrating comics of all kinds that sprang from a partnership between the Billy Ireland Cartoon Library & Museum, comic creator and Columbus native Jeff Smith, comics journalist Tom Spurgeon, and others. What began as a rather humble event to comic convention standards has become a four-day festival that has spread through much of the city with many elements of CXC being held at the Billy Ireland Library, the Columbus College of Art and Design, various bars and restaurants, and the recently-renovated main branch of the Columbus Metropolitan Library (CML). Sadly, Tom Spurgeon, who served as CXC's executive director, passed away in November of 2019.

Hundreds and hundreds of people have entered the library doors thanks to CXC, and CXC has enjoyed an accommodating, accessible, and reliable space to host its guest creators. This mutual beneficial partnership, one that a comics fan may delight in calling a symbiosis, benefits both organizations with little risk and high reward. CML provides the space, dedicating nearly an entire floor of the main branch to the event, along with tables, chairs, and so on, while CXC itself is handled mostly by volunteers. The result is the library enjoying immense foot traffic, providing opportunities for the library to show off its services and materials, and have its good name spread throughout the community, while CXC gets to enjoy the library's PR and marketing resources, too. And the public, the dear, dear public, benefits most of all, with an opportunity to connect to superstar creators like Brian Michael Bendis, Art Spiegelman, Kelly Sue DeConnick, and more, including up-and-comers and emerging talent.

This is one of the best situations that any library that wants to host a comic convention could hope for. CML was fortunate enough to have an outside group who wanted to throw a comics festival and needed space. It was truly fortuitous. Chelsea District Library in Chelsea, Michigan, enjoyed a similar fortunate situation when a local group organized the Kids Reads Comics event, which the library was able to host. Whereas CXC is a more literary, academically-leaning event, Kids Read Comics and its later-incepted counterpart Teens Read Comics are targeted toward younger audiences. The Main Branch of CPL, the same library that hosted the Superman Exhibit, hosted Flaming River Con in 2019, an LGBT fandom convention, because the group organizing the con sought the library's help. A library in a metropolitan area is much more likely to encounter an outside group needing space, naturally, so what is a library to do if it is not as fortunate as Chelsea or Columbus? Even libraries in small areas can find a partnership, but it may simply mean the library has to be a bit more proactive.

If your library hopes to host another organization's comic convention, it may require the partnership to be more 50/50, but that can come with its own advantages. A library can take a look at its community and decide if their patrons are aching for a comic convention. If so, the library can reach out to local groups and plant the seeds of a joint convention. It may be that it's something your community desperately desires and there may be other groups who want to see it happen and who would leap at the chance to make it so. Sometimes, groups that would love to throw a big comics event are simply lacking a few crucial pieces to make it happen, and it is always possible that the library has those crucial pieces that are needed. All that may be needed is someone to reach out.

So, whom to ask? At this point in the book, the first answer should come as no surprise. If your library has an LCS nearby, reach out and gauge its interest. It could be that the comic shop has had a desire to throw a comic convention for quite some time, but being retail, it may lack the space to do so. Some comic shops may leap at the chance to throw a convention, a convention that is on the smaller side but intimate and full of local flavor. It's possible that the comic shop could even be willing to do the bulk of the work for the convention, as it may have more connections to comic creators, other vendors, and materials that could be used to supply the convention with fun and interesting things for the visitors to enjoy. Meanwhile, the library can contribute the space, crafts, programming, and so on. It's possible that this may not take the form of a traditional comic convention and might become something truly unique and more beneficial to your public. Library staff and the comic shop may come up with something that is more unique than what patrons could experience at the average convention, such as the Toronto Comic Art Festival (TCAF), the largest literary-focused comic convention in North America which is held at the Toronto Reference Library and has seen attendance of up to 18,000 people (MacDonald 2014b).

Local cosplay enthusiast groups may also be thrilled to help put on a comic convention or at least a fandom convention. As previously mentioned, cosplay and comics are still intricately tied, but at this point the hobby has taken on a life of its own and there are now many cosplayers who do not actually read comics. Such a group may be more apt to put on a convention that is more cosplay and fandom focused but which can still include comics. If you want another group to do most of the work for the convention while the library mostly just acts as host, be willing to be flexible in the form that the convention could possibly take and be open to ideas from other organizations. Some may find the idea of a strictly comic convention to be too limiting while others may appreciate the focus. A fandom convention may be the direction to go.

Lastly, you can try reaching out to local creators or companies that host comic conventions, such as ReedPOP or Wizard World. Some creators have the same immense connections and resources as a comics retailer, and they may be willing to do some footwork to create a comic convention and spread the love of the medium that provides their income. Regarding the comic convention companies, it is unusual to encounter a library that partnered with one of these companies to host a smaller, separate, and library-centric convention, but it could be worth a shot to ask. Though it seems possible that a library comic convention would be seen as competition to their main attractions, it's always possible they may be more open to the idea of spreading out their brand through multiple venues than we think. Plus, aiding libraries is often seen as positive publicity.

Hosting another organization's comic convention is mostly a matter of luck. It's a matter of your library being in the right location with the right group who happens to want to throw a con and needs the space. Though it may not seem likely if your circumstances aren't exactly right, your library doesn't have to just sit around waiting for the opportunity to arise. Your library's staff members can take the initiative and help put the word out that your library is available and eager for such an endeavor, increasing the odds that a like-minded organization will notice and respond. You may be amazed at the possibilities that can arise when your library's intentions and resources are promoted to the public. And if there is simply no possibility that an outside group will be willing to host a convention at your library, do not despair. There are options to bring a convention to your patrons.

HOST YOUR OWN CON

So, here it is. The ultimate option. Your library wants a convention. After weighing the possibilities of partaking in an already-existing con or inviting an outside group to hold one on library premises, you've come to the conclusion that the best option for your library and your patrons is for the library to host its own. Congratulations, you are in for a lot of work, but an equal amount of fun. Libraries across the United States and beyond are hosting their own comic and fandom conventions to great success, so your library can be the latest to join in a new, lively tradition.

Small Fandom Programs
- Presented with just one or two staff members (and maybe a volunteer)
- Limited budget ($0–$100)

- Up to 2 hours long
- Focused on one fandom/franchise
- Examples include:
  - Trivia competition based on a TV show or franchise
  - Youth program featuring stations with a mix of crafts and activities
    - Including something active is a plus!

Medium Fandom Programs
- Presented with more than two staff members
- Small to medium budget ($100–$500)
- Usually 2–5 hours long
- May feature outside speakers and/or guests
- Focused on one or more fandom/franchise

Large Fandom Programs
- Presented with more than three staff members
- Medium to large budget ($500+)
- Usually 4 or more hours long
- Features outside speakers and/or guests
- Generally focused on a range of fandoms, but may just elaborate on one
- More than 300 attendees

(Dawson et al. 2019)

Even if your library is large, it may be a good idea to start small. Perhaps start with a half-day event that takes up your largest meeting space, depending on the kind of space your library has, and then, if successful, grow the event year-by-year. Even the smallest of conventions is a lot of work, so it's a good idea to get your feet wet with a smaller event and have a convention under your belt before moving on to bigger and better. Even with a small con, you'll need to delegate responsibilities, because most con ideas you come up with will likely require more than one person to coordinate. And it's not just you who needs to get used to running a con and adjusting to one being at the library, but also the rest of the staff and uninterested patrons who may see a big event as an interruption.

Starting small gives your library and your community a chance to get used to the idea and even come to expect it.

Delegating responsibility will be crucial. Regardless of whose idea throwing the convention is, you should assemble a group to make it a team effort. One of the best things to do is create a committee that includes staff who will be instrumental in the planning, who will actually be present and working the convention, someone to represent fiscal matters, and someone who will be responsible for PR. The need for delegation is the most consistent piece of advice that librarians who have thrown cons have to offer. Small cons are still too much for one person to handle, since ideally your convention will be filled with multiple activities and lots of people. You'll need staff to work at give-away tables, to monitor panels and discussions, to be judges for contests, to provide directions, and, of course, for set-up and take-down.

Spotlight on Bryn Wolanski, Teen Librarian for Willoughby-Eastlake Public Library's Willowick Branch, and Coordinator of WEPLcon

Can you tell us the origin of WEPLcon? Whose idea was it?

It was my idea! I pitched the idea of doing a library con during my interview. WEPLcon (pronounced *wee-pull-con,* short for Willoughby-Eastlake Public Library Convention) was always something I thought would be perfect for the Willowick Branch, because they have the space, and it's a centralized location to get the clientele.

How long did WEPLcon last?

The first time was 6 hours, 10 a.m. to 4 p.m. Second time was 11 a.m. to 3 p.m. Next time will be 11 a.m. to 4 p.m. It's a range between 4 and 6 hours.

How would you describe WEPLcon? What kind of convention would you call it?

I market it as a "fandom" convention, which means that no matter what kind of nerd you are, we love and accept you. Come geek out with us. I think it's more inclusive than something more specific like calling it a comic con. We wanted it be a teen program that is intergenerationally friendly (we even had a 50-year-old woman cosplay as Sailor Mercury!), to bring teens into the library, invite them to be comfortable, let them be who they wanted to be, since comics and fandoms are a huge part of who they are. We also wanted to get people into the library who normally might not come, and to connect on a new level, fostering future connections with these people.

What makes WEPLcon different from other conventions?

I want to say that part of it would be our community connections. We reach out to local organizations and ask them to participate. Also, the thoughtfulness of our programming I think helps it stand out, such as using a green screen for photo ops. We take a picture, they pick the background, and we print it off for them. The raffle tickets are also a big hit. Donated books are given away as prizes for the raffle. In the past, we've given *Harry Potter* books, *Hunger Games, Divergent,* as well as comic books, science fiction books . . . we've had prizes for every type of nerd or geek. We also provide gift card prizes for cosplay contests. Dozens of people participate, and we have various categories including adult, teen, judge's choice, etc. We also provide a video game room for gamers. Our convention stands out from others because of its broad theme of "fandom" and welcoming all kinds of interests.

Did you face any resistance from the library authorities or from the public about putting on a convention? If so, what were some of your selling points?

As a matter of fact, the deputy director of the library system was very impressed with the idea. All of the patrons that attended voiced their excitement and support for continuing the program. One of the only obstacles came from ignorance from staff and public who didn't understand what the purpose of a fandom convention is or even *what* a fandom convention is.

What was the budget like for WEPLcon? Does it have its own line or is it taken out of your general teen budget?

Our overall budget for the program was under $500. It was also sponsored by Team IBB (a local business organization), the Boosters (the WEPL Friends group), and we used some remaining

Summer Reading money. We save money by carrying over any prizes that aren't given away into the following year's event.

If you had to guess, how many hours did you spend preparing for WEPLcon?

I'd say about 5 hours for set-up, including preparing crafts, prizes, food, etc., 12–15 hours for planning, and that was with tasks being delegated between multiple employees throughout the system. It was like the teen equivalent of a Summer Reading finale.

How much staff was needed for WEPLcon? How about volunteers? What was the attendance?

We had about 8 staff members present and working that day to assist with the con and fulfill normal library duties. We also had 5 volunteers. 150 attendees each time so far.

Did you have any assistance from vendors or outside organizations?

As I mentioned earlier, Team IBB and our Boosters group donated funds. Local comic shops Comics and Friends and Comic Heaven assisted with prizes and promotions. We also had a local artist, a face painter, and the Boosters selling manga during the event as our vendors.

What were some of the challenges you encountered while preparing for WEPLcon or during the event?

We did not budget time for ourselves to take breaks. In fact, we did not eat at all during the first WEPLcon, nor did I sit for nearly 8 hours. Make sure to take time to take care of yourself and feed yourself. Also, beware of the mess that cosplay can cause. We had a Chewbacca lean against the walls in the meeting room and his fur permanently stained the paint. The marks are still there. Beware of leaning Chewbaccas.

What was the feedback like from the community and library authorities after the event?

Overall, the library administration members were overwhelmingly impressed. They sent a message to the staff and the board thanking them for making it happen. Other branch staff did think the noise was an issue and didn't fully understand what was happening, but after the initial culture shock, they came around.

What would you like to do different for WEPLcon in the future?

I would like to have a more cohesive theme amongst the staff and among the various events that make WEPLcon. I want to always make sure people are taking breaks so we can be a well-oiled machine. I would like to include more local authors and local artists so they can spread their talents and gain notoriety among the locals.

What advice would you give to other libraries who want to throw their own convention?

If you haven't been to a convention, go. I think anyone who is going to be involved should have to go to a convention to get a feeling for and a baseline of what to expect at your own. Also, going to any local conventions can open doors for possible presenters, since that's where the networking opportunities are. Our main presenter for the next WEPLcon speaks at multiple conventions, and we are paying him instead of expecting him to volunteer. Reach out to local organizations and ask questions about what they sell, what is popular right now regarding fandoms, comics, literature, ask them if they want to join. The more local involvement you have, the more successful you will be. Not to mention if you are working with them, you may have a chance for the library to get involved with their events, too. Remember, any businesses you partner with will send their customers to you. Look at what other libraries do at their conventions, such as how we borrowed our cosplay guidelines from another library. Reach out to local radio, podcasters, TV, newspapers. I interviewed on the radio and promoted the event. Ask the PR people to be involved in this process with you. Social media has been very helpful, including Instagram. Don't forget to use hashtags to promote your event! Use the convention as a way to promote other library events and services. For example, we gave bonus raffle tickets out to attendees who checked out YA materials leading to a boost in circulation for the day. Look at what library associations and partners can be of use to you, such as Hoopla. Delegate, delegate, delegate, do not take on the whole project yourself.[4]

Though your con should start small and get larger over time, you'll still have to realistically consider size and space the first time. If your library doesn't have much space, don't be hesitant to look elsewhere for a space to host your con rather than settle on having it crammed. You can reach out to local community centers or schools if you need gymnasium or auditorium-size spaces. To throw a proper con with multiple activities, you'll need one very, very large space that can be segmented into smaller sections or multiple rooms of multiple sizes. You'll need a larger space for vendors and artists, plus multiple smaller spaces for panels and expert talks. You'll find that all the programs mentioned in the previous chapter can all be held at a comic convention, but some staple activities are vendor/artist areas (AKA artist alley), expert panel talks, creator talks, and cosplay contests. Depending on how busy your convention is, some of these events may have to overlap, so they may need their own space.

Remember that even though this is your library's convention, you can't possibly pull it off without help from your community. If the con gets large enough, you'll need volunteers. You'll still want assistance from your local comic shop who may want to be involved as a vendor or involved in putting together some programs to be included. The comic shop can help connect you to creators and comic experts who can give talks and sit on panels. You may want to get in touch with some cosplay enthusiast groups and invite them to participate in programs or be judges for a cosplay contest. You may need food vendors or even some fabulous food trucks. You may want to populate your vendor room with local artists who can present their work. And no doubt you'll want to involve your library's Friends group who may want to provide volunteers, host a booth, donate prizes, or make a financial donation.

Speaking of donations, you'll want to get started seeking donations for prizes early. Comic shops, Friends groups, or other organizations may be able to contribute money or materials that you can give away as prizes throughout the event, such as rewards for contests or door prizes, and local artists may be interested in contributing prizes, as well. Even if all those groups want to donate, it may not be enough depending on the size of your con. But you can ask for donations of comics, manga, movies, and more throughout the year from your patrons, setting aside good copies as prizes. As you weed collections throughout the year, you can set aside any geek stuff that's still in good condition and use those as prizes. You may be surprised how much people love to own retired library books, not to mention you may be able to give away some really spectacular items like Blu-rays, music CDs, and video games.

Before and while your con is taking form, you'll need to pay close attention to your library's policies. You'll need to review your libraries existing policies and how those would apply to your convention. If you plan on having vendors at your event, which you likely will, you will need to have your vendors adhere to your library's board-approved policies regarding for-profit enterprises on library property. Many libraries are forbidden from allowing for-profit sales of any kind on library property, others make exceptions. Some library policies allow the director or board to approve sales temporarily for special occasions. Other libraries allow sales on library property as long as the seller donates a certain portion of sales back to the library. Other libraries only allow their Friends groups to sell on library property, so the Friends may have to sell on behalf of all vendors. These are things you'll need to know before inviting vendors to your con so that you can make appropriate arrangements beforehand with the director, board, and fiscal office.

You'll need to review all safety procedures. Know what to do in case of fire or any other sort of possible calamity to ensure the safety of your staff and visitors. Review the locations of first aid kits, fire extinguishers, and emergency exits. If your con is going to be large enough, you may want to look into asking for police presence or hiring security. Be sure to review all behavior guidelines and run through some possible scenarios that may occur during the convention and how you would best address them. As fun and high spirited as conventions can be, whenever large groups of people cluster together in one place, trouble is always possible, so you'll need to do all you can to be prepared.

Besides reviewing existing policies, you'll need to consider policies that may need to be implemented or tweaked specifically for the convention. Specifically, these would be dress codes and weapons policies for cosplayers. Your library dress code is likely something like "shoes and shirts a must" currently, or perhaps it specifies "no profanity." You'll need to get even more specific for cosplayers, however. You'll need to consider how some of the characters in comics and pop culture dress and how that could possibly appear in physical form on an actual human body of a well-meaning cosplayer. Some cosplay costumes, male and female, can be quite risqué, maybe or maybe not too risqué for a public library, so you'll need to address the issue in concise printed guidelines that are posted publicly and not easy to miss if it is a concern you have. The same could go for profanity as part of costumes and fake blood and prosthetic gore. You'll also need to consider the possibilities of harassment while visitors are in costumes and know how you will address it. Post in your guidelines what is acceptable and unacceptable behavior. A popular convention phrase is "cosplay is not consent."

FIGURE 6.2. The poster for the Brown County Library Comic-Con. (Designed by local graphic designer Carolyn Paplham.)

A very important thing to consider is weapons. Most conventions have weapons policies now, and you will likely need one too. It's important to keep in mind that many cosplayers incorporate weapons into their costumes for the simple reason that many characters in pop culture and speculative fiction carry weapons, as most are action-oriented. These could range from pirate swords to lightsabers, axes and maces, whips, and nearly any other weapon you can name. Guns may be a big sticking point, as guns are very popular in cosplay. We're talking guns that range from the blasters that a Stormtrooper would carry that look nothing like real guns to the hyperrealistic assault weapons of the Punisher. You'll need to consider how you want to approach this issue carefully. A policy on such items could range from a zero-tolerance ban on anything resembling a weapon to allowing weapons with no sharp points or guns that have colorful, plastic tips. You'll need to discuss this issue with library authorities and other staff members for input, perhaps local law enforcement, as well.

Hosting a library comic convention can be a tremendous amount of fun, but it is sure to be an equal amount of hard work. Much time, labor, and money will have to be dedicated to throwing a successful event. Again, it cannot be stressed enough how important delegation will be, as one person alone cannot organize and execute a successful con with a truly con-level attendance. But with ample buy-in and ample preparation, your library's con can bring something truly spectacular to your community, creating an inviting space for slews of community members who may otherwise never set foot in the library. There is potential that your library convention could become an epic, annual event that your community will look forward to, and you may make waves in ways that you never thought possible. You may not only have patrons clamoring to get through the doors, but you may have other community organizations and local artists hoping to get into the convention, too. Put your nerdiest foot forward, and make it happen!

NOTES

1. Be cautious when using the term "comic con," however. It's a popular abbreviation, and it's reasonable for one to assume that it is generic, but in recent years, the San Diego Comic-Con has been suing other conventions who use the phrase. In August of 2018, a federal judge ruled for San Diego Comic-Con and against Salt Lake Comic Con, prohibiting Salt Lake from using "comic con," "comic-con," or "any phonetic equivalent," though an appeal is likely (Gardner 2018). Libraries may be granted permission to use "comic con," but it comes with stipulations; "library" must be as large as "comic con" in your logo and

promotional material and the registered trademark symbol must be used, as well as a specific credit line. If your library decides to host a comic convention, I recommend you avoid using the term "comic con" and instead use another clever use of "con." To learn more, read the article "A 'Comic-Con' by Any Other Name" at *Programming Librarian*, http://programminglibrarian.org/articles /comic-con-any-other-name-or-how-not-commit-trademark-infringement -your-library-comic-event.

2. We'll discuss these events in greater detail in the next chapter.

3. Natalie DeJonghe, email exchange, April 28, 2019.

4. Bryn Wolanski, in-person interview by Jack Phoenix, February 8, 2019.

7

Promoting Comics

Other chapters have mentioned the importance of promoting the comics collection in your library. After all, a comics collection will do your library no good if no one knows that it's there. It's important to get the word about your comics out of the building and into your community. To truly maximize comics circulation, you simply cannot rely only on in-house promotions, though those are still important. You will need to be sure that you are attracting potential patrons from the outside and convincing them to come in. You must find the comics fans where they are and draw them into the library with the promise of reads that are free and fabulous. No matter how dense your library's service area population is or isn't, it's a guarantee there are some potential comic fans out there who are just waiting to become loyal library users. All you have to do is reach them.

This chapter will act as a greatest hits of some of the content already covered in previous chapters, but there may also be some new ideas. It's important to remember that the opportunities to promote your comics collection, and any collection in your library for that matter, are quite literally endless. Comics can be promoted at any event, within any other collection, in nearly any part of your library, as well as any part of your community. If you think comics can only appeal to superhero fans or science fiction and fantasy fans then you are underestimating how broad and inclusive comics really are, for comics is a medium that can include every genre and subject. You may think, for example, that your local senior center would not be a wise place to promote comics. It may be true that the audience could possibly be more resistant to picking up a comic than a younger crowd, but don't forget about all the graphic memoirs and graphic nonfiction titles that exist and may appeal to an older audience, not to mention the possibility that you may have a collection of Sunday morning comic strips in trade form, featuring characters such as Peanuts, Beetle Bailey, and so on, that senior citizens may remember from their youths. Let's take a look at some of the options to promote comics.

SIGNAGE

Never forget, nor ever let your superiors forget, the importance of signage in your library. Signage can be the most fundamental way to promote comics in your building. Make your signage eye-catching but not an eyesore. Ensure that your comics and the directions to them are properly placed to lead your comic-loving or comic-curious patrons to the end of the rainbow. Carefully consider the terminology you want to use to identify your comics (see the conversation on the term "graphic novels" in Chapter 1). Remember, there may be merits and drawbacks to using signs that say "comics," "graphic novels," or a combination thereof.

DISPLAYS

Chapter 4 dives into a variety of display ideas and merchandising techniques for your comics. In his book, Matthew Wood additionally describes three effective types of displays: end caps, mixed displays, and pure comics displays (2018). Mixed displays can be especially effective in attracting new comic readers, since users of all kind of media would be drawn to them and may be tempted to pick up a comic that is about the same subject matter as their favorite prose book or DVD.

PROGRAMMING

Chapter 5 discusses the importance of comic-centric programs and how those programs can double as effective promotion for your library's comic collection.

SOCIAL MEDIA

A strong social media presence is a benefit to any library, and it is crucial for promoting any library service or collection in the 21st century. Your library should promote its comics on social media on a regular basis. Highlight new titles, post pictures of the collection, and make sure that your patrons know that you have the titles that tie-in to the latest big comic book movie. Start an online book club dedicated to comics or invite patrons to post reviews of their favorite comics to your library Facebook page, Twitter page, and so on. A blog attached to your website dedicated to comics can also be a very informative source of hot titles, new and old, that your library has to offer and can keep your patrons abreast of what's happening in the world of comicdom. Look out for any local social media groups that are comic-centric that your library can participate in and post things to. Get them excited for your comics and let their word of mouth do some of your work for you. The best times to post to social media are early mornings, afternoon between noon to 1 p.m., around 6 p.m. in the evening, and around 11 p.m. to midnight; this is when people will be checking their phones when they get up in the morning, take a lunch break, come home from work, and get ready for bed, respectively. There are even apps and mechanisms embedded in some social media services that will automatically post your content at a designated time of day.

PARTNERSHIPS

You've seen a lot of print about the importance of community partnerships in this book. That's because it's not something that can be overestimated. Provide your LCS with fliers and posters advertising your comic collection and events. If you establish a good working relationship with your LCS, you may find the staff there willing to put advising customers to visit the library for additional comics into practice. Keep your eyes and ears peeled for big comic book movie releases and other such events. Make arrangements with your local movie theaters, for instance, so that the library can be present with giveaways during the premier of the next big comic movie.

VENDORS

Contact your library vendors and ask them for promotional materials, such as fliers, bookmarks, posters, and anything they can offer. Don't forget vendors of digital comics, such as Hoopla and OverDrive, both of whom usually keep such swag printed and ready to ship.

POP-UPS AND TRAVELING DISPLAYS

Chapter 6 discusses the benefits of having a booth at a comic convention. It's not just comic conventions that would benefit from a table of comics, though. If your library has pop-up library capabilities, be sure to include some comics wherever it goes. Remember, nearly every genre and subject matter is included in the comics medium, so it's entirely possible to find comics that could theoretically fit any audience. Also think about audiences in your community who would greatly benefit from comics, such as those at hospitals and daycare centers. Offer to bring these organizations some boxes of comics that can be checked out on a special outreach library card for all their charges to enjoy. Your library can even bring comics to be displayed and enjoyed at local doctors' offices, such as pediatricians' or dentists' lobbies and waiting rooms.

LINKED DATA

Linked data allows a library to display thumbnail images of titles, in this case comic cover art, directly on the library website. These thumbnails act as hyperlinks, linking directly to the title in the library's catalog when clicked on by a user. Linked data works for a library's physical and digital titles equally, so a library can display its entire collection. Even better, linked data can be curated, so that specific titles can be added to a particular webpage that fits a theme, just like a traditional, physical book display in the library. If the next big Marvel movie is coming out, a library can curate all of the related comics and display them as linked data under a banner or do the same for comics for kids or comics for adults. The possibilities are quite endless, and linked data can do wonders for circulation, especially since a library can share its linked data all over the internet.

Spotlight on Andrew Tadman, Head of Reference Services for East Baton Rouge Parish Library System

Tell us about you, how long have you been with your library? Are you a comics fan?

I'm the head of Reference Services for the East Baton Rouge Parish Library System in Louisiana, and I've worked here for 11 years. I am a comics fan and a horror fan and sometimes those two passions combine.

Which Linked Data service does your library use?

We use NoveList's Linked Library Service from EBSCO.

When did your library start looking into Linked Data?

Our library was an early adopter of linked data, beginning in 2016.

What were some other Linked Data options you explored? Why did you choose your service?

We actually didn't shop around, because we have a very close relationship with EBSCO.

How much of a measurable impact has Linked Data had on circulation of your comics?

I don't have those specific statistics, but having linked data on our website has been positively received by our patrons. We primarily use NoveList's embed options to create galleries of comics for the InfoGuides (LibGuides) on our site.

Can you detect an increase in clicks when you attach comic-linked data on an event page? How about if you create a collection that ties in to a movie?

I don't have those specific statistics. But the NoveList data allows us, with very little staff effort, to create galleries simply using subject headings. For instance, we can create a gallery of Black Panther comics to highlight just by searching and selecting "Black Panther (Fictitious Character)." This also allows us to easily create galleries of comics using subgenres, as well.

How often do you update the comics-linked data pages?

Galleries are updated roughly once a month, every time new content is submitted to EBSCO. They also offer preformatted galleries that are very useful.

Can e-media be used as linked data in the same way?

OverDrive is included in linked data, but I can't speak for other library e-media services. Anything included in the catalog can show up as linked data. They do show up as different links from physical materials, though, so if there is a print copy and a digital copy of the same comic, it may show as double thumbnails.

Does your linked data appear anywhere else on the web, like on community partners' websites?

Linked data on social media shows as a picture of a generic thumbnail on the page as opposed to the gallery itself, unfortunately, but it's something EBSCO is working on.

What advice would you give to other libraries who want to explore Linked Data to improve their comics circulation?

Just go for it! Having the cover images on your site that people can click on really makes a big difference. It's much more aesthetically pleasing.

What else about you would you like us to know?

We work with a service called KOIOS; as a public library, we are eligible for $40,000 in free Google Ad money. KOIOS manages these ads for the library, so that they show first in a related Google search, similar to sponsored ads, allowing a user who may have been searching for the title to buy instead see that the local library has it. We intend to run one of these ads for comics. KOIOS creates a landing page for the library, and they can see the ranking of search terms in Google so they have the opportunity to create strong lists.[1]

With all the competition facing libraries today, such as Amazon's ability to connect a person to a physical book in just one to two days, promoting library collections is no longer optional. It's not something libraries can afford to do only if they have time and resources, but a necessity to which time and resources, proportionately, must be dedicated. Without promotions, library collections are simply dead trees taking up space. Without effective promotions, libraries will go by the wayside as people turn to booksellers and other avenues, turning potential library circulations into someone else's profits. Thankfully, promoting collections can be (and should be) a lot of fun. As mentioned earlier, the possibilities for promoting comics are limitless, so let your creative flags fly and enjoy it.

NOTE

1. Andrew Tadman, interview via phone by Jack Phoenix, December 7, 2018.

8

Comics and the Curriculum: School and Academic Libraries

School and academic libraries will find their comics situations very similar to those of public libraries, but there are plenty of key differences. All of these libraries can and should purchase and circulate comics for one purpose, and one purpose only, to benefit the communities they serve. The size of their service populations is but the first major difference worth mentioning. The public library may serve an entire town, city, or even county. Its policies, including collection development, are driven by its priorities to support these communities. School and academic libraries may have very different policies and based on different communities, as their main goals may be to support the curriculum, faculty, and student learning. Intellectual freedom and the rights of the reader may be ethical priorities for all three institutions, but their approaches may differ, as, for instance, the staff of a school library may be acting in loco parentis. It's important to remember, while a public library is largely a freestanding entity, a school library and an academic library are organizations within larger organizations and have different stakeholders and hierarchies to whom they answer.

As with public libraries, there are tips, tricks, and best practices that this book can suggest, some fine ideas gleaned from expert school and academic librarians who love comics, but, ultimately, suggestions are all they are. What works well for one school or academic library may not work for others. Staff members of these organizations within organizations will have differing rules to abide by and different resources available. Some of these entities will have vast amounts of wealth and space at their disposal, but others may find themselves in positions of resourcefulness out of necessity. This chapter will take a look at some of the differing ways that school and academic libraries of a variety of sizes can maximize their comics to the betterment of their patrons of a variety of ages.

Spotlight on Raina Telgemeier, Writer, Artist, and Librarian Fan

Raina, you're an Eisner Award winner, and the school/teacher librarians who don't know of you are probably few, but, just in case, would you like to tell the readers about you and your career?

Sure! I'm a lifelong comics fan. I started making my own comics when I was in elementary school, and never stopped. I self-published short autobiographical comics during my college years, before teaming up with the folks behind the burgeoning Graphix imprint at Scholastic. In 2006 they published my first graphic novel: an adaptation of Ann M. Martin's first *Baby-Sitters Club* book! Since then, I've created a series of memoir and fiction graphic novels, and I hope I get to keep doing it for a long time.

Can you tell us about some of your early experiences with comics and graphic novels and how they shaped your imagination? What were your favorites? If not comics, what did you read?

I inhaled comic strips in the newspaper, and illustrated books of all stripes. My dad was a bit of an underground comics fan, so he added titles like *Barefoot Gen* by Keiji Nakazawa (a manga by an atomic bomb survivor) and *Maus* by Art Spiegelman to my reading pile. My favorite prose books were almost always slice-of-life stories. *The Baby-Sitters Club*, everything Judy Blume and Beverly Cleary . . . the late '80s were a great time for girl-centric middle-grade fiction! I phased through light horror and suspense and my mom's adult novels in my teens, but comics were always my first love. Strips like *Calvin and Hobbes, For Better or For Worse,* and *Luann* imprinted on me at a young age and are still my favorites.

Comics has historically been perceived as a male-dominated medium, and creators like you are changing that perception. Are there any female comic creators who have been inspirations to you in your own work?

Lynn Johnston, who created the comic strip *For Better or For Worse*, was my most influential role model. She was one of the few women in the newspaper funny pages, and her work was as real to me as if the characters lived next door. I discovered Lynda Barry in my early teens, and her writing just socked me in the gut with its insight, humor, and crystal-clear voice.

It's such a shame there were so few female cartoonists in the spotlight before the mid-aughts—I can't even imagine how cool it would be to grow up with comics by Tillie Walden, Jen Wang, Marguerite Abouete, Lorena Alvarez, Dana Simpson, and G. Willow Wilson in my library.

Are there any librarians or teachers who are truly memorable from your youth? Did you ever encounter comics or graphic novels in the school library or the classroom?

My first-grade teacher, Miss Stoopenkoff, was one of those teachers every kid remembered as their favorite. We did a year-long journaling exercise, and I still have that little journal: essentially a time capsule of my learning to read and write. I illustrated it, too, and I consider those entries to be my first diary comics! (Good penmanship earned a scratch-and-sniff sticker.)

Although comics weren't part of our curriculum, my fifth-grade teacher, Mr. Abrams (who has a supporting role in *Guts*), noticed my interest and put me in touch with a friend of his, a cartoonist named Bill Amend who had just launched his own syndicated comic strip. That strip was none other than *FoxTrot*, which is still around today! I got to read the first several months of dailies on Xerox printouts, which my friends all begged to borrow. I felt so special. Bill even offered to look over my own early attempts at comics, but I was too shy to send them to him!

It's no understatement to say your work has been an important force getting teachers and school librarians to see comics as valuable and that they have merit. What would you say to any librarians out there who are still reluctant to carry comics in their collections?

I've heard stories of teachers banning graphic novels in their classrooms, because they're "too popular" and it's all students want to read! I say, encourage that enthusiasm. Have kids draw responses to what they're reading or act out scenes as plays. Host book clubs.

Shelve them alongside companion texts to introduce new works and authors of parallel interest. It seems that some of the hesitation comes from gatekeepers who have yet to read or discover the merits of comics for themselves. Gotta try harder than that, folks. Kids like something? It's your job to figure out *why*, and how to harness that excitement in positive ways.

I believe you began with webcomics. How have things changed for you since aligning with Scholastic? Were there any libraries that supported you when you were an independent creator?

Technically, I began with minicomics! (Although *Smile* debuted as a webcomic in 2004.) It feels like the whole world has changed since the late '90s when I was starting out, but I could see glimmers of the graphic novel movement early on. Jeff Smith's collected volumes of *Bone* sat on library and bookstore shelves alongside collections of Watchmen and Batman very nicely. Those, plus the influx of translated manga that took young readers by storm, helped set the stage for what came next.

Early in my own career, I met what I think of as the Super Librarians, comics-loving members of YALSA and ALA eager to stock their shelves with great graphic novels for young readers. Robin Brenner, Eva Volin, Mike Pawuk, Jack Baur, and Scott Robbins were blogging and podcasting and hosting panels at both library conferences and comic conventions, and they quickly became friends and allies who helped integrate the two worlds. Attending my first ALA Annuals (in 2010 and 2011) were life-changing. I had been fighting to get my work noticed at comic conventions for half a decade, and suddenly here was the enthusiastic readership I had been searching for.

You've gotten a lot of attention from libraries and schools, including YALSA and ALA. What are some library events or partnerships you participated in that really stand out?

One of my favorite events is A2CAF, the Ann Arbor Comic Arts Fest. Every June, the Ann Arbor District Library hosts a weekend of events and programming specifically for and about kids' comics. It's free to the public, and the goal is to get kids drawing and thinking and participating in the experience with their favorite cartoonists—including tabling alongside them and selling their own self-published comics! The library partners with organizations and businesses around town: there are workshops at the local 826 branch, and signings at Vault of Midnight, the local comic shop. University of Michigan hosts an educators' day ahead of the festival, and the whole weekend is full of likeminded folks, amazing readers, and delightful energy. The "Library Con" is a template that's used more widely these days, and I love seeing communities join together to create an environment that encourages reading and creativity in young people.[1]

COMICS AND SCHOOL LIBRARIES

If you are a school librarian, hopefully there is an English teacher in your school who embraces comics. Though many educators and librarians may still assume that comics are an easier form of reading, that is far from the case. Comics present an opportunity for students to engage an unconventional type of reading, one that can exercise their comprehensions skills in ways that reading a traditional book cannot, as the very language of visual arts comes into play when reading a comic. Educator and researcher, Drego Little, explains reading comics has three cognitive effects, those being:

closure—the brain's capacity to create complete images out of partial ones, to fill in gaps and construct a sequence where none specifically exists

narrative density—the interpretation of the full range of many layers of information that a single panel can convey

amplification—the ability of pictures and words to scaffold one another to support full comprehension (Little 2005)

In public libraries, there was a prevalent notion that if comics had any value at all, it was as gateway reading. Comics were only seen as valuable if they could lead a child to reading "real" books and were not seen as being valuable reading experiences themselves. As an expert in graphic narratives in education, Ashley K. Dallacqua tells us that "comics are positioned as supporting, but also separate from, traditional literacy work" (2018). Comics can be valuable as supplemental reading material, but they also carry value all their own.

Like the best classroom materials, comics present opportunities beyond just the typical reading and book report model. Dallacqua writes about the positive impact from a project allowing students to study graphic narratives and then compose their own. Comics and graphic novels provide an invaluable form of multimodal text, and the students reported that they were "complicated, difficult work" but "inspired opportunities for students to position themselves as sophisticated, thoughtful, and creative composers" (Dallacqua 2018). A school library should not stock comics just for traditional reading purposes, whether for school or leisure, but because of the many other types of projects and studies such a complex medium can open opportunities for. The potential learning from comics for literacy and visual arts is nothing short of amazing.

School librarian and teacher Jesse Karp, citing Allison and Barry Lyga, experts in comics in school libraries and media centers, explains three types of readers who especially benefit from comics that the Lygas identify.

"Slow visualizers," who have trouble creating mental images from word descriptions (a skill essential to reading) and can be intimidated by long passages of text, benefit from the graphic novel's "visual cueing systems that not only balance the text but also help the student interpret it." (Lyga and Lyga 2004)

"Reluctant readers," who lack motivation to pick up or enjoy books, "don't consider graphic novels to be 'real' books [and so do] not mind reading them." (Lyga and Lyga 2004)

"Visually dependent" students, victims of the all-encompassing visual media that inundates children every day, tend to eschew books because books are too slow moving or have no visual component to keep interest engaged (Lyga and Lyga 2004). Graphic novels, naturally, tend to stimulate interest in these students much faster than books. (Karp 2012)

Comics can not only bring a wealth of entertainment and stimulation to capable readers, but they can be a blessing for readers who are reluctant for many kinds of reasons. Students who are intimidated or bored by prose books can find comics easier to read thanks to the visuals, but also receive the benefit of those same visuals conveying complex ideas. A dyslexic learner may find the visuals and lettering structures easier to follow than a prose book. A student who is learning English as a second language may find following the stories in an English-language comic easier thanks to the visual cues provided, allowing the student to connect the words to the action and images.

Comics may assist these types of readers more than others, but all types of readers can benefit from comics, even the most voracious readers of traditional, prose novels. As other parts of this book have stressed, comics can and should stand on their own merits as a medium that can be consumed by all. Like books or film, comics is a medium composed of all genres and any subject, though there are certainly some genres more popular within comics than others. Because comics are so versatile, there is no reason for a school library not to carry them for student and faculty needs. If students and faculty do not read comics, it may be up to the school librarian or school media specialist to introduce the medium to the school and ensure that the school community sees their value. As school librarian and content specialist for OverDrive, Sheila Heinlein says, "Graphic novels help develop 21st Century Literacy and Future Ready skills by incorporating skills that include creativity and innovation, critical thinking and problem solving, communication and collaboration, as well as media and technology skills."[2]

Though supporting intellectual freedom is a core value of modern librarianship, school librarians and teacher librarians, first and foremost, support the curriculum. School librarians must also act in loco parentis. Due to these reasons, school librarians, arguably, must be even more thorough in their selections and be even more familiar with the content of what they are choosing, or at least be familiar with sources that indicate to you what the content is. A teacher librarian must be thoroughly familiar with a comic's content to ensure that it truly supports the curriculum, whether it ties in with specific lessons in literature, history, and more and that the comic can actively be a part of lesson plans. Since comics is a visual medium, a school librarian must be cautious and know the levels of violence and nudity that exist within the pages.

Spotlight on Jessica Lee, Teacher Librarian for Berkeley Unified School District

How long have you held this position? What credentials do you have and what makes you a comic expert?

I have been a school librarian for 16 years, and I work at the Berkeley Unified School District in California. I did not grow up reading comics. It was not a strong part of my childhood. I got into comics and graphic novels later in life when I took an art course that taught graphic novels. That art class introduced me to creator Art Spiegelman who said that reading a comic is the closest thing to thinking, and that really stuck with me. That's when I saw the value in graphic novels, and I became a fan. I know it's a fuzzy distinction, but I'm really a fan of graphic novels specifically as opposed to comics in general, since I'm not really into superheroes, such as Marvel and DC, and my dyslexia makes reading manga very difficult. But I'm still happy to support any graphic narrative my students love. For my students, I champion graphic novels, manga, and anything that will get them reading. As far as my credentials, I did an article in *SLJ* somewhere between 6 and 10 years ago and I've done some workshops for the CA School Librarian Association.

So, you're not a comics fan yourself?

As I said in the earlier question, I wasn't always a graphic novel fan. I'm more verbal than visual, but I do appreciate how the art works with the story. What really turned the corner for me were my students who were struggling readers and seeing how they enjoyed graphic novels. My very first year teaching, I had a class I was substituting for, and I was working with another teacher's lesson plans. She required a standard book report, and I had this one kid who was a real behavior issue. He wasn't participating in class, he wasn't reading anything, he hated all of that. All he wanted to read was this *Superman* comic. He argued that it has all the things required in the assignment; character, setting, etc., so I agreed to let him use it. He was then suspended for something unrelated, but he was sneaking into school to work on the assignment, and I saw that he had the connection to the text. Because I was willing to meet him where he was, he became a much better student. The school I was in was primarily a school for immigrants, and I also realized how much the images from graphic narratives supported their learning and comprehension. Graphic novels count.

What are some of the key challenges that school libraries have that other libraries do not?

From within the school itself, teachers saying, "this isn't real reading" can be a problem. There's a big push in public education to get kids to read at their level and graphic novels are hard to "level," such as Lexile levels or AR lists. These levels are designated to titles from criteria such as rare word use and sentence length, and graphic novels don't always fit nicely with the criteria. Some will use a great deal of rare words but may have short sentences, because much of the art is also telling the story. Many of these leveling schemes ignore the fact that art can convey complex ideas, so the art component of a graphic novel can still benefit a student intellectually. I even love having students looking at wordless books. And when graphic novels do have words, the research by linguist and educational researcher Stephen Krashen has shown that graphic novels can still enhance a student's vocabulary.

Are there unique challenges to being a librarian acting in loco parentis?

We have to be thoughtful in what we order, and the visuals make it more likely that someone will be offended. There are a few titles that I bought and then retracted from the collection, including *Lone Wolf and Cub* by Kazuo Koike. It felt like it was a good curriculum match for seventh grade since it fits with history and feudal Japan. One day, a parent came to me and raised a concern. We had the most reasonable conversation about a particular scene in the series that might could be construed as an instruction guide to rape. A series will often get more complex or richer as it goes on, and the first couple of books in a run might be fine, so this was one of those situations where I wasn't especially familiar with each entry in the series. I agreed with the parent, and withdrew the title from the collection. Berkeley tends to be fairly liberal so we can get away with a lot, but issues still arise. There are other complications with content, too, for instance *This One Summer* by Mariko Tamaki. It won the Caldecott, which is usually given to books targeted toward a younger audience, but this book is really for high schoolers, though sixth graders are often reading it. Graphic novels can just have an all-ages appeal, even though they aren't intended for all-ages. There are some parents who will tell me they don't want their kids reading graphic novels, and I sometimes have to enforce that.

What sorts of programs or activities have you organized around comics?

I've had graphic novel creators in my school, including Raina Telgemeier, Doug TenNapel, and Jen Wang. Every once in a while, we'll do craft projects including collage art, creating an original comic strip made from other comics that the students cut up strip-by-strip to make a new story, and sometimes we use the button maker to create buttons from old comic pages. We've had the public library visit to do book talks about graphic novels. We've also implemented a program called Book Club in a Box and one of those book club options was "graphic novels for schools." Getting this off the ground required a lot of grant writing, but now our collection is shared by other schools and the public library when they want to do graphic novel programs. We've developed conversation questions for each title in the Box, 4–5 questions per book. We have collected multiple copies of 52 different titles and developed discussion questions for most of them.

What sorts of merchandising methods do you use to increase circulation?

When I first came on board, the graphic novels were on a cart. Now, they are shelved up front and very visible, because they are the highest circulating section. In most of the libraries in this school system, graphic novels are together in their own collection, separated as a format. We mostly keep graphic nonfiction there, too, but, every once in a while, I will keep a graphic nonfiction title in the nonfiction section, if I think it will be useful for a school project, such as a title about King Tut. That way, a student is more likely to find it as they search the other books of a similar topic. This is a book kids will find when doing research to go with the other research books. Graphic novels can get increased circulation through the 30 Book Challenge, which is something our school does. There is a chart with a variety of book genres and formats and the kids have to fill out the chart as they read the corresponding criteria. One of the formats on the chart is Graphic Novel.

Have you received pushback from faculty or administrators about comics?

Interestingly enough, I've never had an issue with administrators. I've had more pushback from other teacher librarians in the district because I pushed so strongly for the materials and their inclusion.

Have you had to push to have comics be accepted into the curriculum or encourage reluctant teachers to use them in the classroom?

I have advocated very strongly to get faculty to recognize that graphic novels can fit in the curriculum, and I have had mostly success. Independent reading, for example, is an important part of the middle school curriculum, so we carry plenty of superhero titles for that purpose. I've even had success outside of the English department. I actually got the art teacher to start teaching sequential art as part of the art program. She even reorganized her program to match the creator visits. Some teachers now create a sort of ratio of balancing the number of graphic novels with prose books so that the reading experience in class maintains some variety.

Which vendors do you order from?

I purchase almost exclusively from Follett. We've been having a conversation about book wear and tear and it always circles back to graphic novels, because they circulate so often and fall apart. We've been looking at some rebinding companies to see if that could be a solution. I don't purchase graphic novel e-books, because we have a partnership with our public library through OverDrive. Our students have access to the public library's graphic novel e-books through the Sora app, and I usually make sure the kids know that when I introduce them to Sora, because they get excited.

Do you have any tips or tricks for selection?

Just buy what you think is good that supports the curriculum. Apply the same consideration to graphic novel choices as you would to prose books, and be mindful of series. Remember, you may only want to carry the first few titles of *Naruto*, but you probably can't afford to carry them all, so see what your students can borrow from other sources, like the public library.[3]

   In her interview, Jessica Lee, teacher librarian of Berkeley United School District, shares a story of the importance of knowing a comic's contents involving a concerned mother and the book *Lone Wolf and Cub* by Kazuo Koike. Situations like this are not uncommon when it comes to a highly visual medium like comics, so it's vital to be as familiar with the contents as one feasibly can. Comics, though, is such a broad and inclusive medium that, just because one title does not fit your curriculum and school appropriately, you may be able to find a suitable substitute with the help of annotated reading lists that you can find online, in books, or in journals.

English classes will be the most obvious and likely classrooms that your comics will be supporting, but do not take for granted just how rich comics are and the diversity of subject matter that composes the medium. Science courses, music, and even mathematics have comics that will aptly support their lessons. Of course, never forget the visual aspect of comics and how that can be useful for an art course. See the interview with Jessica for an excellent example of how a teacher outside of English curriculum found a way to make comics work for her lessons. Anyone would be hard pressed to truly find an area of school life where comics wouldn't be a benefit.

Supporting a curriculum is a process that must be taken seriously, but that does not mean that there is not the opportunity for making fun selections that you simply think students might enjoy. You can still select titles that don't directly support particular lesson plans, because most school curricula have independent reading as a major component. This means most school and teacher librarians will be able to carry comics that are simply "fun" that students will enjoy, even if their value in the classroom as sources of learning may be questionable, which could include fantasy and superheroes. Thanks to independent reading, school libraries have the opportunity to connect students to popular materials they can enjoy rather than only those assigned as homework by their teachers.

When it comes to physical placement of the comics and graphic novels in the school library, many of the merchandising techniques found in Chapter 4 may still apply. Comics are likely to be one of the most highly circulating forms of media in the school library, so placing them in front may be a good idea. Placing them in the back may also be a good idea, so that students must enter the library and pass other materials they may find enjoyable on the way, but this option should only be implemented if your students are already aware of the comics collection and eager for it. While public libraries will generally sort their comics into three broad age groups, juvenile, teen/YA, and adult, school libraries and media centers tend to get much more specific. These entities are often concerned with grade level and reading level, as well as intended audience, including AR lists and Lexile levels. Each of these can be a factor into how the comics can be merchandised most usefully for students.

Comics and graphic novels can be, unfortunately, very difficult to assign levels. Some methods of leveling books, for instance, must fit certain criteria. These criteria can include the frequency in which "rare words" appear and average sentence length, as Jessica Lee explains. This can be difficult to apply to comics, since often the medium may use visuals to convey complex ideas rather than prose. There are resources that can help with comics levels, such as commonsensemedia.org (which is also useful for content), but this also highlights the importance of carrying comics that students can pick up for fun. Just because a comic doesn't perfectly fit a curriculum or perfectly fit a level, that comic doesn't necessarily have to be excluded from a school library collection. Knowing why a comic is in the collection, however, is very important for being able to justify its presence, its usefulness, and its purpose.

Having your comics placed properly by reading level and organized by grade level are two things you will find necessary to do if you want comics in your school library, but if you really want to maximize their impact, make sure to take a look at the other chapters of this book and see how those strategies can be applied. As mentioned before, shelving will be important, and you'll have to decide if you want to shelve them in front in the spotlight or in the back of the library. Either way will have its advantages. You'll have to decide if you want to organize them in an unorthodox but browser-friendly fashion, such as organizing them by publisher, series title, and franchise. What would be ill-advised, regardless, is shelving your comics interfiled within fiction or nonfiction where they are less likely to be discovered, though a case could be made for keeping comics that may be valuable for a student's research project interfiled with other nonfiction books where the student may easily come upon it.

Don't forget the importance of programming in order to boost your comics circulations. Depending on your time and budget, your school library could benefit from a comic book club, manga club, comic crafts, or a creator visit. Check out Chapter 5 on comics programming for some ideas and remember that most of the resources available to public libraries are also available to school libraries. Your school library will have the benefit of a plethora of activities happening throughout your building or district in various classrooms, and if any of them are comic related, you'll have a chance to show off the collection and boost your circulations. Just remember that, even if your collection of comics is small, it can have a big impact on your students and faculty, and you, a school or teacher librarian, are in the perfect position to turn a student into a lifelong comics lover.

COMICS AND ACADEMIC LIBRARIES

In some ways, academic libraries will find themselves with more freedom (and likely with larger budgets) than a school library, but they still have a mission to fulfill. Comics have been springing up at academic libraries for the past few decades or more, and more and more academic libraries find themselves embracing the medium each year. Comics have a strong presence at Ivy League universities like Columbia and at state universities such as the Ohio State University, through its affiliation with the Billy Ireland Cartoon Library & Museum and the Comic Art Collection at Michigan State University, and others. That's not even mentioning the various art colleges that have strong sequential art programs with library collections to support them or a center such as the Institute for Comics Studies. Like public and school libraries, academic libraries have largely come around to embrace the comics medium and recognize its value.

Unlike most public or school libraries, these academic libraries are likely to have a librarian who is a dedicated comics expert, so, if you truly love comics and have an immense appreciation for them as a source of study, perhaps it's not too late to point your eye to academics. Having a dedicated professional with comics expertise means that an academic library can establish a rich collection that supports casual learning, leisure reading, and rigorous study. This means the assortment of comics that an academic librarian can justify purchasing can be incredibly diverse, including pop culture materials like superheroes, but also nonfiction, biographies, and memoirs, collections of comic strips, comics from countries outside of the United States and in languages other than English, and even rare materials for archives, like original pieces of illustration.

An academic library is sort of a blend between a public and school library, as it is likely to have a larger budget for the materials but also must adhere to its goal of supporting the research needs of faculty and students. But a collection is only as good as its use, and it may be up to the specialist comics librarian to make sure that students and faculty know the collection is available to them. This means that, just like the other two types of libraries, an academic library must promote its collection to the college or university and do all that is necessary to keep the collection as accessible as possible. As the title of this book suggests, even an academic library with a specialized collection must find a way to maximize its impact.

Just like with school libraries, the other chapters of this book may be helpful when it comes to ideas for boosting circulations, which can be easily tweaked for an academic setting. An academic library will have to consider the same cataloging and organizational issues as a public library. The LCC, much like the DDC, is not well-equipped to appropriately organize the comics medium. If comics are shelved in strict adherence to LCC standards, then they will end up separated on the shelves and buried amidst the other materials where they may be difficult for students to find, since, according to Columbia University's Karen Green, Curator for Comics and Cartoons at the Rare Book & Manuscript Library, "The Library of Congress has three separate approaches for classifying graphic novels and comics," with the largest percentage going in the Ps for Literature, some in the Ns for Fine Arts, and some classified by subject matter (Green 2010). A librarian may need to consider going against LCC rules and separating the items into their own collection or otherwise finding a method to highlight them, similar to what Green is doing at her library. You can see her interview in this chapter for more details. Creating an in-house classification system may be useful, along with unique call numbers, or a library could choose to use other, simpler methods such as effective displays, or even shelf-talkers and signs, not something as frequently used in academic libraries. See Chapter 4 for ideas.

Spotlight on Karen Green, Curator for Comics and Cartoons at Columbia University's Rare Book & Manuscript Library

How long have you been in your current position?

I have been the Curator for Comics and Cartoons at Columbia University's Rare Book & Manuscript Library since 2017. Before I had that title, I was the Librarian for Ancient & Medieval History for Butler Library, starting in 2002. I also worked at Columbia's library during my graduate studies, so I have had a very long relationship with that library and university.

What qualifies you as an expert on comics in libraries?

I sort of stumbled into being a comics expert. In 2005, I realized that the university would benefit from a collection of cartoons and comics for research purposes, since—among other reasons— it was a medium getting greater scholarly attention. After initiating this collection, comics became an increasingly prominent focus, giving short shrift to my original responsibilities—and eventually they became the sole focus of my career. Comics have led me to some fantastic places and have had a powerful impact on my life. I am very proud of the collection here and the work that I've done, and we have some amazing material, such as the Chris Claremont archives, which were the origin of my expansion into special collections.

What challenges have you faced, from university authorities, students, or other stakeholders/decision makers regarding comics in an academic setting?

Honestly, none. My superiors have been very supportive since the beginning; our former University Librarian used to enjoy saying that our Ancient & Medieval History Librarian was also our comics librarian. Something very exciting I have in the works is a chance to move the comics into their own rooms and keep them all together. At Butler Library, three of the rooms with our undergrad collections had become empty. I had the idea that those three rooms would make a wonderful space for the comics, and I got permission from my superiors to make it happen.

Do you personally have a passion for comics or is your passion for them strictly professional?

Like many kids, I loved to read the comics in the newspaper. I also read *Archie* and other comics that my pediatrician and orthodontist had on hand in their waiting rooms. I've been a fan of comics and cartoons my entire life, although I never quite got into superheroes. That often surprises people, since superheroes have traditionally dominated the comics industry, but that is less and less the case of the industry overall. Often, when a critical conversation is happening concerning comics in general, it's clear that the speakers are referring to the superhero genre, specifically. People will complain, for instance, that comics have too few female creators, but that's actually more likely in superhero comics; other comics genres feature plenty of female creators.

What do you love about having comics in your library? What do you not like?

I love what comics have done for the stacks. Years ago, when I first began working in the library, when the digital catalog wasn't quite what it is now, students would be in the stacks, browsing and searching them. After online catalogs, I stopped seeing that happen. But now, thanks to the comics collections, I see students browsing the stacks again, exploring them the way they were meant to be explored.

Do you promote the comics collection in your academic setting? If so, how?

I host events and promote them on social media. The events are often successful; however, I've noticed that they tend to be attended more by the general public than by students or Columbia affiliates. Still successful, but perhaps not in the way I would intend them to be. I find a challenge for an academic library such as Columbia's is reaching the students about the collection and events promoting the collection. The Columbia community is so busy, there's so much going on for faculty and students, that sometimes it can be difficult to find an effective way to connect with them.

You have spoken about the challenges in cataloging, classification, and organization of comics in libraries. Would you mind, generally, telling us what some of those challenges are, particularly pertaining to DDC or LCC systems?

I can't speak much about DDC, but the unfortunate thing about LCC is that it provides neither a physical nor a digital mechanism for browsing the entire collection. The bulk of the collection is in Literature, but there are significant portions in Art or Children's Literature, and then there are certain titles, such as biographies, that are shelved by subject. Because there is neither a single classification nor a unifying Library of Congress Subject Heading, there's no way to browse the collection effectively or efficiently. This is what the abovementioned move will address. At last, the entire collection will be together. I wrote an article about this for *Publishers Weekly* ("Whaddaya Got? Finding Graphic Novels in an Academic Library," November 9, 2010) and that would be a good source to look at to see why exactly this is a problem.

Do you know of any recent efforts to alter cataloging standards to be more conducive with comics? If not, do you know of any discussions on the horizon?

No, I really don't.

Would you say there are ample professional development opportunities for academic librarians regarding comics?

There are, but you have to know where to look. It can be challenging for academic librarians at the ALA Annual Conference, which often seems geared more for public libraries, but comics have an increasing presence there. The Graphic Novels & Comics in Libraries Round Table is also a promising development. But look at comics conventions that happen around you, look for local comics enthusiast groups through social media, and look for local creators and publishers around you who can help inform you about the medium. In my career with comics, I've even been able to travel to international events with European comic vendors, because I don't solely collect American comics. Reach out to the vendors and talk to them, and they will be eager to guide you to sources of education and professional development, as well.

Is there something more you would like to see academic libraries doing for comics and the comics industry?

I want to see them buy comics. That's what they can do for the industry. I want to see more academic libraries creating comics collections and I want to see more institutions of higher learning embracing the medium.

Is there something more you would like to see the comics industry do for academic libraries?

Honestly, I just want the comics industry to keep putting out quality material. That's the best thing they can do for academic libraries. I'm not just talking about Eisner Award winners and other industry awards, I'm talking about comics that are so good that they win literary awards and are reviewed by the *New York Times* and other prestigious media outlets. Those are the titles that are going to get the attention of faculty and make it into academic libraries. The more quality comics there are that get such critical attention, the easier it is to open the door for other titles.

What advice would you give to an academic library that wants to build a comics collection?

Just go for it and know that I'm proud of you. Reach out for help when you need it, and, remember, if you build it, they will come.[4]

Speaking of in-house systems, it would be remiss of me to discuss academic libraries without mentioning a true pioneer of comics in libraries, Randall Scott. Scott literally wrote the book on the topic titled *Comics Librarianship* in 1990. Yes, one of the first efforts to truly dissect and analyze library practices as applied to comics began in an academic setting, as Scott spearheaded Michigan State University's organization of their Comic Art Collection.

Because it's a special collection rather than a public one, Scott has taken many liberties to create an index[5] organized by "Creators," "Settings," "Chronology," "Nationalities," and much more, which can be cross-referenced. As Rachael Bild points out, "And c'mon, what other library has a list of comics they hold that take place on balconies?"[6] Scott's work with organizing comics has had a tremendous impact on how the profession approaches the medium.

It would be a good idea for your academic library to host programs and events to promote your comics, and an academic setting can open ample opportunities. Creator visits will be especially valuable, and perhaps even easier to arrange, for an academic library. Don't think that just because it's an institution for higher learning that your students wouldn't benefit from a stress-relieving comic trivia night or mini comic convention. Reedley College, a rural college in the San Joaquin Valley in California, has held a successful con thanks to librarian Shivon, who had this to say:

> I always wanted to put together a comic-con on our campus. I pitched the idea to the library and other faculty on campus. I quickly got buy-in and several individuals wanted to help make it a reality. We formed a committee comprised of campus faculty, staff, and students that met once a month and followed up via email or Canvas. Duties and programs were divvied up amongst members. Programs included an artist alley, STEM demos, geek trivia, cosplay contest, gaming, and more. The Reedley College Comic-Con had about 200 in attendance. We used donations from faculty, staff, and local businesses for prizes and materials. Additional funds were contributed by the library and the Associated Student Government (ASG). The total dollar amount for the event was roughly $1,000 with at least 500 combined labor hours. We promoted via flyers, email, library displays, student-created teaser posters, display monitors across campus, and word of mouth. It generated a lot of interest from students both years. One of the major challenges was choosing a date and time. We're a rural college so most of our students leave in the late afternoon during the weekday. For the first year, we tagged along for one day with an already established campus-wide 3-day program with the aim to increase student engagement. The next year, we considered a weekend. However, this proved difficult since the

campus is pretty much closed on the weekends. We decided to move our event to its own day during the weekday before spring break.[7]

Even if an activity, such as a craft, may seem too immature for college-age individuals, it's worth noting that early adults these days are more open to relaxing activities from childhood. Remember, though, that colleges and universities are busy, bustling places, and you'll have to, metaphorically speaking, shout very loudly to get through the din of other activities, events, and work that consumes campus life. You'll need to utilize your campus resources to get the word out; marketing department if there is one, bulletin boards, campus publications, asking faculty to spread the word, and, of course, social media. See Chapter 7 for tips on some effective social media use.

Regardless of which kind of library or librarian, the goal is for this book to be useful. What can work for a public library, can work for any library, though it may require just a bit of modifying, whether its organizing, merchandising, or programming. A comics collection, regardless of library type, deserves a degree of care and attention to keep it flowing, to and fro, through your library doors. Comics can be educational, comics can improve reading comprehension, comics can improve vocabulary, comics can improve cultural literacy, and be useful for all kinds of research; quite frankly, the value of comics in education and higher education centers cannot be overstated. They can only reach their useful potential, however, if a librarian takes an active role in getting them into the hands of students, faculty, and researchers.[8]

On the rise: Graphic Medicine! "Graphic medicine" is a term coined by Dr. Ian Williams to denote the various ways that comics can be used for healthcare purposes. This can include a comic's use in the study of healthcare, delivery of healthcare information to a comic's reader, a comic being used for therapy, and much more. This concept is something the library world should keep its eyes on, especially academic, medical, and special libraries, as librarians are on the frontlines of this trend, including medical librarian Matthew Noe and Alice Jaggers of the University of Arkansas for Medical Sciences Library. Articles about graphic medicine have been appearing with more frequency in publications like *Publishers Weekly* and panels about the topic have been popping up in more and more library conferences. To learn more about graphic medicine, visit www.graphicmedicine.org.

NOTES

1. Raina Telgemeier, interview via email by Jack Phoenix, April 22, 2019.

2. From OverDrive professional development handout, 2018.

3. Jessica Lee, interview via FaceTime by Jack Phoenix, March 26, 2019.

4. Karen Green, interview via phone by Jack Phoenix, February 18, 2019.

5. You can browse the index here: http://comics.lib.msu.edu/rri/classdex .htm.

6. Rachael Bild, email exchange, April 5, 2019.

7. Shivon, email exchange, June 10, 2019.

8. A great new book was released in 2019 which academic librarians will find valuable. Piepmeier, Olivia, and Stephanie Grimm, eds. *Comics and Critical Librarianship: Reframing the Narrative on Academic Libraries.* Sacramento, CA: Litwin Books, 2019.

9

Comics as Professional Development

If you think a comic convention could never be a legitimate form of professional development (PD), you need to rewire your neural pathways more than Doc Ock. Sure, comic conventions can be massive fun with countless collectibles, frenzied fans, and crazy cosplay, and writers, artists, and celebrities galore. But along with such gleeful sights, you may be surprised just how much of an educational experience a comic convention can be. Nearly every comic convention will host panels, presentations, and lectures to educate the public on the comics industry, genres, upcoming releases, and so on. There is never a lack of news and content to make for some interesting discussions in the world of comics.

Beyond general comics information, many conventions, especially the larger ones, have been hosting educational events that are specifically targeted toward educators and librarians. These range from events lasting an entire day to single presentations, but the comics industry has realized that librarians and educators are a key demographic that would benefit from the information best obtained at a comic convention. At a comic convention, librarians and educators can attend panels about readers' advisory, collection development, supporting diversity in comics, trends to watch, comics for the curriculum, even the occasional presentation about cataloging. At a comic convention, librarians and educators can have the opportunity to speak directly to comic creators, and vice versa, allowing the possibility for productive dialogue about the value that libraries see in comics and the value that the comics industry sees in libraries.

This chapter will briefly explore the ways that professional librarians and library support staff can benefit from attending comic conventions and what can be expected. Attending comic conventions as PD can come with challenges that you may need to find ways to overcome. But if you are able to successfully attend a comic convention, you may be thrilled at just how valuable of a PD opportunity it can be, possibly more valuable than a traditional library convention, especially for those librarians who are focused on the comics medium. Member of ALA Council, the GNCRT, and a coordinator for convention Pop-Up Libraries, Natalie DeJonghe explains, "Graphic novels circ very well in many libraries. It's vital for library staff to be able to provide readers advisory and programming around these collections to help highlight them for current graphic novel fans and to introduce them to possible new fans. Professional programming at comic conventions provides the resources staff need to do these things. Also, since many attendees are local to the area, it's an amazing way to let fans of comics and graphic novels know that the library has these books available."[1]

So, where should you look for PD opportunities if you are a comics librarian, aspiring comics librarian, or a librarian who just cares about comics? There are all kinds of places to look. Some of them you'd be expecting, as they are more traditional library sources. But others may surprise you, since they would be unorthodox sources, ones that many librarians may otherwise overlook. Hopefully, the ideas below will be helpful to you as you pursue PD opportunities, perhaps also helpful to your staff, and in convincing your library superiors that these are perfectly legitimate sources to improve your knowledge, skillset, and ability to serve your communities.

PROFESSIONAL ORGANIZATIONS

The most important PD activity for you to engage in is joining a professional organization. Such organizations can guide you to the opportunities being presented hence and then some. Besides leading you to additional PD opportunities, you'll find that professional organizations are the best way to keep abreast of the conversations and trends happening within comicdom. Not all of these organizations are for librarians, per se, but by simply following the organizations, following the conversations taking place, from articles circulating, to memes going viral, to reading any output of literature from these groups, you can keep your finger on the pulse of comics. There may be those who still think comics are just for kids or for a niche crowd, but there are professional and scholarly organizations composed of very educated experts who would disagree. The members of these organizations have dedicated their time, energy, and critical minds to proving that comics deserve to be taken seriously and are an artistic and literary force worthy of attention. Comics studies has become an accepted field of academics in many colleges and universities around the world. Here are just a few.

- **American Library Association Graphic Novels & Comics Round Table (GNCRT):** This group is formally known as the Graphic Novels Interest Group but successfully obtained true Round Table status in 2018. The GNCRT advocates on behalf of comics in libraries to ALA and beyond. They'll host events and meetups at library conventions and comic conventions and promote PD as much as they can. Following this group on social media alone provides a wealth of information about what's happening in the world of comics, libraries, and comics in libraries. You can often find some GNCRT presence at major comic conventions, often times a booth. "One of the things that I find most exciting about the creation of the RT is how many opportunities for mentorship and fellowship that it supports," says DeJonghe. "We're working to create reading lists, awards, tool kits, etc. All of which provides opportunities for library workers, both RT members and non-members, to participate and to access tools they need to support these collections in their libraries." You can join the group by adding the Round Table to your ALA membership here, http://www.ala.org/rt/gncrt/membership, follow them on Facebook here, https://www.facebook.com/groups/ALAGNMIG, or follow them on Twitter and Instagram using the handle @libcomix.
- **Comics Studies Society (CSS):** This group of educators, scholars, writers, medical and mental health professionals, and others is dedicated to studying comics and all things comics-related, including essays and books about the topic. They publish *Inks: The Journal of the Comics Studies Society* through Ohio State University Press (see Chapter 3 for a list of scholarly sources).
- **Comix-Scholars Discussion List:** The University of Florida is a prominent school for comics studies and they offer a listserv for any and all comics scholars and professionals. http://www.english.ufl.edu/comics/scholars/index.shtml
- **National Cartoonists Society (NCS):** A society composed strictly of cartoonists, animators, and comic creators.
- **Scottish Centre for Comics Studies:** Located at the University of Dundee, this entity seeks to bring comics professionals, educators, and students together to teach, learn, and advocate for comics studies.
- **Siegel & Shuster Society:** This group is dedicated to carrying on the legacy and spreading the good names of Jerry Siegel and Joe Shuster, creators of Superman and patriarchs of the superhero. The group

spearheads projects and fundraisers for the sake of preserving artifacts and historical sites connected to the pair as well as events celebrating their contributions to the world.

LIBRARY CONVENTIONS AND CONFERENCES

Most library-centric conferences and conventions hold a presentation or two about comics these days, as many more librarians find information about comics useful. At any given conference, you'll find panels about collection development, readers' advisory, and more as they pertain to comics. Sometimes, experts outside of librarianship are also brought in as presenters or keynote speakers. Scour any and all library conferences you can find and seek out comic-related programs. Though they are usually relegated to YA blocs, there are plenty of discussions regarding juvenile and adult comics, as well.

- **American Library Association Annual Conference & Exhibition:** The ALA Annual is the most well-known and well-attended library conference. Happening in the summer, you can count on a plethora of networking opportunities, educational presentations and panels, informative literature, and more, all pertaining to comics. Many of the major comics publishers, like DC, as well as many smaller publishers, are present at booths, providing previews of the upcoming titles on their dockets. ALA is one of the largest conventions for librarians in the world, so it's not an understatement to say that the amount of comics knowledge you can obtain at this event is staggering. ALA Annual is likely to have events pertaining to comics in other types of libraries besides public, especially school libraries. Keep your eye on the ALA Midwinter Meeting & Exhibits, as well.
- **Public Library Association Conference:** The PLA is a division of ALA, and the PLA Conference is held biannually. It offers many of the same types of comic programming opportunities as ALA Annual, but with a focus on public libraries.
- **American Association of School Librarians National Conference & Exhibition:** The AASL is another division of ALA, and this conference is also held every 2 years. This is the only national conference exclusively for school librarians, and this often presents a perfect opportunity to learn about supporting a curriculum with comics. Comics publishers are often present that cater to school libraries, such as First Second, often giving presentations as well as running booths.
- **State Level Conventions and Expos:** If national level conferences are too far or too expensive for you, don't forget about the valuable PD

opportunities awaiting in your own state. If you are not a member of your state's library organization, it is something you need to consider, whether you are professional or support staff. State level organizations such as the Ohio Library Council or Illinois Library Association host annual conferences and expos and presentations on comics, such as graphic novels and manga, have become fairly standard fare. Many such organizations will still allow you to attend the conference or expo even if you are not a member, though often at a higher rate.

COMIC CONVENTIONS

As already discussed, many comic conventions have become valuable resources for PD, as many now offer panels, presentations, and meet-ups for those who are affiliated with libraries and education. Some of these conventions now offer programming tracks or even entire days dedicated to librarians and teachers, as many comic conventions have learned to embrace members of those fields. Some of these conventions also offer special rates for librarians and educators that are far less expensive than the standard ticket prices. Currently, C2E2, NYCC, SDCC, and Emerald City Comic Con (ECCC)[2] allow professional registration for librarians.[3] Do not overlook comic conventions as PD opportunities, as you may find them more valuable than the usual library convention. Here are some examples of prominent comic conventions and what they can offer.

- **Chicago Comics & Entertainment Expo (C2E2):** The first day of this convention, traditionally a Friday, has special events for librarians and educators. Some examples of offerings for C2E2 2019 included a "Librarian Networking Session," "Revolutionary Ideas: Fan Days, Cons and Large Scale Interactive Programs for Libraries," and "Get It Sorted: Keeping Collections Browse-able @ Your Library." ALA and GNCRT are often present with a pop-up library booth, and C2E2 offers professional badges for librarians and educators for only $30 for a 3-day pass or professionals can get a single-day badge for the professional and educator day for free.
- **New York City Comic Con (NYCC):** Like C2E2, this convention recognizes the importance of librarians and educators and offers them a special day of distinct programming. Unlike C2E2, this special day is held outside of the convention center at the New York Public Library. The first day of the convention is known as NYCC @ NYPL and one can find a multitude of programs about comics in

libraries, as well as a likely keynote speaker who is a professional in comics. Some examples from 2018 included "Graphic Novels, Mental Health and the Challenges that Inspire Authors," "#RepresentationMatters in Your School Library," "What's It Worth? Adult Graphic Novels Are an Investment," plus Marjorie Liu, creator of the comic *Monstress,* as the keynote speaker. NYCC @ NYPL is actually completely free to librarians and educators who apply and are approved to attend, but the rest of the convention can also be attended at a discounted rate for professionals.

- **San Diego Comic-Con (SDCC):** Also known as Comic-Con International or simply Comic-Con, this is a sacred pilgrimage for geek culture, the ultimate convention and the most famous in the world. SDCC partners with the San Diego Public Library to offer Comic Conference for Educators and Librarians (CCEL), a 5-day conference held at the library during SDCC full of programs and events for librarians and educators. These include workshops for teachers, library panels, publisher panels, a Comics and Libraries Fair, and more. The day before Comic-Con @ the Library, there is even an event called Pre-Con @ the Library with additional opportunities for games and programs. Though this event is free for librarians and educators, registration is required as space is limited. Wondercon, in Anaheim, CA, is another convention held by the same organization as SDCC. Wondercon also offers professional registration for librarians.

- **Toronto Comic Arts Festival (TCAF):** Though outside of the United States, this is still useful and shimmering with opportunity, so perhaps professionals near the Canadian border would be interested to know that TCAF offers professional registration for librarians and educators during its Librarian & Educator Day. The event is held at the Toronto Reference Library, and 2019's event hosted sessions on Comics Advocacy, Comics Cataloguing Best Practices, and so on, as well as Raina Telgemeier as keynote speaker (Beguiling 2019).

- **Local Comic Conventions:** If you can't make it to one of these larger conventions in these major cities, fret not. With a quick Google search, you can possibly find that one of the smaller conventions held in your state offers opportunities for librarians. Most major cities in every state have at least one comic convention annually, and some have more than one. Columbus, Ohio, for example has CXC, which is held at the Main Branch of the Columbus Metropolitan Library and offers plenty of opportunities for librarians to learn. It also has a Wizard World and a few other smaller conventions throughout the year. Take note that Wizard World conventions, as of this writing, do not make any special arrangements for librarians or educators as far as programming or ticket prices. Look for similar opportunities at smaller conventions like CXC in your state, and, if you have no luck, then perhaps you can be the one to spearhead such an idea and make it happen! (See Chapter 6 about partnering with comic conventions).

LITERATURE

There is now a wealth of literature about comics in libraries written by fellow librarians, which are invaluable if you are hoping to maximize your comics services. You may also find reading academic and historical works about comics useful, and some of these may be already in your library's collection. See the bibliography at the end of this book for reading recommendations that you may find helpful.

WEBINARS

Webinars are one of the simplest, commitment-free forms of PD. You can often watch them at your own pace at a time that's convenient for you and your employer. There are a multitude of webinars about comics offered every year from multiple sources. Sometimes there is a fee for webinars, but many webinars are completely free or complementary with a membership to a professional organization, such as ALA. Webinars can be just as lively as an in-person discussion, since many allow the participants to engage in live-chat with the panelists and leave room for Q&A. If you can't attend a webinar when it casts live, most can be archived and viewed later at your leisure. Below are some places on the internet to keep your eye out for comics webinars.

- **Library Journal Webcasts:** Library Journal and School Library Journal frequently provide webinars or webcasts. See the webinar from 2019 titled "Spring Graphic Novels" featuring a panel of speakers including representatives from Diamond, Marvel, and Viz Media, for instance. Most Library Journal webcasts are usually free to those who work in libraries, especially if your library has a subscription to *Library Journal*.
- **ALA Webinars:** ALA always has a slew of webinars available on-demand on a variety of topics, including comics and graphic novels. The major drawback to this resource is the price tag. ALA webinars usually come at a cost and, even for ALA members, are rarely free and only available at a discount at best.
- **Library Vendors:** Many vendors offer free webinars to their library clients about upcoming titles and their offerings that are currently

available. Digital vendors, such as Hoopla and OverDrive, are often reliable when it comes to offering webinars and webcasts on a regular basis, usually with information straight from the publishers. Many of these include comics and graphic novels.

- **Webjunction:** This is a very popular source for library webinars. What makes this especially nice is the webinars are free for those currently employed by a library. Unfortunately, there aren't any webinars exclusively dedicated to comics or graphic novels currently available, though the material pops up in discussion in many of them. It's still a good idea to keep your eye on this resource, as that can change at any time.

- **State Level Organizations:** As mentioned earlier, don't underestimate what opportunities can be offered at the state level. Local library organizations are quite likely to offer webinars and webcasts and some of those just might deal with comics. For example, the Northeast Ohio Regional Library System (NEO) has an archived webinar titled "Graphic Novels for All Patrons."

MAKING YOUR CASE

You shouldn't be surprised if your library superiors and decision makers are not one hundred percent on board with the idea of you using comics as PD, so it may become necessary to do some convincing. Making your case for using comics as PD is really no different than making your case for any other form of PD, but you may have the added obstacle of the ones who control your library's pocketbook not taking comics very seriously. If you want to attend a comic convention for PD, for instance, you'll have to prove that you aren't just going for fun. Just like attending any other event on work time, you'll need to firmly establish the PD you will receive and how that will in turn benefit your library and your community. Here are just a few things to keep in mind as you prepare your proposal.

- If you want to read comics or books about comics as PD, you may be able to convince your library to purchase copies for you. Be prepared with professional reviews of the titles you want to read as well as their prices.

- For a webinar, be sure to know how much the webinar will cost, if anything. Know the time and date and make sure it works with your schedule. Pay attention to whether or not the webinar will be archived in case there is a conflict.

- If you want to join a professional organization, your library likely has a policy in place for paying for those memberships. But in case your library is unwilling to pay your fee for ALA or GNCRT, for example, set aside some money of your own as best you can and be prepared to pay for the membership yourself for at least a year. Be active and engaged with the organization for a year and return to your decision makers with a list of benefits and accomplishments you can attribute to your participation. They may be willing to change their minds for the following year.

- If you want to attend a comic convention, be willing to put in a lot of research, because you'll essentially plan the trip, knowing full well those plans may not be followed. Find ticket prices, the cost of transportation, a reasonably priced hotel, budget for food, and so on. Look up the previous year's convention's library-focused programs and show them to the ones you have to convince; instill confidence in them that the convention has worthwhile, substantive programs that will leave little doubt that they will benefit you professionally.

- No matter what PD opportunity you wish to pursue, remember that the most important thing to do is to articulate, concretely, what benefits will be derived from these PD opportunities. You'll need to convey to library authorities and stakeholders that comics are not just fun and enjoyable but are a benefit to the community. You'll need to establish how and why, exactly, these PD opportunities will benefit you, so you can benefit your library, so your library can benefit your community.

NOTES

1. Natalie DeJonghe, in email exchange, April 28, 2019.
2. C2E2, NYCC, and ECCC are all run by the ReedPOP company.
3. Natalie DeJonghe, in email exchange, April 28, 2019.

10

Conclusion

As you can see from this book, comics can be very tricky for librarians. Hopefully, though, it's also become clear that this is mostly due to the perfectionist nature of librarianship; we librarians prefer our materials to follow strict order and fit within easily replicable systems so we can reduce the amount of subjective judgment calls we have to make. A place for everything, everything in its place; all those places should be easy to determine. Comics, however, that unique and positively bonkers medium, is simply not conducive to such order and needs just a touch of chaos to be treated properly. My hope is that this book has been helpful to you. I hope it's not too preachy, but rather grants you permission to tamper and tinker with your comics to find the right way to provide your communities access to them.

Despite highlighting how frustrating it can be to fit comics into libraries, I hope this book has equally highlighted how important it is for libraries to embrace them. Librarians cannot erase the mistakes of the past, but the truth is, comics should have been carried in libraries from the beginning. The important thing is to look forward. Libraries have evolved, librarians have evolved, and so have comics. There needs to be a willingness to acknowledge the changes over the decades, rather than resist them, and to acknowledge that more changes are yet to come. Comics and libraries are, hopefully, destined to be bedfellows and will need to support each other. Be creative to find the best possible way to support comics and comic readers, and do what you can to encourage the comics industry to support libraries and library patrons, as well. Once all the details are ironed out, it's easy to see how libraries and comics are simply made for each other. It's more than the notion that comics are just another type of reading material, but the cultural and intellectual benefits that the comics medium uniquely provides in its own way is directly in line with the mission of most libraries.

Of the sordid history between comics and libraries, it's reinvigorating to know that comic creators, at a near wholesale level, see libraries as a positive force for the comics industry, for their careers, and for the world in general. Take advantage of this. Know that, in all likelihood, these great, brilliant creators probably look up to you just as much as you look up to them. That's something I learned from writing this book, since every comic creator I contacted in regards to this book expressed an eagerness to help librarians in any way they could, even if they didn't have time for an interview. All displayed respect for what librarians do and the resources libraries provide. You, as librarians, hold more power and respect than you may realize. Use it to serve your communities even more.

This book took me to many places, from Chicago to New York to Toronto, and to many different kinds of libraries. I met dozens of librarians of various kinds of various backgrounds. They had commonalities. They all recognized the same problems and challenges inherent with having comics in libraries. They all experimented and created in-house solutions to deal with those problems. They all had to negotiate buy-in from their authorities in order to implement those in-house solutions. Most had to try multiple methods, trial and error, before settling on a system that worked. What they don't share, however, is a love for comics. That's right, not all of the librarians I spoke to who deal with comics are fans or readers of the material, but they are all, regardless of level of personal affinity for the material, dedicated to connecting their patrons to comics and comics to their patrons. It was nice to learn that there are more involved in the battle for comics' respectability than just fans.

As mentioned in Chapter 9, there is a plethora of professional development opportunities when it comes to comics, since discussions about the topic of comics in libraries are present at nearly every library conference, in every library publication, and at many comic conventions. While writing this book, I attended professional development events at C2E2 in Chicago, ALAAC in Washington, DC, NYCC in New York, and countless webinars. Each had sessions on overcoming the challenges that comics present and how to best connect them to the readers. Only some of the information I gathered from these events made it into this book, because there is just so much. For further learning, I advise you to attend such events in your part of the country where you will learn that your challenges and love for comics are not unique and you will find kindred spirits for sharing ideas. There is no shortage of opinion and information about comics in libraries in the library world.

I do hope you have found this book helpful, and I encourage you to add your voice to the topic. Go to PD sessions, host PD sessions, write about your challenges, solutions, and love for the medium. Do whatever it takes to get comics into the hands of those who love them and those who do not yet know they love them. Be a champion of comics within your library building and without. Comics can be, and should be, for everyone, and librarians are the ones who can put that theory into practice by proving to your communities that the comics medium is worth respect. Present at conferences, write the blogs, submit the articles to professional publications, and, of course, write a book if you are so inclined. Heck, why not write a comic about comics in libraries? It could be a hit.

Before we part, I'd like to end at the beginning and share with you my history with comics. When I was a child, I stayed home from school with the chicken pox, and saw an episode of the *X-Men* cartoon series on Fox Kids.[1] The episode was titled "Enter Magneto," and it dealt with bigotry, marginalization, politics, and many other things not typically found in a children's show at the time. I felt that this story, and these characters, were not talking down to me for once, and it made me feel, in a way, like a grown-up. Later, I was at the local drug store and saw a bunch of comics on a spinning rack. I recognized some of the characters on the cover of a particular issue from the cartoon, and so I bought my first *X-Men* comic book and my first comic ever. The pages within dealt with the same heavy, real-world issues in a fantastic, exciting, easily digestible way, and, once again, I felt like the writer was trusting me, a little kid, to understand those issues. This began my comics journey, which has seen me through joy and woe, with comics as constant companions through the tumultuous teenage years, the college years, and they are still with me as an adult and professional. The comics medium has been a hobby, passion, and point of professional interest. When I entered libraries, I knew I wanted to do whatever I could to help support comics in libraries. After all, like Stan Lee said, ". . . comic books should be in every library."

NOTE

1. Eric Lewald, the headwriter for the *X-Men* animates series, wrote a book giving fans a behind-the-scenes look at the show's interesting and tumultuous production titled *Previously on X-Men* (2017), which I highly recommend.

Appendix A

Love Comic Books? Then Take This Survey!

Hello, my name is Jack Phoenix, employee here at the London Public Library. I am conducting a research project to improve the ways that public libraries help connect readers of comics and graphic novels to the materials they love. I hope to make finding these materials in the library easier for readers like you. If you would like to help, please answer the following questions below to the best of your ability. Please be advised that no name or other information used to identify you will be collected. Your answers will be shared with others in the library profession, but not your identity. Survey must be completed by 10/31/15 to be included in the research project. Please return to the front desk staff when finished.

If you would like to answer these questions from a distance to help us with our study, you may do so via email. Please be advised that your answers will be duplicated to a document, but your email address will not be recorded, and the email correspondence will be deleted. Please email your answers to sphoeni1@kent.edu

Please answer the questions below. Please do not include your name. This survey is to be completed by adults 18 and over.

1. How do you most often find comics in the library?

a) Browsing the shelves

b) Searching the catalog from home

c) Searching the catalog at the library

d) Asking library staff for assistance

2. When you look for comics in the library, do you look by:

a) Series title

b) Creator name

c) Character name

d) Story arc title or subtitle

3. How often would you say you check out comics or graphic novels from the library?

a) Weekly

b) Monthly

c) Yearly

d) I read them at the library

4. Where do you get most of your comics?

a) Book stores

b) Comic shops

c) Library

d) Subscription

5. Are you loyal to a particular comic publisher?
If so, which one?

6. Which would you say is more convenient for comics?

a) Comic shops

b) Libraries

Why?

7. Comic shops often organize their comics by publisher. Does this make a specific comic easier to find?

a) No

b) Yes

c) I don't know

8. Is there a difference between a "comic" and a "graphic novel" to you? If so, what is the difference?

9. If I asked you to find out if the library had *The Killing Joke*, what is the first thing you would do?

a) Look in the online catalog from home

b) Search the library shelves

c) Ask library staff

d) Look in the online catalog at the library

e) Other

If you answered "e", what would you do?

10. If I asked you to find out if the library had *The Dark Phoenix Saga*, would you:

a) Check the online catalog for "Dark Phoenix Saga"

b) Check the online catalog for "X-Men"

c) Check the online catalog for "Chris Claremont"

d) Ask library staff

e) Other

If you answered "e", what would you do?

11. If I asked you to find out if the library had *Maus*, would you:

a) Check the online catalog for "Maus"

b) Check the online catalog for the author

c) Search the library shelves

d) Ask library staff

e) Other

If you answered "e", what would you do?

12. Is there a particular comic creator(s) that you follow?

13. Is there a particular character(s) you follow?

14. How do you learn about new comics coming out that you would like to read?

a) Internet websites

b) Ads in magazines or other comics

c) Comic shops

d) Library

15. If I asked you how you would expect public libraries across the country to organize their comics, would you say:

a) They organize them by Dewey Decimal System

b) They divide them by fiction or nonfiction, shelved with other books

c) They are separated in their own collection

d) They are separated in their own collection and divided by reading level

16. How do you think libraries SHOULD choose to organize their comics?

a) They should organize them by Dewey Decimal System

b) They should divide them by fiction or nonfiction, shelved with other books

c) They should be separated in their own collection

d) They should be separated in their own collection and divided by reading level

e) Other

If "e", how would you like to see them organized?

17. What would you like to see this library do to make finding comics and graphic novels for you to read easier? Please answer with as much or as little detail as you wish.

Appendix B

Arlington Heights Memorial Library Project Proposal

Project Name: *Teen Graphic Novel collection reclassification project*

Created by: *Jon Kadus and Alice Son*

Statement of Problem or Need: *In order to make the Teen Graphic Novel (GN) collection more browsable and better arranged to serve the needs of teens who use that collection, we would like to propose creating a new classification scheme which divides the collection into three genres: GN, Manga, and Superhero. Presently all of the Teen GNs (fiction, non-fiction, superheroes, and manga) are interfiled with the call number TEEN/GN/cutter which makes browsing the collection for a specific genre of GN a bit difficult and time-consuming. After reclassification, call numbers will be TEEN/GN/Cutter (both fiction and nonfiction Teen GNs which are not Manga nor Superhero will be placed here); TEEN/MANGA/Cutter; TEEN/SUPERHERO/Cutter. Circulation of the collection has been declining this year. Reorganizing this collection may make it more appealing for teens to browse and use.*

Strategic Context: *To better serve the needs of our teen customers who are a priority audience in alignment with AHML's Vision, Values & Priorities.*

Project Deliverables and Customer Benefit: *By reclassifying the collection into three distinct genres:*

GN, *Superheroes, and Manga, we will be arranging the collection to be more user-friendly and browsable to teens who are interested in a specific genre of graphic novel. Presently, all three genres are interfiled and teens must browse the entire collection if looking for Manga titles for example. If reclassified, Manga series would all be together and teens could browse a smaller collection to more easily find items that are of interest to them. Another possible benefit may be better use of the graphic novel shelving. Manga books are generally shorter than other types of graphic novels. By grouping them together, we may be able to add shelves to the Manga sections and free up more space in the other two genres.*

Project Evaluation/Measurement of Success: *Possible increase in circulation of collection. Possible better space allocation of existing shelving units.*

Project Scope: *If approved, Jon and Teen Services staff will review existing collection to determine what to retain, what to withdraw, and what to order. Presently, the collection contains approximately 2,100 items. Shelving and space limitations will keep the collection between 2,000 and 2,500 items. Jon will then create a standardized cutter list for Superheroes and Manga to ensure that all like materials are not only shelved together but under what is the most logical choice (i.e. series name for Manga as opposed to author name, etc.). Items will be recataloged/reprocessed one genre (i.e. Manga) at a time in order to try to minimize confusion and disruption as well as to allow the collection to be shifted and shelved more easily. Materials Handling will need to shift the collection as needed during the project.*

Outside of Project Scope: *Adult and Kids World GN collections.*

Background, References, and Testimonials (*if applicable*): *Trixie Dantis, Teen Services Supervisor, first suggested this arrangement back in 2015 after hearing of other libraries utilizing a similar classification scheme. Additionally, Teen staff have also remarked that they have noticed that many teen users prefer a specific type of GN (usually Manga or Superhero). Grouping them together instead of having them interspersed throughout the collection would make browsing easier. Tom Spicer, Margaret Jasinski, Trixie Dantis, and Jon Kadus met to discuss the project and all felt that it was a worthwhile undertaking. Other projects in the workflow prohibited work on this project at that time.*

Project Start Date and Completion Date: *TBD*

Project Timeline/Schedule: *Two weeks to one month depending on other workflow issues/projects in cataloging or processing.*

Stakeholders: (add as needed)
   Department: *Collection Services*
   Level of Project Involvement: (High, Medium, Low): *High*

   Department: *Teen Services*
   Level of Project Involvement: (High, Medium, Low): *Medium*

   Department: *Materials Handling*
   Level of Project Involvement: (High, Medium, Low): *Medium*

Project Team:
   Sponsor: *(Dept. Manager/s) Margaret Jasinski and Trixie Dantis*
   Project Lead: *Jon Kadus*
   Project Team Members: *Teen Services staff, cataloging staff, processing staff*
   Other: *Materials Handling*

Communication Plan: *Once project has begun, Jon will inform Customers Services staff of the project and the expected timeline via email. Jon will keep Teen Services and Materials Handling supervisors updated on progress of project.*

Estimated Project Costs: *Staff time and labor.*

Project Risks: *While the collection is being recataloged, etc. portions will be unavailable for customers for a day or so. Collection will be in minor disorganization as items are being shifted so Hub staff may need to assist teens searching the collection and explain the new organization.*

Approvals *(LST use only)*

LST Date:
LAT Date:

Appendix C

Recommended Comics

Here is a list of recommended comics titles[1] for collections of various sizes: a library collection that is just getting started, a library collection that is well-established, and a library collection that is large and already has all the well-known stuff. This is a very light list, since this book was not intended as a resource for reader's advisory, as most library science books about comics and graphic novels are. I advise you to take a look at some of those books, many of which are listed in the bibliography, for more thorough lists and additional ideas. Some of these titles have been selected with upcoming movies and other trends in mind. For the first tier, you would want to add mainly first volumes of a series to give your patrons a proper jumping point, but don't forget to add the remaining volumes if the first circulates well. Don't forget to check out the bibliography of cited sources at the end of this book for examples of excellent books *about* comics.

"My library's comics collection is just starting."
Great! Make sure it has these:

CHILDREN'S

Baltazar, Art. *Tiny Titans, Volume 1: Welcome to the Treehouse*. New York: DC, 2009.

Cook, Katie. *My Little Pony: Friendship Is Magic, Volume 1*. San Diego: IDW, 2013.

Davis, Jim. *Garfield at Large: His First Book.* New York: Ballantine Books, 2001.

Holm, Jennifer, and Matthew Holm. *Baby Mouse, Volume 1: Queen of the World.* New York: Random House, 2005.

Kanata, Konami. *The Complete Chi's Sweet Home, Part 1.* Tokyo: Kodansha, 2015.

Monster, R. Sfè. *Minecraft, Volume 1.* Milwaukie: Dark Horse, 2019.

North, Ryan. *Adventure Time, Volume 1.* Los Angeles: kaBOOM! Studios, 2012.

Pearson, Luke. *Hilda and the Troll.* London: Flying Eye Books, 2015.

Pearson, Ridley. *Super Sons, Book 1: The PolarShield Project.* Burbank: DC, 2019.

Peirce, Lincoln. *Big Nate, Volume 1: From the Top.* Kansas City: Andrews McMeel, 2010.

Pilkey, Dav. *The Adventures of Captain Underpants.* New York: Scholastic, 1997.

Reed, MK. *Science Comics: Dinosaurs: Fossils and Feathers.* New York: First Second Books, 2016.

Runton, Andy. *Owly, Volume 1: The Way Home & the Bittersweet Summer.* Marietta: Top Shelf, 2004.

Telgemeier, Raina. *Smile.* New York: Graphix, 2010.

Yoshino, Satsuki. *Barakamon, Volume 1.* New York: Yen Press, 2014.

TWEEN AND TEEN

Aaron, Jason. *Avengers, Volume 1: The Final Host.* New York: Marvel, 2018.

Aaron, Jason. *Thor, Volume 1: The Goddess of Thunder.* New York: Marvel, 2016.

Bendis, Brian Michael. *Superman—Action Comics, Volume 1: Invisible Mafia.* Burbank: DC, 2019.

Bendis, Brian Michael. *Superman, Volume 1: The Unity Saga: Phantom Earth.* Burbank: DC, 2019.

Coates, Ta-Nehisi. *Black Panther, Volume 1: A Nation Under Our Feet.* New York: Marvel, 2016.

King, Tom. *Batman, Volume 1: I Am Gotham.* Burbank: DC, 2017.

Kinney, Jeff. *Diary of a Wimpy Kid.* New York: Amulet Books, 2007.

Lewis, John. *March, Book 1.* Marietta: Top Shelf, 2013.

Liu, Marjorie. *Monstress, Volume 1: Awakening.* Portland: Image, 2016.

Reeder, Amy. *Moon Girl and Devil Dinosaur, Volume 1: BFF.* New York: Marvel, 2016.

Satrapi, Marjane. *Persepolis: The Story of a Childhood.* New York: Pantheon Graphic Library, 2004.

Smith, Jeff. *Bone, Volume 1: Out from Boneville*. New York: Scholastic, 2005.

Spencer, Nick. *The Amazing Spider-Man, Volume 1: Back to Basics*. New York: Marvel, 2018.

Telgemeier, Raina. *Drama*. New York: Graphix, 2012.

Wang, Jen. *The Prince and the Dressmaker*. New York: First Second Books, 2018.

Wilson, G. Willow. *Ms. Marvel, Volume 1: No Normal*. New York: Marvel, 2014.

Wilson, G. Willow. *Wonder Woman, Volume 1: The Just War*. Burbank: DC, 2019.

Yang, Gene Luen Yang. *American Born Chinese*. New York: Square Fish, 2006.

ADULT

Backderf, Derf. *My Friend Dahmer*. New York: Abrams, 2012.

Ferris, Emil. *My Favorite Thing Is Monsters*. Seattle: Fantagraphics, 2017.

Gorman, Zac. *Rick and Morty, Volume 1*. Portland: Oni Press, 2015.

Kirkman, Robert. *The Walking Dead, Volume 1: Days Gone Bye*. Portland: Image, 2013.

Mignola, Mike. *Hellboy, Volume 1: Seeds of Destruction*. Milwaukie: Dark Horse, 2004.

Moore, Alan. *Watchmen*. Burbank: DC, 1987.

Posehn, Brian, and Gerry Duggan. *Deadpool, Volume 1: Dead Presidents*. New York: Marvel, 2013.

Spiegelman, Art. *Maus: A Survivor's Tale, Book I: My Father Bleeds History*. New York: Pantheon Graphic Library, 1986.

Thompson, Craig. *Blankets*. Marietta: Top Shelf, 2003.

Vaughan, Brian K. *Saga, Volume 1*. Portland: Image, 2012.

Walker, David F. *The Life of Frederick Douglass: A Graphic Narrative of a Slave's Journey from Bondage to Freedom*. Berkeley: Ten Speed Press, 2019.

Ware, Chris. *Jimmy Corrigan, the Smartest Kid on Earth*. New York: Pantheon Graphic Library, 2000.

"My library's comic collection is awesome!"
Go, you! Add these, if you haven't already:

CHILDREN'S

Bell, Cece. *El Deafo*. New York: Abrams, 2014.

Holm, Jennifer L., and Matthew Holm. *Squish, Number 1: Super Amoeba*. New York: Random House, 2011.

Jamieson, Victoria. *Roller Girl*. New York: Dial Press, 2015.

Kibuishi, Kazu. *Amulet, Book 1: The Stonekeeper*. New York: Scholastic, 2008.

Krosoczka, Jarrett J. *Lunch Lady and the Cyborg Substitute*. New York: Knopf, 2009.

O'Malley, Kevin. *Captain Raptor and the Moon Mystery*. London: Bloomsbury, 2005.

Thummler, Brenna. *Sheets*. St. Louis: Lion Forge, 2018.

Varon, Sara. *Robot Dreams*. New York: First Second Books, 2016.

Yang, Gene Luen. *Avatar: The Last Airbender: The Promise*. Milwaukie: Dark Horse, 2013.

TWEEN AND TEEN

Kishimoto, Masashi. *Boruto: Naruto Next Generations, Volume 1*. San Francisco: Viz Media, 2017.

Kohei, Horikoshi. *My Hero Academia, Volume 1*. San Francisco: Viz Media, 2015.

Libenson, Terri. *Invisible Emmie*. New York: Balzer + Bray, 2017.

Piskor, Ed. *X-Men: Grand Design, Volume 1*. New York: Marvel, 2018.

Rucka, Greg. *Batwoman: Elegy*. New York: DC, 2010.

Tamaki, Mariko. *Harley Quinn: Breaking Glass*. Burbank: DC, 2019.

Waid, Mark. *Daredevil, Volume 1*. New York: Marvel, 2013.

ADULT

Aguirre-Sacasa, Roberto. *Afterlife with Archie, Volume 1: Escape from Riverdale*. Mamaroneck: Archie, 2014.

DeConnick, Kelly Sue. *Bitch Planet, Volume 1: Extraordinary Machine*. Portland: Image, 2015.

Ennis, Garth. *The Boys, Volume 1: The Name of the Game*. Runnemede: Dynamite, 2007.

Fraction, Matt. *Sex Criminals, Volume 1: One Weird Trick*. Portland: Image, 2014.

Gillen, Kieron. *The Wicked + The Divine, Volume 1: The Faust Act*. Portland: Image, 2014.

Hajime, Isayama. *Attack on Titan, Volume 1*. Tokyo: Kodansha, 2013.

Morrison, Grant. *All-Star Superman: Black Label Edition*. Burbank: DC, 2018.

Palmiotti, Jimmy. *Harley Quinn, Volume 1: Die Laughing*. Burbank: DC, 2017.

Smith, Jeff. *RASL*. Columbus: Cartoon Books, 2013.

Snyder, Scott. *The Batman Who Laughs*. Burbank: DC, 2019.

Wilson, Chris, Rob DenBlayker, Matt Melvin, and Dave McElfatrick. *Cyanide & Happiness: Punching Zoo*. Los Angeles: BOOM!, 2014.

Way, Gerard. *The Umbrella Academy, Volume 1: Apocalypse Suite*. Milwaukie: DC, 2008.

"My library's comics collection is huge, and we have everything, we don't need your help."
Okay, okay, but let me try anyway. Double-check your collection for these:

CHILDREN'S

Barks, Carl. *Walt Disney's Donald Duck, Volume 1*. Seattle: Fantagraphics, 2016.

Eliopoulis, Chris. *Franklin Richards: Son of a Genius: Ultimate Collection, Book 1*. New York: Marvel, 2010.

Faller, Regis. *The Adventures of Polo*. New York: Roaring Book Press, 2006.

McCay, Winsor. *Little Nemo in Slumberland, Volume 1*: CreateSpace, 2016.

Simpson, Dana. *Phoebe and Her Unicorn*. Kansas City: Andrews McMeel, 2014.

Takeuchi, Naoko. *Sailor Moon, Volume 1*. Tokyo: Kodansha, 2011.

Tan, Shaun. *The Arrival*. New York: Arthur A. Levine Books, 2007.

Winnick, Judd. *Hilo, Book 1: The Boy Who Crashed to Earth*. New York: Random House, 2015.

TWEEN AND TEEN

Claremont, Chris. *New Mutants Epic Collection: Renewal*. New York: Marvel, 2017.

Dorkin, Evan. *Beasts of Burden: Animal Rites*. Milwaukie: Dark Horse, 2018.

Franklin, Tee. *Bingo Love, Volume 1*. Portland: Image, 2018.

Grace, Sina. *Iceman, Volume 1: Thawing Out*. New York: Marvel, 2018.

Kuper, Peter. *Spy vs. Spy: The Top Secret Files!* New York: MAD, 2011.

Larson, Hope. *Chiggers*. New York: Atheneum Books for Young Readers, 2008.

Morrison, Grant. *Wonder Woman: Earth One, Volume 1*. Burbank: DC, 2016.

O'Neil, Dennis. *The Question, Volume 1: Zen and Violence*. New York: DC, 2007.

Walden, Tillie. *On a Sunbeam*. New York: First Second Books, 2018.

Whitley, Jeremy. *The Unstoppable Wasp, Volume 1: Unstoppable!* New York: Marvel, 2017.

Zdarsky, Chip. *Jughead, Volume 1*. Mamaroneck: Archie, 2016.

ADULT

Burns, Charles. *Black Hole*. New York: Pantheon Graphic Library, 2008.

Czerwiec, MK, Ian Williams, Susan Merrill Squier, Michael J. Green, Kimberly R. Myers, and Scott T. Smith. *Graphic Medicine Manifesto*. University Park: Penn State University Press, 2015.

Duffy, Damian. *Octavia E. Butler's Kindred*. New York: Abrams, 2018.

Grace, Sina. *Nothing Lasts Forever*. Portland: Image, 2017.

Isabella, Tony. *Black Lightning: Cold Dead Hands*. Burbank: DC, 2018.

Kobabe, Maia. *Gender Queer: A Memoir*. St. Louis: Lion Forge, 2019.

Moore, Terry. *Strangers in Paradise, Pocket Book 1*. Abstract Studios, 2004.

Powell, Eric. *The Goon: Bunch of Old Crap*. Nashville: Albatross Funnybooks, 2019.

NOTE

1. You'll find this list organizes these titles by writer only. I mean no disrespect to the many illustrators, inkers, colorists, and other members of the creative teams, but to keep this list as simple as possible, and to keep it from taking up too much paper and ink, I do not list the illustrator unless the writer is also the illustrator or if the distinction is not specified between two creators listed in the book. I hope I can be forgiven this route of laziness, as I would prefer to see library bibliographic records be a bit more thorough.

Bibliography

Ackerman, Spencer. "Captain America's Creator Spent a Lifetime Punching Nazis." *The Daily Beast.* August 26, 2017. https://www.thedailybeast.com/captain-americas-creator-spent-a-lifetime-punching-nazis.

Aoki, Deb. "'My Hero Academia' Manga Mania at San Diego Comic-Con 2018." *Publishers Weekly.* July 26, 2018. https://www.publishersweekly.com/pw/by-topic/industry-news/comics/article/77611-my-hero-academia-manga-mania-at-san-diego-comic-con-2018.html.

Arrant, Chris. "DC Replacing All Imprints with Age Labeling System–Goodbye Vertigo, Zoom, Ink. *Newsarama.* June 21, 2019. https://www.newsarama.com/45716-dc-elminating-all-imprints-including-vertigo-zoom-ink-shifting-organizational-approach-to-age-labels.html.

Baker, Brandon. "Through Comics, Profs Draw Path to Visual Literacy." *Penn Today.* January 23, 2019. https://penntoday.upenn.edu/index.php/news/through-comics-profs-draw-path-visual-literacy.

Baume, Matt. "How Libraries Are Making Comic Conventions Accessible." *Vice.* March 22, 2017.

Beguiling. "TCAF Is for Teachers & Librarians." TCAF, 2019. http://www2.torontocomics.com.

Boucher, Geoff. "Superheroes Are Thriving in Movies and on TV—But Comic Books Lag Behind." *Los Angeles Times.* July 14, 2018. http://www.latimes.com/entertainment/herocomplex/la-ca-mn-superheroes-comic-books-20180714-story.html.

Cavna, Michael. "Why 'Maus' Remains 'The Greatest Graphic Novel Ever Written,' 30 Years Later." *The Washington Post.* August 11, 2016. https://www.washingtonpost.com/news/comic-riffs/wp/2016/08/11/why-maus-remains-the-greatest-graphic-novel-ever-written-30-years-later/.

Cedeira Serantes, Lucia. "Reading Comics." In *Reading Still Matters.* Edited by Catherine Sheldrick Ross, Lynne E. F. McKeehnie, and

Paulette M. Rothbauer, 124–128. Santa Barbara, CA: Libraries Unlimited, 2018.

Chute, Hillary, and Marianne DeKoven. "Introduction: Graphic Narrative." *MFS Modern Fiction Studies* 52, no. 4 (Winter 2006): 767–782.

Cornog, Martha, and Timothy Perper, eds. *Graphic Novels Beyond the Basics: Insights and Issues for Libraries*. Santa Barbara, CA: Libraries Unlimited, 2009.

Dallacqua, A. K. "When I Write, I Picture It in My Head: Comics and Graphic Novels as Inspiration for Multimodal Compositions." *Language Arts* 95, no. 5 (May 2018): 273–286.

Dawson, Gillian, Clare Kindt, Andrea West, and Dave Powers. "Revolutionary Ideas: Fan Days, Cons, and Large Scale Interactive Programs." PowerPoint presented at C2E2, Chicago, IL, March 22, 2019. https://tinyurl.com/BCLc2e2.

Dewey. "Comic-Book Conundrum: Cracked." *025.431: The Dewey Blog*. February 2, 2006. https://ddc.typepad.com/025431/2006/02/comicbook_conun.html.

Diamond Bookshelf. "The Graphic Novel Resource for Educators and Librarians." Accessed November 14, 2018. http://www.diamondbookshelf.com/Home/1/1/20/163.

Dickinson, Gail. "The question . . . Where should I shelve graphic novels?" *Knowledge Quest* 35, no. 5 (2007): 56.

Ehrlich, Lara. "Graphic Novels 101." *BU Today*. July 24, 2014. http://www.bu.edu/today/2014/graphic-novels-101.

Enis, Matt. "KKR Acquires OverDrive." *Library Journal*. December 26, 2019. https://www.libraryjournal.com/?detailStory=KKR-Acquires-OverDrive.

Fee, William T. "Do You Have Any Ditko?: Comic Books, MARC, FRBR and Findability." *Serials Review* 34, no. 3 (2008): 175–189.

Fee, William T. "Where is the Justice . . . League?: Graphic Novel Cataloging and Classification." *Serials Review* 39 (2013): 37–46.

Gardner, Eriq. "Judge Issues 'Comic-Con' Injunction." *The Hollywood Reporter*. August 24, 2018. https://www.hollywoodreporter.com/thr-esq/judge-issues-comic-con-injunction-1137235.

Gearino, Dan. *Comic Shop: The Retail Mavericks Who Gave Us a New Geek Culture*. Athens: Swallow Press, 2017.

Goldsmith, Francisca. *Graphic Novels Now: Building, Managing, and Marketing a Dynamic Collection*. Chicago: ALA Editions, 2005.

Goldsmith, Francisca. *The Readers' Advisory Guide to Graphic Novels*. Chicago: ALA Editions, 2017.

Goldsmith, Francisca. "What's in a Name: Nomenclature and Libraries." In *Graphic Novels and Comics in Libraries and Archives: Essays on Readers, Research, History, and Cataloging*. Edited by Robert G. Weiner, 185–192. Jefferson, NC: McFarland and Company, Inc., 2010.

Gray, Brenna Clarke. "Graphic Novels, Graphic Schmovels: It's All Just Comics." *Book Riot.* October 6, 2014. https://bookriot.com/2014/10 /06/graphic-novels-graphic-schmovels-its-all-just-comics.

Green, Karen. "'Whaddaya Got?' Finding Graphic Novels in an Academic Library." *Publishers Weekly.* November 9, 2010. https://www.publishers weekly.com/pw/by-topic/industry-news/comics/article/45109-whad daya-got-finding-graphic-novels-in-an-academic-library.html.

Griepp, Milton. "ICv2 Interview: DC Co-Pubs on Comics and Graphic Novel Market Trends, Walmart, Management Changes, and the AT&T Acquisition." *ICv2.* 2018. https://icv2.com/articles/news/view/41000 /icv2-interview-dc-co-pubs-comics-graphic-novel-market-trends-wal mart-management-changes-at-t-acquisition.

Hanley, Tim. *The Many Lives of Catwoman.* Chicago: Chicago Review Press, 2017.

Hanley, Tim. *Wonder Woman Unbound: The Curious History of the World's Most Famous Heroine.* Chicago: Chicago Review Press, 2014.

Herald, Nathan. *Graphic Novels for Young Readers: A Genre Guide for Ages 4–14.* Santa Barbara, CA: Libraries Unlimited, 2011.

Holston, Alicia. "A Librarian's Guide to the History of Graphic Novels." In *Graphic Novels and Comics in Libraries and Archives.* Edited by Robert G. Weiner, 9-16. Jefferson, NC: McFarland & Company, 2010.

IDW. "Marvel and IDW to Create New Comic Books for the Next Generation of Readers." *IDW Press Release.* July 17, 2018. https://www .idwpublishing.com/marvel-and-idw-to-create-new-comic-books-for -the-next-generation-of-readers.

Karp, Jesse. *Graphic Novels in Your School Library.* Chicago: ALA Editions, 2012.

Lee, Nathaniel. "Marvel Will Release New Stories on Innovative E-Book Platform." *Bookstr.* March 1, 2019. https://bookstr.com/article/marvel -will-release-new-stories-on-innovative-e-book-platform.

Levitz, Paul. *Will Eisner: Champion of the Graphic Novel.* New York: Abrams, 2015.

Little, Drego. "In a Single Bound: A Short Primer on Comics for Educators." John Hopkins University School of Education: New Horizons for Learning, 2005. https://www.vashonsd.org/cms/lib/WA01919522 /Centricity/Domain/143/Importance%20of%20Comics.doc.

Lyga, Allyson A. W., and Barry Lyga. *Graphic Novels in Your Media Center: A Definitive Guide.* Westport, CT: Libraries Unlimited, 2004.

MacDonald, Heidi. "Comics, the King of Libraries." *Publishers Weekly.* May 12, 2017. https://www.publishersweekly.com/pw/by-topic/industry -news/libraries/article/73599-comics-the-king-of-libraries.html.

MacDonald, Heidi. "Eventbrite Research: Younger Con Attendees 50/50 Male to Female." *Comics Beat.* July 23, 2014a. http://www.comicsbeat .com/eventbrite-research-younger-congoers-5050-male-to-female.

MacDonald, Heidi. "How to Throw a Comic Con at Your Library." *Publishers Weekly*. April 18, 2014b. https://www.publishersweekly.com/pw/by-topic/industry-news/comics/article/61940-how-to-throw-a-comic-con-at-your-library.html.

McCarthy, Helen. *A Brief History of Manga*. London: Ilex Press, 2014.

McCloud, Scott. *Understanding Comics: The Invisible Art*. New York: William Morrow Paperbacks, 1994.

McNary, Dave. "Film News Roundup: Valiant Comics' 'Faith' Superhero Movie in Development at Sony." *Variety*. June 28, 2018. https://variety.com/2018/film/news/valiant-comics-faith-superhero-movie-sony-1202861346.

Miller, Steve. *Developing and Promoting Graphic Novel Collections*. New York: Neal-Schuman, Inc., 2005.

Moviebob. "In Bob We Trust: The Real Marvel Agenda." *YouTube* video, 8:02. Jan 23, 2017. https://www.youtube.com/watch?v=pmXA08jzUfc.

Nyberg, Amy Kiste. "How Librarians Learned to Love the Graphic Novel." In *Graphic Novels and Comics in Libraries and Archives: Essays on Readers, Research, History, and Cataloging*. Edited by Robert G. Weiner, 26–40. Jefferson, NC: McFarland and Company, Inc., 2010.

OCLC. "Graphic Novels in DDC: Discussion Paper." OCLC, 2014. https://www.oclc.org/content/dam/oclc/dewey/discussion/papers/graphic_novels.pdf.

Osicki, Jody. "Graphically Speaking: Titles Based on Sequential Art Continue to Proliferate in Libraries and Beyond." *Library Journal* 15 (June 2018): 34–42.

Pawuk, Michael. *Graphic Novels: A Genre Guide to Comic Books, Manga, and More*. Westport, CT: Libraries Unlimited, 2007.

Pera, Mariam. "Newsmaker: Stan Lee." *American Libraries*. May 19, 2014. https://americanlibrariesmagazine.org/2014/05/19/an-interview-with-stan-lee.

Phoenix, St. John. "Comics Are Not Books, and That's Okay: Exploring Common Problems and Solutions to User Access to Comics and Graphic Novels." (Masters research project, Kent State University, 2015).

Pizzino, Christopher. *Arresting Development: Comics at the Boundaries of Literature*. Austin: University of Texas Press, 2016.

Pyles, Christina. "It's No Joke: Comics and Collection Development." *Public Libraries* 51, no. 6 (2012): 32–35.

Raviv, Dan. *Comic Wars: How Two Tycoons Battled Over the Marvel Comics Empire—and Both Lost*. New York: Broadway, 2002.

Ricca, Brad. *Super Boys: The Amazing Adventures of Jerry Siegel and Joe Shuster—The Creators of Superman*. New York: St. Martin's Press, 2013.

Riggs, Ben. "Why Reading Comics Makes You Smarter." *Geeks and Sundry*. February 15, 2016. https://geekandsundry.com/science-proves-reading-comics-makes-you-smarter.

Robert Kirkman's Secret History of Comics, "The Mighty Misfits Who Made Marvel." Episode 1. Directed by Rory Karpf. AMC. November 12, 2017.

Rogers, Veneta. "Is the Average Age of Comic Book Readers Increasing? Retailers Talk State of the Business 2017." *Newsarama.* February 2, 2017. https://www.newsarama.com/33006-is-the-average-age-of-comic-book-readers-increasing-retailers-talk-state-of-the-business-2017.html.

Romo, Vanessa. "Oscars Drops 'Popular Film' Category." *NPR.* September 6, 2018.

Scott, Randall. *Comics Librarianship: A Handbook.* Jefferson, NC: McFarland and Company, 1990.

Serchay, David S. *The Librarian's Guide to Graphic Novels for Adults.* New York: Neal-Schuman Publishers, Inc., 2010.

Superheroes: A Never-Ending Battle. "A Hero Can Be Anyone." Episode 3. Directed by Michael Kantor. PBS. October 15, 2013.

Tarulli, Laurel. "Cataloging and Problems with Dewey: Creativity, Collaboration and Compromise." In *Graphic Novels and Comics in Libraries and Archives: Essays on Readers, Research, History, and Cataloging.* Edited by Robert G. Weiner, 213–222. Jefferson, NC: McFarland and Company, Inc., 2010.

Tilley, Carol L. "Comics: A Once-Missed Opportunity." *Journal of Research on Libraries and Young Adults.* May 5, 2014. http://www.yalsa.ala.org/jrlya/2014/05/comics-a-once-missed-opportunity.

Toon Books. "Toon into Reading." Accessed December 27, 2019. https://www.candlewick.com/book_files/0979923824.kit.1.pdf.

Van Lente, Fred, and Ryan Dunlavey. *The Comic Book History of Comics.* San Diego: IDW, 2012.

Weiner, Robert G. "Graphic Novels in Libraries: One Library's Solution to the Cataloging Problem." *Texas Library Journal* 84, no. 1 (Spring 2008): 8–16.

Weiner, Robert G. "An Example of an In-House Cataloging System." In *Graphic Novels and Comics in Libraries and Archives.* Edited by Robert G. Weiner, 222–226. Jefferson, NC: McFarland & Company, 2010.

West, Wendy. "Tag, You're It: Enhancing Access to Graphic Novels." *Libraries and the Academy* 13, no. 3 (2013): 301–324.

Wiegand, Wayne A. *Part of Our Lives: A People's History of the American Public Library.* New York: Oxford University Press, 2015.

Wood, Matthew Z. *Comic Book Collections and Programming: A Practical Guide for Librarians.* New York: Rowman & Littlefield, 2018.

Index

Note: Page numbers followed by *t* indicate tables and *f* indicate figures.

Aaron, Jason, 63

Academic libraries, 181–182, 193–200; cataloging in, 194–195, 197, 199; collection development in, 194; events at, 197, 199–200

Accelerated Reader (AR), 188, 192

Action Comics, 4, 7–8; *Action Comics #1*, 13, 33, 54. *See also* Superman

Active participation, 131. *See also* Programs

Advance reading copies (ARCs), 20

Age appropriateness, 20, 32–33, 83–84, 86, 189. *See also* Children

Alvarez, Lorena, 183

Amazon, 61, 78–79, 133, 178

Ambaum, Gene: *Library Comics*, 63; *Unshelved*, 65

Amend, Bill, 183; *FoxTrot*, 183

American Association of School Librarians (AASL), 206; National Conference & Exhibition, 206

American Library Association (ALA), 184, 205, 209; Annual Conference & Exhibition, 184, 198, 206, 211, 214; Graphic Novels & Comics Round Table (GNCRT), xv, 28, 93–94, 158, 198, 204, 205, 207, 211; Library Bill of Rights, 49; Webinars, 209

Amplification, 185

Anglo-American Cataloguing Rules (AACR2), 97–98

Ann Arbor Comic Arts Fest (A2CAF), 184–185

Ann Arbor District Library, 184–185

Archie (comic), 23–24, 33, 35, 68 n.2, 196

Archie Comics (publisher), 23–24, 43, 58

Archival Quality (Weir), 63

Arlington Heights Memorial Library (AHML), 79, 119–122, 221–223
Artists, 12, 95, 97, 167
Audio comics, 92 n.6
Authors, 59; in cataloging, 95, 97, 106, 113. *See also* Creative team
Awards, 84. *See also names of individual awards*

The Baby-Sitters Club (Martin/ Telgemeier), 182
Baker & Taylor (B&T), 77–78
Barbara Gordon. *See* Batgirl
Barefoot Gen (Nakazawa), 42, 182
Batgirl, 64*f,* 65, 67
Batman, 35; *The Dark Knight Returns* (Miller), 8, 39; films, 43. *See also Detective Comics*
Baur, Jack, 67, 184
Bechdel, Alison, 31, 148; *Fun Home,* 8, 148
Berkeley Unified School District, 187, 189
Bestseller lists, 84
"Big Two." *See* DC Comics; Marvel Comics
Bild, Rachael, 199
Bill Finger Award, 28
Billy Ireland Cartoon Library & Museum, 158–159, 194
Black Lightning, 135–136
Black Panther, 37, 42, 139
Blade (film), 47 n.26
Boise Library Comic Con, 153
Bone (Smith), 7, 16*f,* 25, 82
Book clubs, 131–132, 175, 183, 190, 193
Book talks, 132–133, 190
Booklist, 85

Bookstores and booksellers, 6, 51, 58, 60, 178. *See also* Amazon
Brenner, Robin, 184
The Bronze Age of Comics, 38–39, 45 nn.12–13, 57
Browsing, 59, 95, 108, 112–113, 114, 123, 193, 196–197. *See also* Cataloging; Shelving
Buffy the Vampire Slayer (Whedon), 65
Butler Library, 195–196
Button making, 140–141, 189–190

C2E2, 93–94, 158, 207, 214
Cable and X-Force, 40, 98–100
Caldecott Medal, 189
California School Librarian Association, 188
Captain America, 37, 123–124, 137
Carol and John's Comic Shop, 72, 144, 146
Cartoon Crossroads Columbus (CXC), 158–159, 208
Cartoons. *See* Comic strips
Cartoons and Comics in the Classroom (Thomas), 52
Cataloging, xviii, 93–104, 112, 194–195, 197; authorship, 97; cataloging standards for comics, 98, 114, 127 n.6, 197; comics as serials, 94, 96, 103*t;* examples of, 99–101, 99*t,* 100*f,* 101*f;* series titles, 97–98, 101–102, 103*t;* standards, 98–99 (*see also* Anglo-American Cataloguing Rules; MARC; RDA); subject headings, 52, 104*t,* 177, 197; titles and subtitles, 97–98, 102, 103*t,* 110; volume numbering, 96–97. *See also* Classification

CCEL@SDCC (Comic Conference for Educators and Librarians at San Diego Comic Con), 21, 208

Cel Walden, 63

Censorship, 34, 49, 183; patron challenges, 88, 89f, 189, 214. *See also* Comics Code; Gatekeeping

Central Library Consortium (CLC), 98–99, 101, 104–105

Chelsea District Library, 159

Chicago Comics & Entertainment Expo. *See* C2E2

Children: association of comics with, 6, 33, 49–50, 197; negative effect of comics on, 34, 50, 185 (*see also* Comics Code); positive effect of comics on, 13–15, 27, 66, 215 (*see also* Reluctant readers); selecting comics for, 85–88. *See also* Age appropriateness

Circulation, 42, 122t, 190; digital circulation models, 80–81 (*see also* Digital comics); improving circulation of comics, 71, 102, 108–109, 112, 114, 117, 129, 166, 173, 176–177, 190, 193–194; wear and tear, 61, 79, 90, 191

Claremont, Chris, 194–195; *The New Mutants,* 148

Classification, 102–109; by age level, 32–33, 118, 120, 123; by author, 106, 115, 120, 124; call numbers, 111, 114–125, 124f; by chronological order, 113, 117–118; Dewey Decimal Classification (DDC), 102, 104–106, 112, 115, 119; by franchise or character, 110–111, 113–114, 116–117, 119, 122, 123; by genre, 119–120, 222; in-house classification systems, 109–127; Library of Congress Classification (LCC), 107, 112, 195; nonfiction comics, 106–107, 115; planning reclassification, 126; by publisher, 110–118; reclassification, 221; by series title, 106, 111, 123; spine labels, 118f, 119f, 121f, 122f, 125f; stickers, 108–109, 111; by subseries, 123–124; by title, 106, 123; by volume number, 110–111, 117, 123. *See also* Cataloging; Shelving

CLC. *See* Central Library Consortium (CLC)

Cleveland Public Library (CPL), 54–56, 73, 132, 137, 144, 145, 159

Closure, 185

Collecting comics, 40–41, 57–58. *See also* Comic shops

Collection development, 51, 69–92, 146; for academic libraries, 194; through Amazon, 79; budgeting, 86–88; through comic shops, 71–74; through direct distribution, 76–77; through library vendors, 77–78; policies, 88–90, 181; review sources, 84–86; for school libraries, 187; subscription services, 79; suggested titles for, 225–230; weeding, 90–92. *See also* Digital comics

Colorist, 12. *See also* Creative team

Columbia University, 6, 194–195, 197

Columbus College of Art and Design, 159

Columbus Metropolitan Library, 159, 208

Comic Art Collection at Michigan State University, 194, 199

Comic book movies, xviii, 43–44, 91, 108–109, 139, 175, 176–177

Comic Book Resources (CBR), 85, 91

Comic books, 3–4; versus graphic novels, 6–10, 30–31, 51–52; history of, 33, 34f, 49–50; sales of, 32, 44, 60, 74–75. *See also* Comics; Graphic novels

Comic Con. *See* Comic conventions; San Diego Comic Con (SDCC)

Comic conventions, 153–170, 184; at academic libraries, 199; anime and manga conventions, 42; booths at, 157–158; fandom conventions, 153, 156, 159–160, 163–164; hosted by libraries, 53, 153–156, 161–170, 184–185, 199; independent comics at, 67, 78; libraries participating in, 156–166, 205; libraries providing space for, 158–161; local, 160–161, 166, 208; professional development at, 19, 53, 157, 198, 203–205, 207–209, 211, 214. *See also names of individual conventions*

Comic shops: decline of, 54, 56, 58–59, 74–75, 139; history of,

57–58; organization of, 58–59, 75–76, 110; partnership with libraries, 59–60, 71–73, 76, 134, 142–143, 160, 165, 167, 175, 185. *See also* Distribution; Free Comic Book Day

Comic strips, 2–3, 6–9, 25, 33, 35, 52, 174, 182–183. *See also* Webcomics

Comic swap, 134

Comics: artistic and literary merit of, 21, 27, 40, 84, 107–108, 144, 185, 187, 192, 194, 200, 205; formats, 1–11, 27, 30, 32, 42, 60, 95, 106–107, 149 (*see also names of individual formats*); as medium, 2, 7–10, 21–22, 29, 42, 60, 70, 94, 149, 173, 186–187; as multimodal text, 186; sexuality in, 34, 39–40, 42, 46 n.16, 187; violence in, 32, 34, 39–40, 42, 187, 189; as visual medium, 15, 29–30, 83–84, 187–191, 193. *See also* Comic books; Digital comics; Distribution; Graphic novels

Comics and Sequential Art (Eisner), 52

Comics Code, 34–35, 37–39. *See also* Wertham, Fredric

Comics Librarianship: A Handbook (Scott), 52–53, 199

Comics Plus: Library Edition, 82

Comics Studies Society (CSS), 205

Comics Worth Reading, 85

Comix, 12, 41

Comixology, 61–62. *See also* Digital comics

Comix-Scholars Discussion List, 205

Common Sense Media, 193

Conferences. *See* Comic conventions; Library conferences

A Contract with God and Other Tenement Stories (Eisner), 51

Conventions. *See* Comic conventions; Library conferences

Cosplay, 133, 155, 157, 165, 167–168; groups, 160; workshop, 141

Cost Per Circ (CPC). *See* Digital comics

Create your own comic, 140

Creative team, 12, 95, 97. *See also* Artists; Authors; Writers

Creator visits and appearances, 18, 20, 134, 199. *See also* Expert visits

Creator-owned comics, 12, 17, 23–24, 43

Crossover, 11, 40

Curriculum, 54, 181, 183, 189–193. *See also* School librarians; School libraries; Teachers

Dallacqua, Ashley Kaye, 185–186

Dark Horse Comics, 24

The Dark Knight Returns (Miller), 8

Darth Vader (Soule), 65

Davis, Jim, *Garfield,* 8

DC Comics, 17, 33, 135–136; imprints for young readers, 61, 75; and Marvel Comics, 17; subscriptions, 79, 85; Walmart exclusives, 61, 149

DC Entertainment Studios. *See* DC Comics

DC Ink. *See* DC Comics

DC Zoom. *See* DC Comics

DDC. *See* Dewey Decimal Classification (DDC)

DeJonghe, Natalie, 171, 204, 205, 211

Detective Comics, 17. *See also* DC Comics

Dewey Decimal Classification (DDC), 102, 104–106, 112, 115, 119. *See also* OCLC

Diamond BookShelf, 76. *See also* Diamond Distributors

Diamond Distributors, 58, 76–77, 142–143. *See also* Distribution

Digital comics, 11, 60–62, 80–83, 140; Digital Rights Management (DRM), 62; lending models, 62, 80–82; reading methods, 80–83. *See also names of individual vendors*

Direct market, 12, 26, 57. *See also* Distribution

Disney, 17, 43

Displays, 71*f,* 107–109, 116–117, 122, 174, 176

Distribution, 12; history of, 30, 57–58; small distributors, 78; subscriptions, 58. *See also* Comic shops; Diamond Distributors; Publishers

Ditko, Steve, 36

Diversity, 23, 30, 42–43, 74, 135–138

Dudas, John, 72–76

Dyslexia, 186, 188

East Baton Rouge Parish Library System, 176

EBSCO, 85, 176–178

Eisner, Will, 6–7, 28, 40, 51–52, 233; *Comics and Sequential Art,* 52; *A Contract with God and Other Tenement Stories,* 51

Eisner Awards, 28, 198

Elmwood Park Public Library, 123–126

Emerald City Comic Con (ECCC), 207

Emerald City Distribution, 78

English language learning, 186, 188

Escapism, 13, 26, 50

Expert visits, 139. *See also* Creator visits and appearances

Faith (Valiant Comics character), 24

Fandom, 155. *See also* Comic conventions

Fantagraphics, 25, 80

Ferris, Emil, *My Favorite Thing Is Monsters,* 7

Finger, Bill, 28, 65

First Second Books, 25

Flaming River Con, 159

The Flash, 35–36

Floppies. *See* Comic books

Follett, 191

For Better or For Worse (Johnston), 182–183

FoxTrot (Amend), 183

Fraction, Matt, *Sex Criminals,* 63

FRBR, 95

Free Comic Book Day, 141–144

Fun Home (Bechdel), 8, 148

Funnies. *See* Comic strips

Gaiman, Neil, *Sandman,* 65

Galleys, 20

Game night, 133–134

Garfield (Davis), 8

Gatekeeping, 10, 49, 50, 184, 188

Gateway reading, 15, 22, 52, 185

Genre, 1–2, 9, 13, 21–22, 29, 34–36, 42, 149, 196; subgenre, 45 n.6, 177

The Golden Age of Comics, 32–35, 37, 38–39, 49–51

Good Comics for Kids, 85. *See also School Library Journal*

Google Ads, 178

Grand Comics Database, 97

Grants and grant writing, 146, 190

Graphic medicine, 200

Graphic novels, 5–10, 12, 22, 32, 44, 53, 108; versus comic books, 6–10, 30–31, 60–61, 149; and Will Eisner, 6, 40, 51–52. *See also* Cataloging; Comic books; Volume

Graphic Novels and Comics in Libraries and Archives (Weiner), 112, 114

Graphix, 25, 182

Green, Karen, 6, 8, 195–198

Green Lantern, 36, 38

Guts (Telgemeier), 183

Hanley, Tim, 10, 24, 56–57, 139–149

Hardcover, 7, 24–25, 60–61, 77. *See also* Trade paperbacks

Harvey Awards, 24, 28

Heinlein, Sheila, 13, 187

Hickman, Jonathan: *House of X,* 65; *Powers of X,* 65

Hoopla, 81–82. *See also* Digital comics; Vendors

House of X (Hickman), 65
Humanoids, 25, 32

IDW Publishing, 24
Ignatz Awards, 28
Illinois Library Association, 207
Image Comics, 17–23, 41, 43
In loco parentis, 181, 187, 189.
    See also School librarians
Independent comics, 12, 41,
    66–67, 78, 182, 184–185
Independent participation, 131.
    See also Programs
Independent reading, 191–192
Indicia, 97, 111
Indie comics. *See* Independent
    comics
Inge, M. Thomas, 51–52
Ingram, 78
Inker, 12
Inkpot Awards, 28
*Inks: The Journal of the Comics
    Studies Society,* 205
Institute for Comics Studies,
    194
Intellectual freedom, 15, 49, 181,
    187
Into the Spider-Verse (film), 91
Iron Circus Comics, 78
Isabella, Tony, 135–139
Issue numbers, 4, 27, 95–96.
    See also Cataloging; Volume

Jaffe, Violet, 79, 119–122
Jaggers, Alice, 200
Jefferson Pierce. *See* Black
    Lightning
Jocasta Nu, 65
Johnston, Lynn, *For Better or For
    Worse,* 183
*Journal of Graphic Novels and
    Comics,* 145–146

Kadus, Jon, 221–223
Karp, Jesse, 186
Kirby, Jack, 36–37
Kirkus, 84–85
Koike, Kazou, *Lone Wolf and
    Cub,* 189, 191
KOIOS, 178
Krashen, Stephen, 189
Kurtzman, Harvey, 28

Larson, Hope, 65–68
LCS (Local Comic Shop). *See*
    Comic shops
Lee, Jessica, 187–191
Lee, Jim, 44
Lee, Stan, 36–37, 215. *See also*
    Marvel Comics
Lexile levels, 188, 192
Libby app. *See* OverDrive
LibGuides, 177
Librarian (X-Men character), 65
Librarians: comics characters that
    are, 63–65; opposition to
    comics from, xv–xvi, 22, 29,
    31, 49–52, 58, 66, 138, 213;
    support for comics from, 19,
    49–50, 52–53, 67
Library Bill of Rights, 49
Library Comics (Ambaum/
    Coleman), 63
Library conferences, 184,
    206–207. *See also names of
    individual conferences*
Library Journal, 51, 53–54,
    84–85, 209; Webcasts, 209
Library of Congress Classification
    (LCC), 107, 195
Limited series, 4, 5
Linked data, 176–178
Little, Drego, 185
Liu, Marjorie, 208; *Monstress,*
    21

London Public Library (LPL), 79, 115–117
Lone Wolf and Cub (Koike), 189, 191
Lord High Librarian, 63
Lubbock Public Library, 113–115
Lucien, 65
Lyga, Allison, 186
Lyga, Barry, 186

Makerspace programs, 140–141
Manga, 10, 41–42, 85, 110, 184, 188; female characters in, 42
MARC, 95, 98, 102, 103*t*, 104*t*
Marston, William Maulton, 37, 46 n.16, 148
Marvel Comics, 11, 17, 36–38, 41, 43–44; and DC comics, 17; digital copies, 62; subscriptions, 58, 79. *See also* Timely Comics
Marvel Studios. *See* Comic book movies; Marvel Comics
Maus (Spiegelman), 8, 40, 52, 182
Maxiseries. *See* Limited series
McCloud, Scott, xvi, 44; *Understanding Comics*, 53
McFarlane, Todd, 44
Meadowvale Public Library, 154
Medical comics. *See* Graphic medicine
Metadata, 97
Metered Access. *See* Digital comics
Michigan State University, 52, 194, 199
Miller, Frank, *The Dark Knight Returns*, 8, 39
Minicomics, 184
Miniseries. *See* Limited series
Misnomers, xviii
Mod podge, 140

The Modern Age of Comics, 39–45
Moldoff, Sheldon, 65
Monstress (Liu), 208
Monthlies. *See* Comic books
Moore, Alan, *Watchmen*, 39
Movie night, 134
Ms. Marvel, 42, 138–139, 146
Multimodal text, 186
My Favorite Thing Is Monsters (Ferris), 7
My Hero Academia (Kohei), 42

Nakazawa, Keiji, *Barefoot Gen*, 42, 182
Narrative density, 185
Naruto (Kishimoto), 191
National Book Award, xviii, 84
National Cartoonists Society (NCS), 205
The New Mutants (Claremont), 148
New York City Comic Con (NYCC), 93, 157, 158, 207–208, 214; NYCC @ NYPL, 207–208
New York Times, 6, 198
Nimona *(Stevenson)*, xviii
No Flying, No Tights, 85
Noe, Matthew, 200
Northeast Ohio Regional Library System (NEO), 210
NoveList, 85, 176–178

Oak Park Public Library (OPPL), 77, 117–118
OCLC, 104–105. *See also* Dewey Decimal Classification (DDC)
Ohio Library Council, 207
Ohio State University Press, 205
One Copy/One User. *See* Digital comics
One-shot. *See* Limited series

Ongoing series, 4
Online Computer Library Center (OCLC). *See* OCLC
Organization. *See* Classification
Original graphic novels (OGN), 5–7, 32. *See also* Graphic novels
Ornaments, 141
Otaku USA Magazine, 85
Outreach, 175–176. *See also* Programs
OverDrive, 80–82, 177, 187, 191, 209–210. *See also* Digital comics; Vendors

Partnerships, 166, 175, 184–185; with colleges and universities, 144, 146, 149; with comic conventions, 157–161, 208; with comic shops, 60, 71–76, 142–143, 160, 175; with comics creators, 66; with cosplay groups, 160; with Diamond Distributors, 76–77, 143–144; with publishers, 21
Passive participation, 131. *See also* Programs
Pawuk, Michael "Mike," 53, 71, 184
Pencillers. *See* Artists
Plotters. *See* Authors
Policy: collection development, 69–70, 84, 88–92, 90*f*; for conventions, 157, 168, 170; weeding, 90–91
Political cartoons, 28, 37, 105
Pop-up library, 158, 175–176
Powers of X (Hickman), 65
Previews (catalog), 77. *See also* Diamond Distributors
Professional development, 19–21, 53, 93, 197–198, 203–211, 214–215; for academic librarians, 197–198; advocating for, 210–211; at comic conventions, 203–204; literature, 209. *See also* Professional organizations
Professional organizations, 204–206, 209–211. *See also* *names of individual organizations*
Programs, 129–134, 139–144, 150; at academic libraries, 197, 199–200; budgeting for, 130; passive programming, 131; in school libraries, 189–190. *See also names of individual programs*
Promotion and advertising, 77, 146, 158, 166, 169*f*, 175, 199, 200. *See also* Social media
Proposal, 221
Public Library Association (PLA), 206
Public Library Association Conference, 206
Publishers, 15–25, 31–32, 34, 37, 41, 53, 67; and comic shops, 57–59, 76; and Free Comic Book Day, 142; local, 198. *See also* Cataloging; Digital comics; Distribution; *and names of individual publishers*
Publishers Weekly, 85–86, 197, 200
Pulitzer Prize for Editorial Cartooning, 28
Pulitzer Prize for Literature, 40
Pyles, Christina, 112–113

Ramos-Peterson, Chloe, 18–23, 134
Rare Book & Manuscript Library, 6, 195. *See also* Columbia University

RBdigital, 80, 82
RDA, 97, 98
Readers, 26; accessibility for, 83;
    age of, 14f, 15, 26; diversity
    of, 42, 137; expertise of,
    26–27, 59, 113; gender of, 10,
    42; loyalty to publishers,
    16–17, 110; new, 27, 44, 61,
    69, 75, 83, 108–109, 174.
    See also Browsing; Children;
    Reluctant readers
Readers' advisory, 11, 21–22,
    59–60, 68 n.1, 72, 133, 146,
    158, 204, 225–230. See also
    NoveList
Reading level, 32–33, 188,
    192–193
Reedley College, 199
ReedPOP, 161, 211 n.2. See also
    Comic conventions
Relaunch, 91, 95, 96
Reluctant readers, 13, 108,
    183–184, 185, 186, 188.
    See also Children
Reuben Award, 28
Rex Libris, 63
Rex Libris (Turner), 63
Robbins, Scott, 184
Run, 12, 118, 189
Rupert Giles, 65

Salt Lake Comic Con, 170 n.1
San Diego Comic Con (SDCC),
    153, 157, 208; Comic
    Conference for Educators and
    Librarians (CCEL@SDCC),
    21, 208. See also Comic
    conventions
San Diego Public Library, 21
Sandman (Gaiman), 65
Scholarly organizations. See
    Professional organizations

School librarians, 187–190,
    192–193. See also Teachers
School libraries, 29, 181, 185–193
School Library Journal, 53, 86,
    188; Webcasts, 209
School media specialists. See
    School librarians
Scott, Randall, 97, 118; Comics
    Librarianship: A Handbook,
    52–53, 199
Scottish Centre for Comics
    Studies, 205
Seduction of the Innocent
    (Wertham), 51
Self-published comics. See
    Independent comics
Seniors, 133, 173–174
Sequential art, 1–2, 6, 33, 191,
    194. See also Comics and
    Sequential Art (Eisner)
Series, 11, 191. See also
    Cataloging; Limited series;
    Ongoing series
Sex Criminals (Fraction), 63
Shelf talkers, 108–109. See also
    Displays
Shelving, xviii, 60–61, 63, 93,
    108, 110–112, 116, 119–120,
    190, 192–193; at comic shops,
    58–59, 76; interfiling, 106–
    108, 193, 221; keeping like
    items together, 106, 116–118,
    123–124, 184, 194–195,
    197; size considerations,
    78, 86. See also Cataloging;
    Classification; Displays
Shivon (no last name provided),
    90, 199–200
Shojo, 10, 42. See also Manga
Shonen, 10, 42. See also Manga
Siegel & Shuster Society, 205
Signage, 174. See also Displays

The Silver Age of Comics, 35–38, 45 nn.12–13, 51

Six-Gun Gorilla (Spurrier), 63

Slow visualizers, 186

Smile (Telgemeier), 184

Smith, Jeff, 159; *Bone,* 7, 16*f,* 25, 82

Social issues, 13, 33, 38–39, 42–43, 137. *See also* Diversity

Social media, 166, 174–175, 178, 197, 198, 200; for professional development, 206

Son, Alice, 221–223

Sora (app), 191

Soule, Charles, *Darth Vader,* 65

Spider-Man, 110; *The Amazing Spider-Man,* 15, 38–39, 96, 98; *Spider-Verse,* 91

Spiegelman, Art, 8, 15, 40, 52, 148, 159, 182, 187, 227; *Maus,* 8, 40, 52, 182

Spurgeon, Tom, 159

Spurrier, Simon, 63

Stevenson, Noelle, *Nimona,* xviii

Story arc, 11, 98, 113

Story time, 133

Subtitle, 97–99, 102, 106. *See also* Cataloging

Superheroes, 13, 29, 31, 33–41, 43–44, 196; of color, 37, 38, 42, 135–136, 138–139; deconstructions of, 39; female, 24, 37–38, 40–42; with human problems, 36, 38–39; and social justice, 37. *See also* DC Comics; Marvel Comics

Superman, 7–8, 13, 33–35, 37, 41, 137, 188; "Superman: From Cleveland to Krypton" exhibit, 54–56, 74. *See also Action Comics*

Surveys, 110, 115, 117, 126, 217

Suzie *(Sex Criminals),* 63

Symposium, 144, 146, 150

Tadman, Andrew, 176–178

Tamaki, Mariko, *This One Summer,* 189

Tarulli, Laurel, 95, 112

Teachers, 21, 185, 187–188, 190–192; comics characters that are, 135; opposition to comics from, 50, 183, 188. *See also* School librarians

Telgemeier, Raina, 182–185; *The Baby-Sitters Club,* 182; *Smile,* 184

This One Summer (Tamaki), 189

Thomas, James, *Cartoons and Comics in the Classroom,* 52

Thor (Aaron), 63

Timely Comics, 36. *See also* Marvel Comics

Titles. *See* Cataloging; Series

Toronto Comic Arts Festival (TCAF), 160, 208

Toronto Public Library, 154

Toronto Reference Library, 160, 208

Trade paperbacks, 4–5, 7, 59, 91, 98. *See also* Hardcover

Trivia, 133

Turner, James, *Rex Libris,* 73

Understanding Comics (McCloud), 53

University of Arkansas for Medical Sciences Library, 200

University of Dundee (Scotland), 205

University of Florida, 205

University of Michigan, 185

Unshelved (Ambaum), 65

Valiant Comics, 24
Vault of Midnight, 185
Vendors, 157, 191, 209–210; at
    comic conventions, 167–168,
    175; of digital comics, 62,
    80–83, 191; of library
    products, 108; of print comics,
    71–72, 76–79, 191, 198;
    webinars from, 209–210.
    See also Comic shops; *and*
    names of individual vendors
Visually dependent students, 186
Voices of Youth Advocates
    (VOYA), 53
Volin, Eva, 184
Volume, 12, 106; numbering,
    5, 95, 96–97, 99, 102, 111.
    See also Cataloging
VOYA. *See Voices of Youth*
    Advocates (VOYA)

Waid, Mark, 28–32, 45, 142, 228
The Walking Dead, 45
Walmart, 61, 149
Watchmen (Moore), 39
Webcomics, 10–11, 29, 66–67,
    184
Webinars, 209–210, 214
Webjunction, 210
Weiner, Robert, 53, 112–115;
    Graphic Novels and Comics
    in Libraries and Archives,
    112, 114
Weir, Ivy Noelle, *Archival*
    Quality, 63
WEPLcon, 163–166
Wertham, Fredric, 34; *Seduction*
    of the Innocent, 51. *See also*
    Comics Code
Whedon, Joss, *Buffy the Vampire*
    Slayer, 65

Will Eisner Comic Industry
    Awards. *See* Eisner Awards
Will Eisner Hall of Fame, 42
Williams, Ian, 200
Willoughby-Eastlake Public
    Library, 154, 163–166
Wizard World, 158, 160–161, 208
Wolanski, Bryn, 163–166
Women in comics: characters,
    37–38, 39–40, 42; in comic
    shops, 19, 73; creators, 138–
    139, 182–183, 196. *See also*
    Diversity; Superheroes; *and*
    names of individual characters
Wonder Woman, 35, 37–38, 135;
    symposium at the Cleveland
    Public Library, 74, 144, 146
Wondercon, 208
Wood, Matthew Z., 49, 78, 86, 174
Writers, 12, 106; opinions on
    libraries, 138, 214. *See also*
    Authors; Creative team

X-Force. See Cable and X-Force
X-Men, 37–38, 65, 215; *The New*
    Mutants, 148
X-Men (cartoon series), 215
X-Men (film), 43

YALSA (Young Adult Library
    Services Association), 84,
    184. *See also* ALA (American
    Library Association)
Yellow Kid, 45 n.14
Yellow Kid, The (Outcault), 33
Young Adult Library Services
    Association. *See* YALSA
    (Young Adult Library Services
    Association)

Zullo, Valentino, 13, 145–150

About the Author

JACK PHOENIX is a librarian in Cleveland, Ohio. He earned his MLIS from Kent State University and his MA in English from Ohio Dominican University. He has presented on the topic of comics in libraries at library conferences and is a member of the American Library Association, the Graphic Novels & Comics Round Table, the Ohio Library Council, and the Comics Studies Society. Follow his musings about comics, libraries, and other nerdy things at jackphoenix.com.

CPSIA information can be obtained
at www.ICGtesting.com
Printed in the USA
BVHW032028291022
650670BV00013B/146

9 781440 868856